THE ULTIMATE GUIDE TO
DOG TRAINING

Teoti Anderson, CPDT-KA, KPA-CTP

COMPANIONHOUSE
BOOKS

The Ultimate Guide to Dog Training

CompanionHouse Books™ is an imprint of Fox Chapel Publishing, Inc.

Project Team
Director of Product Development and Editorial Operations: Christopher Reggio
Editor: Heather Russell-Revesz
Copy Editor: Amy Deputato
Design: Mary Ann Kahn
Index: Elizabeth Walker

Library of Congress Cataloging-in-Publication Data
Anderson, Teoti.
   The ultimate guide to dog training : puppy training to advance techniques plus 25 problem behaviors solved / by Teoti Anderson.
      pages cm
   Includes index.
   ISBN 978-1-62187-090-6 (alk. paper)
   1. Dogs--Training. 2. Dogs--Behavior. I. Title.
   SF431.A527 2014
   636.7'0835--dc23
                              2014015365

This book has been published with the intent to provide accurate and authoritative information in regard to the subject matter within. While every precaution has been taken in the preparation of this book, the author and publisher expressly disclaim any responsibility for any errors, omissions, or adverse effects arising from the use or application of the information contained herein. The techniques and suggestions are used at the reader's discretion and are not to be considered a substitute for veterinary care. If you suspect a medical problem, consult your veterinarian.

CompanionHouse Books
1970 Broad Street
East Petersburg, PA 17520
www.facebook.com/companionhousebooks

Printed and bound in China
17 18 19 20   5 7 9 8 6

PART I

THE
BASICS OF
DOG
TRAINING

CHAPTER 1

WHY TRAIN YOUR DOG?

You are awesome. Just by picking up and reading a book on training your dog, you have already proven yourself to be a responsible, caring pet parent. Congratulations! You have one lucky dog.

Dogs Bring Unconditional Love ... and Responsibilities

There are responsibilities to having a dog as a family member. You need to ensure that he gets proper health care. You need to make sure that you feed him quality nutrition. You also need to help him understand how to live with humans and, specifically, how to live with your family as a good companion.

As much of an affinity as most dogs have for humans, they are not born knowing how to live with us. Dogs are a different species than humans, and they come with their own species-specific behaviors. These behaviors can often clash with our human expectations of proper behavior.

Did You Know?

TRAINING IS MUTUALLY BENEFICIAL

A well-trained dog is easy to live with and often welcome in other places. If you want to travel with your dog, even if it's just to a relative's house, he will need to have manners so he doesn't embarrass you or cause problems. Training your dog will build your relationship as you learn to better understand each other. And the nice compliments you get on your dog's behavior are a bonus!

As you were growing up, you were taught life skills by adults. Some of those adults may have been better teachers than others, but you grew up learning how to behave in the home and out in public. What was acceptable in your environment may have differed slightly from what was acceptable in your neighbor's environment, but, in general, you learned basic good-citizen skills. Now, you need to teach similar skills to your dog.

Your dog doesn't inherently know that he's not supposed to pee on your carpet or jump on you and knock you over. He doesn't have a manual explaining that he can't chew on your favorite shoes or the bed skirt. He has no clue what an "indoor voice" is. He also doesn't realize that he can't just run up and get in another dog's face or dig in your neighbor's prized rose garden. You need to teach him all of these things, and you can!

Part of being a responsible pet parent is teaching your dog good family manners, cleaning up after him when you're out in public, and ensuring he that isn't a public nuisance. By training your dog using reward-based, positive methods, you are fulfilling these responsibilities.

Establishing Goals

There's nothing wrong with setting goals for your dog. You may have dreams of raising an agility champion or sharing your dog with others as a therapy dog. Learn what's required to achieve those goals and start training your dog to reach them. You will work on getting there together.

Another responsibility that you have is to accept your dog for what he is. Realize that not every dog is suited for every task. Every dog is different. He can never compare to any past dogs you've had, and you will never have another dog like him again.

Dogs are lifetime companions. Your dog is special in his own way, even if he never does turn out to be that agility champion or therapy dog. You may find that you need to adjust your goals as you start your training program and learn more about your dog's strengths and

You need to help your dog understand how to live with your family as a good companion.

challenges. While changing your expectations can be very disappointing initially, you will always have something wonderful in your favor—your dog. Your dog will love you no matter what you achieve, and that is truly something to be treasured.

Making Time to Train

There is no set, defined time when training is best. What works for you? What works for your dog? Are you a morning person? Then train your dog when you first get up. Are you a night owl? Then train your dog in the evenings. Your training program can be just as flexible as you need it to be. The most important thing is to just get started and then keep it up every day.

Most people are very busy. Many don't realize how much work a dog, especially a young puppy, is to train. When you use positive methods, you don't need a lot of time to train your dog—just fifteen minutes a day will do the trick, and not even fifteen minutes in a row. Each training session should be only a few minutes long, so it's easy to squeeze in fifteen minutes throughout the day, especially because you can train during your everyday routine.

For example, you have to take your dog outside on leash each morning as part of your house-training program. You can train the Wait cue at the same time you do this. The Wait cue means that your dog has to wait in place until you tell him to do something else, and it's a very handy behavior to help prevent your dog from bolting out the door. If you train Wait as you go inside and outside for all of your dog's potty breaks, you'll get in many repetitions, in

Your training program can be as flexible as you need it to be.

HOW SMART IS YOUR DOG?

Is a Border Collie smarter than an Airedale Terrier? Just how smart is your dog? There are many theories, but it's very difficult to get a consistent measurement of canine intelligence in the scientific community. Experts can't even decide on a consistent way to test human intelligence, and less study has been devoted to canines.

What does it take to prove intelligence, anyway? The ability to use tools? A great memory? The ability to solve problems? An IQ test? And do we bias any measurements by looking at the results through our human eyes rather than focusing on a different species?

You could argue that a Basset Hound that sits by the pantry door waiting for you to get his dinner is as smart as the Golden Retriever that figures out how to open the door himself. Maybe the Golden has more initiative, but the Basset knows that he's going to be waited upon!

In general, dogs are fairly smart creatures. According to psychologist and canine researcher Stanley Coren, PhD, a dog's mental abilities are equivalent to those of a two- to two-and-a-half-year-old human child. The average dog can learn approximately 165 words, including signals. Dogs can also learn how to count up to about five and understand errors in simple computations.

Just as with people, some individual dogs are going to be smarter than others. You may find that your dog has difficulty learning some behaviors, or you may find that you need to scramble to stay ahead of your dog!

short bursts, throughout the day. Before long, waiting at the door for you to tell him he can go through will become a habit for your dog.

Following House Rules

It's best to determine house rules before you bring your dog home because it can be very confusing for your dog if you teach him one set of actions and then decide later that they are unacceptable. What are your house rules? Do you want your dog on the furniture? In the bedroom at night? Is it OK if he jumps on you? Is it OK if he kisses your face? Where do you want him to eliminate? If you have other dogs in your home, how do you want him to interact with them? For example, if you have a senior dog and are bringing home a puppy, what will you consider acceptable behavior with your older dog?

Set some boundaries and train your dog to follow them. Be consistent. Make sure your family or roommates are on the same page, or it will be very difficult to train your dog. He won't understand if you don't let him up on the bed but your roommate does when you're out of town.

CHAPTER 2

UNDERSTANDING
HOW DOGS LEARN

Dogs are a different species than we are. Behavior that you find unacceptable in a person is often normal in canine terms. Imagine waking up one morning surrounded by people who use a language you don't understand and who have unfamiliar customs. You can learn the new language and what this community finds acceptable and unacceptable, but someone is going to have to teach you in terms that you can understand. This is your role with your dog.

Understanding Instincts

Dogs instinctively dig and jump and chase and bark and perform other behaviors typical of their species. These are normal dog behaviors. If you are taking a lovely stroll down the block and your dog sees a squirrel, he may instinctively bolt after it. This doesn't mean that you have to tolerate behaviors that you don't like, but it helps to understand what behaviors are normal for dogs.

Some breeds were purposely bred to do specific things. Some dogs were fine-tuned to chase livestock, while others were developed to follow scent. These behaviors are now ingrained in those breeds, so it's natural for them to do them. Your dog is not being stubborn or defiant if he's just answering to his DNA.

Feelings and Emotions

Anyone who has ever loved a dog will tell you that dogs have feeling and emotions, and a recent study has shown that dog lovers have been right all along. Gregory Berns, a professor of neuroeconomics at Emory University in Atlanta, Georgia, completed research demonstrating that dogs use the same area of the brain as humans do to feel. Berns found similarities in structure and function of a region of the brain called the caudate nucleus. In people, the caudate nucleus responds in anticipation of things that we enjoy, such as love, food, and money. In dogs, Berns's research found that the caudate nucleus responds to hand signals indicating food and to the smells of familiar humans. Preliminary tests also showed that the caudate nucleus reacted to the return of a dog's owner after the owner had momentarily stepped out of view.

What the study basically showed is that dogs have about the level of sentience as a human child, which is no surprise to anyone who has ever loved a dog. What else can you describe other than happiness when your dog greets you after an absence? If you've ever seen those heartwarming videos of servicemen and servicewomen returning from deployment to greet their ecstatic dogs, how could there be any doubt? If you've ever lost one dog of several, don't the others appear to mourn?

Dogs are feeling, emotional beings, whether or not science has caught up with what we know to be true.

This is important when it comes to choosing a training program. If dogs can feel, do you want to hurt them to train them? Of course not. And you don't have to—there are positive ways to train your dog to do what you want.

Breeds Make a Difference

Your dog's breed or mix of breeds will have an impact on his behavior. Humans have selectively bred dogs to perform different tasks over time, eventually coming up with defined breeds. There are hundreds of breeds of dog in the world. If you have a mixed-breed dog, you may have to take a guess at who his parents are if you don't get a chance to meet them. Sometimes, you can tell by looking at a dog, but you can also look at your dog's behavior.

If your purebred dog exhibits breed traits that you don't like, who can you blame? You're the one who chose the dog. This doesn't mean that you have to put up with excessive chasing or barking or hunting, but please don't get angry with your dog for doing what he was bred to do.

The American Kennel Club (AKC) puts dog breeds with similar traits together into groups. Let's take a look at some of the traits of these groups.

Pet parents know that dogs do have feelings and emotions.

Herding Breeds

Herding breeds were created to move livestock. There are some breeds that specialize in cattle, others sheep, and some multiple species. Some move livestock by barking at them, while others nip at their charges' heels. In essence, herding breeds are really good at chasing things and rounding them up. Often, people complain that their herding dog chases their children or the family cat.

Herding breeds are usually very agile and fast, and they do really well at speed sports, such as agility. They are often energetic dogs, and they do best when you give them healthy options for channeling that energy. Breeds in this group include the Collie, Corgi, Shetland Sheepdog, Australian Cattle Dog, and Puli.

Sporting Breeds

Sporting breeds were designed to work with hunters. Some flush game, some retrieve, and some point to where the game is hiding. Some excel at working in the water, and others are best in fields. Still others perform multiple tasks.

Sporting-breed dogs usually have a lot of energy, especially as puppies and adolescents. They generally work very well with people and are popular family dogs. Breeds in this category include the Labrador Retriever, English Setter, Golden Retriever, Portuguese Water Dog, and Brittany.

Hound Breeds

Hounds were bred to hunt. Some (such as the Basset Hound) specialize in following scent, and some (such as the Whippet) hunt by sight. These breeds are persistent and have stamina. Some also bay. Breeds in this category include the Greyhound, Bloodhound, Beagle, Irish Wolfhound, and Afghan Hound.

Terrier Breeds

Terriers were bred to hunt and kill vermin. They are persistent, with lots of energy, and can be feisty. Most have wiry coats that require special grooming, called stripping, to keep up their appearance. You may notice that your terrier likes to "kill" his toys by shaking them. Breeds in this category include the West Highland White Terrier, Parson Russell Terrier, Rat Terrier, Cairn Terrier, and Bull Terrier.

From left to right: West Highland White Terrier (Terrier Group); Siberian Husky (Working Group); Border Collie (Herding Group); Brittany (Sporting Group).

Toy Breeds

These little dogs were created to be companions. As a result, they are very attached to their people and often follow them everywhere. Their small size makes them ideal for apartment living, but don't bother telling a Toy breed dog that he is little. He won't believe you! Breeds in this category include the Papillon, Chihuahua, Maltese, Pomeranian, and Pug.

Working

Working dogs were bred to perform jobs, such as guarding property, pulling sleds, and other duties. Because all of the jobs vary, so do the individual dogs. In general, these dogs are usually strong and committed, and some are very large. Breeds in this category include the Siberian Husky, Saint Bernard, Great Pyrenees, Samoyed, and Great Dane.

Non-Sporting

The Non-Sporting Group is kind of a catchall for a variety of breeds, so the dogs in it are all across the map in terms of size and behavior traits. For example, the Shiba Inu is a small Japanese dog bred to hunt small wild game, boar, and bear. The Chow Chow is a medium-sized Chinese dog used for hunting, protection, pulling, and herding. Other breeds in this category include the Schipperke, Bichon Frise, and Poodle.

Miscellaneous

The AKC also has a Miscellaneous Class. This group is for purebred dogs that are "on deck" for admission to the rosters in a regular group. In order to graduate to a regular class, breeds must have an active parent club and "serious and expanding breeding activity over a wide geographic area." These breeds may already be recognized in other countries; there are many breeds active in other countries that aren't yet AKC-registered, possibly because they are not as popular in the United States as they are in other countries.

From left to right: Greyhound (Hound Group-Sighthound); Basset Hound (Hound Group-Scenthound); Pug (Toy Group); Bichon Frise (Non-Sporting Group).

Puppy Development

AGE	DEVELOPMENT
Newborn	Puppies are born without teeth. They are blind and deaf, and they can't regulate their body temperatures. They can only pee and poop when their mother stimulates them. They do have a sense of smell and touch.
Birth to 2 Weeks	Puppies are sleeping most of the time. Their legs can't yet support their weight, but they can move by paddling and crawling.
2–4 Weeks	Eyes and ears start to open. Puppies start to stand and take their first real steps. They start to gain a little independence from their mother. They play with their littermates. Their baby teeth start to come in. They also start moving away from their sleeping area to eliminate.
4–12 Weeks	Puppies start weaning from their mother at about four weeks. They are deep in their socialization period, learning good and bad things about everything around them.

Understanding Puppy Development

Puppies are learning soon after birth, so it's important to understand what goes on during those critical first weeks of life.

Puppies learn so many lessons from their mothers and siblings. Mothers have to lick puppies in order for them to urinate and defecate, and they also lick the pups clean afterward. This is how puppies learn to stay clean. If they don't have this experience with Mom because they are removed from her too soon, they may have trouble learning house-training later; this is often a challenge with puppies bought from pet stores.

Puppies learn bite inhibition, meaning not to bite down too hard, from playing with their siblings. When puppies play, if one chomps down too hard on another, the recipient will yip or snap and stop playtime. The chomping puppy doesn't want to stop playing, so he learns to lessen the intensity of his bite. Puppies learn bite inhibition from their mother, too, especially as she wants to start weaning them. Puppies also learn to share with their littermates. They learn about competition for resources, such as toys or their mom's milk. These are important social lessons that are critical at this age, which is why it's important not to take puppies away from their families too soon. Good breeders and rescue organizations will keep puppies with their families for at least eight weeks.

When a mother dog has only one puppy in the litter, called a singleton, he is at a disadvantage. He may not learn bite inhibition very well because he doesn't have brothers or sisters to teach him when he bites too hard. This could prove to be a problem for you because the pup could be very mouthy. He also never has to share or compete for anything, so he may find it very frustrating when he suddenly doesn't get everything he wants when he comes to your home. You will need to spend extra effort in training a singleton puppy.

Some people want to get two littermates or young puppies at the same time. This is certainly appealing, because the puppies will spend a lot of time together and be playmates, but it can cause several problems. Puppies raised together can become overly dependent on each other because they spend all of their time together, especially if they are crated together, so they never learn to be alone. Then, when one of them has to go to the veterinarian or gets to go somewhere without the other, the puppy left behind becomes traumatized. Too much dependence is not healthy.

Another challenge of raising littermates is that, because they spend so much time together, they bond more closely with each other than with you or other members of your family. Dogs bond most closely with whomever they spend the most time in positive experiences. During the critical socialization window, if a puppy spends the majority of his time with another puppy, then that's who he'll bond with. You'll likely find that they don't listen to you, especially as they mature, which will make training them a greater challenge.

Some littermates also can develop aggression toward each other as they get older. Sometimes, aggression may develop to the point where it is not healthy or safe to keep both pups together any longer, which is heartbreaking.

Raising littermates or young puppies together can be done, but it requires a lot of extra work and dedication. You will need to ensure that each puppy has his own crate and own bowl. You must separate them daily for individual bonding time with you and other members of your family. You'll need to train them individually and take turns taking each one on trips and adventures. With all that you need to do to raise a puppy right, the extra effort may prove to be a greater challenge than you are prepared to tackle. This is why so many professional trainers do not recommend getting littermates.

A Long Way from Wolves

In the past, common theory was that dogs evolved from wolves. Modern research has shed some doubt on this. The more we learn about dogs, the more we realize that their past may not be as closely aligned with wolves as previously thought.

Puppies learn bite inhibition from playing with their siblings.

Whether dogs started out as wolves or not, they are now a long, long way from *Canis lupus.* Can you imagine a pack of Pugs taking down a caribou? Not likely. Humans have shaped dogs, for better or worse, into the domestic animal we know and love today.

Why is this important to understand? Because if you think that your dog is behaving like a wolf, and you try and respond accordingly, you will be way off base. Wolves are pack animals. A pack has a nuclear family consisting of a breeding pair and its offspring. Males take part in raising the young. There is generally a hierarchy, from an "alpha" male and female at the top to the lowest "omega."

Experts used to think that dogs were pack animals, but as they study village dogs all over the world, they are starting to realize that this is not likely the case. Village dogs are dogs that may have once been owned by people but came to be strays, or they are descendants of previously owned dogs. They sometimes are claimed by local people who feed them on occasion, but they are not in-home pets like the dog that you've brought home.

Such dogs have fallen into a natural state, living near dumps and in cities where they forage for food. They don't form packs. Instead, they form transitional acquaintances, sometimes teaming up with one or two other dogs for a brief period of time and then moving on. Males do not help in rearing pups. The village dogs do not team up to hunt together. Instead, they are mainly scavengers. It is not in the best interest of a scavenger to team up with buddies.

People who try to treat their dogs like wolves are barking up the wrong tree. For example, your dog growls at you when you reach for his collar, so you assume that he is jockeying for an alpha position. You flip him upside down in an "alpha roll" and hold him until he stops struggling. Big mistake. A dog may growl at a collar grab because the gesture has been

Unlike domesticated dogs, wolves are pack animals.

associated as a negative experience or because he is afraid. Now that you've forced your dog into a frightening position and held him there, you've convinced him that he was right all along! Hands around his head are now really scary to him. Your dog may growl at you sooner next time. What you thought was a play for rank was really something else altogether, and now you have a worse problem on your hands.

Your dog knows that you're not a wolf or another dog. You don't look or smell a thing like a dog, so trying to act like one will just confuse or startle him. Your dog won't understand any message that you're trying to convey, and you could create some serious problems in the delivery.

THE DOG FAMILY TREE

It used to be common theory that primitive humans took wolf cubs into their families and raised them. This led to the domestication of the wolf, which evolved into the dog that we know today.

Modern scientists dispute this theory. It's exhausting to raise domestic puppies properly. How could primitive families find it easy to raise wolf cubs, who are not naturally social with man? Weren't these families busy trying to survive from day to day? Wolves are naturally fearful of man, are extremely challenging to confine, and can be very dangerous, especially during mating season. It does seem unlikely that wolf cubs fit naturally into the ancient family unit.

Biologist Ray Coppinger believes that wolves domesticated themselves at the end of the last Ice Age, when people started forming settlements. Villages created garbage, which the wolves would then scavenge. The wolves with the least "flight distance"—the ones who stayed the closest to the villages without running off in alarm—survived, and they passed on the trait to their descendants.

Recent studies of wolf and dog genomes show that wolves are more closely related to each other than dogs. This suggests that modern dogs and gray wolves descended from an older, common ancestor.

As more studies unfold, no doubt we will learn more about our canine friend's family tree!

Early Training and Socialization Benefits

The sooner you can start training a dog, the better. You'll stop bad habits from developing and becoming ingrained. If you properly socialize a puppy during his critical socialization period (up until about sixteen weeks of age), you'll help prevent serious behavior issues later.

You can start training your puppy as soon as you bring him home. This goes for adolescent and adult dogs, too. It's never too late to start training a dog. Some people worry that their puppies are too young to start or that their adult dogs are too old. Neither is the case.

It is true that your puppy may not be able to attend a group class until all of his vaccinations are complete, depending on the class. But you don't have to wait for a class—start training him at home. Puppies are clean slates, and they tend to learn fairly quickly. Older dogs are not too far behind, however. They may already have some habits that you want to fix, but they also have much better attention spans than easily distracted puppies. Once you teach your older dog how much fun positive training can be, he'll become a stellar student.

CHAPTER 3

COMMUNICATING
WITH YOUR DOG

In order to train your dog successfully, you need to communicate with him. Sounds easy, but it's not always easy to communicate with animals that don't think like we do.

The most common problems between dogs and humans are based on poor communication. You want Fido off the couch, but he thinks that the couch is a convenient perch for looking out the window. You want him to potty outside, but he thinks that you let him outside to chase squirrels. You expect one thing to happen, but your dog may have a completely different idea.

You may think that what you're telling your dog is crystal clear, but it's likely he doesn't have a clue what you're saying. Dogs don't speak English. They can learn your words, but you have to teach them. You need to communicate to him in terms that he can understand. So, if you say, "Fido, Come!" and he doesn't run to you, it's not surprising. Repeating the cue over and over again won't help him learn it any faster. Saying it louder or in a stern voice won't help, either. He can hear you, but he just doesn't understand what you're saying. You have to train him to understand what "Fido, Come!" means. This book will help you!

You do not need to yell at your dog or use a mean tone of voice for him to perform. Who wants to have to yell at their dog all the time? It's just not necessary, especially if you use positive methods to train. You could whisper the cues and he would respond happily.

Get the Behavior First and then Add the Cue

Since dogs don't understand your verbal language, it's more effective in training to get your dog to do the behavior first, before putting a verbal label on it. If you try to teach

Your dog may be able to hear you, but that doesn't mean that he understands what you are saying.

your dog a verbal cue when you are first training a behavior, it just clutters the situation and can confuse your dog. You're going to want to talk to your dog—it's a human thing to want to do! Just remember that your words mean very little to your dog until you teach him.

Once a behavior is reliable, then you'll attach a cue to it. It will take many repetitions for your dog to understand that when he hears a cue, he should perform a behavior. It's harder for dogs to learn verbal signals, so it will take him a while to connect them to the correct behaviors. This doesn't mean that you should run boring, repetitive drills when training. Training sessions should be very short—only a few minutes at a time. You want to leave your dog wanting more, not bore him so he loses interest.

Using Effective Cues

To get the best results, here are some things to keep in mind when communicating with your dog:

- Keep cues short, and they will be easier for your dog to understand. Saying, "Come!" is more effective than saying, "Come over here!"
- Use one cue to mean one action. If you use the cue Down when you want your dog to stop jumping on you, don't also use Down to tell him to lie down on the ground. This is too confusing for your dog. How is he supposed to know which Down you mean?
- Be consistent with your cues. If you say, "Come!" once, and then, "Come here!" another time, and later "Come on!", you will just make it harder for your dog to learn what you want. Pick one cue for each specific action. Make sure that everyone who interacts with your dog, such as other family members, uses the same cues.
- Use a friendly voice. Some people make the mistake of delivering every cue in a stern "no-nonsense" voice, but this is not necessary and can even make it harder to train a shy or fearful dog. Dogs don't understand your language, but they do understand your tone. If you say all of your cues in a stern voice, your dog could interpret it to mean that you are unhappy with him. Even happy, bouncy dogs don't need you to sound like a military drill instructor. Save your stern voice

Be consistent with your cues.

What a Dog Says

DOG VOCALIZATIONS CAN MEAN DIFFERENT THINGS

Whine—Whining could mean excitement, stress, or fear.

Bark—Dogs bark because they're bored, excited, afraid, or alert to something. Dogs bark when they want something. They bark to get attention, and they bark when they want something scary to go away. Some breeds, such as the Miniature Schnauzer and Shetland Sheepdog, tend to bark more than others. Other breeds, such as the Basenji, don't bark at all.

Growl—Dogs growl when they are playing, stressed, or angry. If your dog is playing, and he growls, it's normally nothing to be concerned about. If your dog growls over food or toys, or at other dogs and people, it's best to get professional help. What you don't want to do is punish him for growling! A growl is communication—the dog is telling you something important. Punishing him for growling will just make him stop warning you—it won't get rid of the problem. You want a dog to warn you before he feels the need to bite!

for when your dog is doing something really bad … and if you train your dog, those times will be few and far between!

It's sometimes helpful to use your dog's name right before a cue, such as "Fido, Sit" or "Fido, Down." It can be especially good if you have more than one dog and need to get an individual dog's attention. Keep in mind, however, that if you don't assign a behavior to the dog's name, then the name itself doesn't mean anything other than to get the dog's attention and indicate that you are talking to him.

For example, in the pet-supply store, you see a frazzled-looking woman with a bouncy Boxer puppy lunging at the end of his leash. She yells, "Buster! Buster! Buster! BUSTER! BUSTER!!" This is just a name, not an action. What does she want the dog to *do*? If she hasn't trained the dog specifically to do something at the sound of his name, then repeating it over and over again isn't helpful or communicative.

Now, say, for example, that the owner had taught Buster that when he hears his name, he should look at her. That would be a good way to get the puppy's attention, and saying his name would mean something to him.

When you say a cue, try to say it one time only. Repeating it won't help your dog perform the cue any faster, and you'll just be teaching him that you're going to say something a dozen times before you expect him to respond. This can be a very hard habit for people to break. If you want your dog to respond the first time that you cue him to do something, you have to cue the behavior just one time.

The Body Tells the Tale

If you really want to better understand what your dog is saying to you, his body language will tell you just about everything. Dogs have an intricate, expansive vocabulary of body language; it's how they communicate best with each other. Dogs know a friendly dog by what he does, what he looks like, and how he acts. They also recognize a hostile dog in the same way. Dogs show that they are afraid by their body language. By communicating with body language, a dog can diffuse a potentially tense situation and avoid fights. By better understanding a dog's body language, you will better understand your dog.

Ears

When a dog's ears lay flat, it can indicate fear. Ears forward indicate interest or excitement. Note that some dogs have ears that don't allow them to show a lot of expression. For example, Cocker Spaniels have beautiful, long ears that naturally lay flat and won't stand erect.

Eyes

A soft, sweet expression indicates friendliness or contentment. Your dog's eyes might even squint. If your dog looks at you with a friendly or alert expression, it's perfectly fine. Some people worry that if a dog looks them in the eyes, it's a challenge or the dog is trying to assert himself. Hardly! Your dog is likely just making a friendly connection or trying to read your own expression. Eye contact *is* a sign of confidence, which is not the same thing as defiance. This is why shy or nervous dogs will often look away from you.

A soft, sweet expression in your dog's eyes indicates friendliness or contentment.

Mouth

Some dogs smile, and it's exactly what you think it is—a sign of happiness. A tense, closed mouth is a sign of stress. The lips may be pulled back at the corners. Depending on the context, panting can indicate stress. A dog that has been running will pant, and it doesn't mean that he's upset, but a dog that's afraid of thunderstorms will often pant as the storm begins. Dogs may pant if they are in pain. Also, if a dog is panting and closes his mouth, it can indicate increased stress. For example, if a dog is panting at the veterinarian's office and he suddenly stops when the veterinary technician approaches with a thermometer, the dog's stress has just increased.

When a dog is warning you or another animal to stay away, his lips may move forward over his teeth so that they look puffy. His lips can also curl up in a snarl and retract to expose his teeth; this may be accompanied by a growl. This is different from a submissive grin, which is often mistaken for a snarl. In a submissive grin, the dog's lips pull up vertically to expose the front teeth. It's almost always accompanied by a submissive body posture—curved body; low, wagging tail; frequent looking away; and squinty eyes.

Tail

A tail tucked under is an indication of fear. A wagging tail is often mistaken for a sign of friendliness, but this could be a serious mistake. Just because a dog is wagging his tail doesn't mean that he is social or that he wants you to pet him. A tail that is very low and wagging rapidly can indicate stress or fear, and it can also indicate excitement. A tail that is held very high and wagging indicates high arousal. The dog could be excited to greet you, or he could be getting agitated and contemplating lunging or even biting. In general, a mid-level or low, swishy tail wag is a sign of happiness or friendliness. Some dogs get so happy and excited that their tails go around in big circles.

Did You Know?

CURLY TAILS

Not every dog will display a wide range of communication with his tail. Some dogs have tightly curled tails that don't often move out of position, no matter what they're feeling.

Overall Body Posture

A dog's overall body posture can tell you a lot about his intentions and what he is feeling. A dog that puts most of his weight on his hindquarters is trying to increase distance between himself and something. He could be unsure or afraid. When his weight is balanced forward, he's trying to decrease distance. He is interested or eager. For example, a puppy who is unsure of a tall man may lean backward, away from the man. When he decides that the man is OK, he will lean or move toward him. If a dog is conflicted, he'll shift his weight back and forth. He could be afraid yet interested at the same time.

A curved body posture indicates friendliness or appeasement. Some dogs seem to wiggle and wag with their entire bodies! When a dog lifts his paw, it also indicates appeasement and could be an invitation to play. When a dog lowers his head and bends his elbows, but his rear remains up, this is called a play bow. It's an invitation to play and a way for a dog to indicate that he is not a threat.

When a dog lowers his head, stiffens his body, and affixes a hard-staring "lock and load" expression, his intent is to threaten. It doesn't necessarily mean that the dog will bite, but he is definitely telling you to go away. If pressed, he could escalate to a bite. You may see the fur on the back of his neck or all down his back rise up. This is called "piloerection."

Signs of Stress

Just as a dog's body language will tell you whether he's happy or aggressive, it will also tell you if he's stressed or afraid. These are important signals to learn. If your dog is showing signs that he is nervous or fearful while you are training, for example, you'll need to stop your training session and address your dog's distress. It's much harder for a dog to learn when he is upset. Imagine trying to learn a complicated math equation if you were afraid—it would be challenging! If you want your training sessions to be successful, learn the canine signs of stress so that you can monitor your dog's emotional state. Stress signals are also critical to learn when you are socializing a young puppy as well as to help your dog throughout his life.

This is a play bow.

If your dog displays one or two of the following behaviors, it doesn't necessarily mean that he is stressed or fearful. Take account of his body language as a whole, and consider the context. For example, if you take your dog into a pet-supply store and he yawns a bit and licks his lips, but he is stepping brightly and pulling you to explore, he likely is excited. But if he yawns, licks his lips, tucks his tail, and cowers and presses against you, then he is stressed.

Here are signs of stress to look for:

- Licking lips
- Yawning
- Cowering
- Quivering, trembling
- Whining
- Shaking off (similar to what dogs do when they are wet, but in this case they are dry)
- Tucking tail
- Turning away, avoiding, trying to get away
- Flattening ears
- Wet pawprints (dogs sweat through their pawpads)

Yawning can be a sign of stress.

Sometimes a dog will display a behavior out of context. It's a normal behavior, but it's odd for the situation. This is called a "displacement signal" or "cutoff signal" and can indicate stress. For example, your friend brings her new puppy over to meet your dog. As the puppy comes into the house, your dog rushes over to greet him. The puppy suddenly starts sniffing the floor. It's not unusual for a puppy to sniff at a floor, but it does seem an odd priority with another dog barreling into his personal space. The sniffing is a displacement signal. The puppy could be signaling to your dog that he is not a threat by avoiding direct eye contact. He could also be indicating he is stressed at your dog's boisterous greeting.

Your Body Language

Just as your dog communicates with you using body language, your body language sends communication signals to your dog. Sometimes, you could be sending messages that you don't really mean. For example, if you bend or loom over a dog, you could unwittingly intimidate him. Some dogs won't mind it at all, but sensitive or fearful dogs could be frightened.

Your body language affects your training. If you bend over at the waist and call your dog to come to you, he may come but sit at a distance from you so that you are not looming over him. If you bend at the knees and crouch down to call him, he may come more enthusiastically because you have lowered your body and are less intimidating.

When you are angry or upset, your body language changes. Always be sure that you are in a good mood and full of patience when you train your dog; otherwise, he will sense when you are upset. Your body will be stiffer, your hands may clench, your jaw might tighten, your voice may sound different. You may think that you're acting the same as you usually do, but your dog is very perceptive and will notice even the slightest change. Your dog may be less likely to respond to your cues when you are tense or upset. He may even start bouncing around and acting silly, trying to reduce the tension! This will likely just make you tenser, so it ends up being a frustrating training session.

Staring a dog in the eyes intently is very assertive, and some dogs may find it a challenge. This can be especially troublesome with children. Some children like to cradle a dog's face, get close, and stare into in his eyes. They mean it affectionately, but do not allow this! While some dogs will tolerate this, others will not. And in this position, the dog's proximity to a child's face is extremely dangerous. Even if your dog doesn't mind, children don't often understand that what one dog likes, another dog will not. So if your child should try to get too close to a dog that is less tolerant, there could be a tragedy.

Your body language changes when you are angry or upset.

Hands Over Words

Because dogs are so in tune to body language, it is easy to teach them hand signals. It's easier for them to learn hand signals or other physical cues than it is for them to grasp verbal cues. They can learn verbal cues, of course, but it just takes a bit longer.

It's important to be consistent when you use hand signals or other physical cues with your dog, just as with other aspects of dog training. If you motion downward with your hand pointed when teaching your dog to Down, but then one day you keep your hand by your side, your dog may not respond. He's not being defiant, he's just confused. He's learned that your hand pointing downward means you want him to lie down, and you didn't make that motion. This doesn't mean that you always have to make exaggerated hand signals in order for your dog to perform. You can "fade" hand signals to make them smaller, you just have to do it gradually.

A Dog's Senses

A dog's senses are much more acute than a human's. That's why your dog is so good at reading your body language. It also explains why dogs can be distracted during training, or when you take them for walks, or in new locations. They can perceive things that you can't!

The All-Knowing Nose

A dog's sense of smell is uncanny. Scientists have not been able to pinpoint exactly how powerful it is, but they estimate that it is 10,000 to 100,000 times more acute than ours. Dogs have up to 300 million olfactory (scent) receptors in their noses. We have about six million. Dogs also have a significantly large part of their brains dedicated to analyzing smells—about 40

It's easier for dogs to learn hand signals than verbal cues.

percent more than we do.

When we inhale, we smell and breathe through the same pathways in our noses. When dogs inhale, a fold of tissue within their noses separates the air into two pathways: one is for smelling, and the other is for breathing. Researchers have determined that about 12 percent of the air goes to a recessed part in the back of the dog's nose that is dedicated to smelling. The rest goes into the lungs.

Did You Know?

THERE'S MORE TO A NOSE WIGGLE THAN MEETS THE EYE

A cool thing that dogs can do that we can't is wiggle their nostrils independently of each other. The aerodynamic reach of each nostril is smaller than the distance between the nostrils. What this means is that a dog can tell which nostril an odor enters, which helps him track scent.

When we exhale, we send air out the way it came in—through a single pathway. When dogs exhale, the air goes through slits in the sides of their noses. When this air rushes out, it swirls new odors into the dog's nose. It also lets a dog sniff almost continuously.

As if this wasn't enough to make them superb smelling machines, dogs have a part of anatomy that we don't. It's called the Jacobson's organ. It's at the bottom of the dog's nasal passage, and it senses pheromones, which are the chemicals that animals produce to attract other animals, especially their mates. The pheromone molecules that the Jacobson's organ detects don't mix with the other odor molecules. The Jacobson's organ has its own nerves, which lead to the part of the brain that is dedicated to analyzing pheromones.

It's no wonder that dogs are so distracted by smells! They're very good at smelling because of

Dogs have far superior scenting ability than we do.

their anatomy. Some breeds and individual dogs are better at scenting than others, but all dogs have far superior scenting ability than we do. Dogs excel at scent sports, such as tracking and K9 Nose Work®. They also serve people by working in search and rescue, cadaver detection, and more. Some have been trained to detect termites, bed bugs, and even cancer by scent.

The Eyes: Not Just Black and White

We used to think that dogs could see in only black and white, but recent research indicates otherwise. Dogs may actually have some color vision. How an eye perceives color is based on the presence of cone photoreceptors in the eye's retina. The cone photoreceptors work in bright light. The central region of a human's retina consists of 100 percent cone photoreceptors, while only about 20 percent of the photoreceptors in the same region in dogs are cone photoreceptors. So while we're able to see a broad range of colors, dogs can see only a few. Researchers have conducted behavioral tests in dogs indicating that dogs can tell the difference between red and blue but have difficulty telling the difference between red and green.

Dogs can hear sounds at significantly higher frequencies than we can.

Where eyes are placed on the head determines what kind of peripheral vision an animal has, as well as the size of the visual field that the two eyes can see at one time. Dogs' eyes are on the sides of their heads, which means that they have a visual field of 240 degrees, whereas humans have a visual field of 200 degrees.

Binocular vision is used to judge distances. Dogs have about half of the binocular vision as humans do. Thus, dogs have better peripheral vision than we do, but they need to be closer to objects than we do to see them clearly.

What Can Dogs Hear?

Puppies are born deaf. Their ears don't open until they are about two weeks old. Some dogs have floppy ears, either short or long. Some have prick ears. No matter what shape or size, there are about eighteen muscles in the ear that move it in different directions to help a dog hear sound. Dogs' ears can move independently of each other.

Dogs can hear sounds at significantly higher frequencies than we can.

A dog's ear canal is different from a human's. People have ear canals that are horizontal to the ear drum. In dogs, the ear canal is L-shaped. It's vertical toward the jaw, and then it takes about a 90-degree turn horizontally near the ear drum. This shape makes the ear canal difficult to examine without special equipment. It also makes the ear a host for bacterial and yeast infections, especially in drop-eared dogs, where the ear flap covering the ear canal provides a moist environment.

Taste and Touch

Dogs do not have as many taste buds as we do, which means that they can't taste the range of flavors that we can. This may explain why some dogs appear to eat anything! Dogs can taste sweet, salty, sour, and bitter tastes, but they smell more than they taste. Their powerful sense of smell compensates a bit for their lack of taste buds.

Dogs do have a great sense of touch. Mothers immediately lick their newborns, and very young puppies huddle together for warmth. They have touch-sensitive hairs, called vibrissae, above the eyes, on the muzzle, and below the jaw. The vibrissae can detect air flow. A dog's entire body, including his paws, has touch-sensitive nerve endings.

Just because a dog can feel touch doesn't mean that he finds all petting pleasurable. Individual dogs can develop individual preferences. For example, one dog may love having you scratch behind his ears while another will maneuver himself so you scratch his rear. Some dogs don't really enjoy petting at all. They may not have been conditioned to find it a positive experience as puppies, or it may just be a personal preference.

CHAPTER 4

ACCENTUATE THE POSITIVE!

Positive training based in science is powerfully successful. It works with all types of dogs, even those considered "stubborn" or "challenging." It works great with fearful and shy dogs. It also works with big dogs, little dogs, puppies, seniors, bouncy dogs, and couch potatoes—this is because it follows the fundamental laws of learning. You can train any species using positive training. Many wild animal trainers use positive training to get large, potentially dangerous animals to perform behaviors. If they can train elephants to willingly offer their feet for care, or if they can train tigers to sit patiently for blood draws, then you can train your dog without using force or intimidation.

Here are some benefits to using positive training:

- You don't have to rely on physical strength to train your dog. It doesn't require you to muscle your dog into position or push or pull him to do what you want. It opens up training to a much broader range of people with different physical capabilities and enables them to train bigger dogs, too. It also means that your kids can train your dog (with supervision).
- It's efficient. With positive training, sessions are very short. A couple of minutes are all you need for one session. Short sessions work best for dogs, especially young puppies with short attention spans! It's also great for anyone with a busy schedule. You can always squeeze a couple of minutes in, and if you do that a few times a day, you'll see great progress.
- It gets fast results. Your dog will look forward to your training sessions and be more engaged with you, so you'll be able to teach him faster.
- You'll get your dog to want to work for you, rather than be afraid to disobey you. This forges a strong relationship.
- It's fun! Training your dog doesn't have to be a chore. By using positive methods, you and your dog will both enjoy the learning experience.

Just because you use positive methods to train does not mean that you let your dog get away with whatever he wants. "Positive" does not mean "permissive." You should establish rules and boundaries for your dog. You should have realistic expectations for his behavior and train him to work within those guidelines. You can absolutely do this and still train positively. You don't have to be mean to your dog to teach him what you want him to learn.

Did You Know?

THE PENALTIES OF PUNISHMENT

The laws of learning state that a behavior that is punished reduces in frequency. Punishment in training can work. The catch is, it can come with a lot of baggage. By using harsh, physical techniques to train your dog, you could create more problems than you're trying to solve. For example, if you spank your dog for chewing on your shoe, he could start taking your shoes and hiding from you to chew them. You still end up with chewed shoes, except now it's harder to catch your dog in the act. Or, he could get really frightened and start growling at you. Now you have an aggression problem, which is much worse—and harder to fix—than a chewed shoe.

Another problem with punishment is that it doesn't teach your dog what you want him to do—only that you don't like what he's doing. For example, spanking your dog for chewing on your shoe doesn't teach him that you want him to chew on his chew toys. So how is he supposed to learn what to do? You have to train him. It would be more effective to use a Leave It cue to get him to drop the shoe, and then give him one of his toys and praise him for chewing on that instead. You still get him to do what you want, and you avoid the potential negative side effects!

Understanding the Scientific Principles of Training

The positive training methods in this guide are based in science. They are based on learning theory from the works of psychologists, behaviorists, and more. If you've ever taken a psychology class, these principles may be familiar to you. Because these methods are based in science, they have held up time and time again to scientific scrutiny. They work. They work on any animal with a nervous system.

Scientists have used these training methods with laboratory animals—if an animal performs a task correctly, he gets a piece of food. The animal begins to perform the task correctly more frequently.

Wild animal and marine mammal trainers use these techniques. They teach performance behaviors, but, more and more, they are also training animals to perform husbandry behaviors that make it easier to care for the animals and attend to their medical care. Examples include teaching a whale to roll to an upside-down position so a technician can perform an ultrasound, teaching a wolf to hold still to receive treatment on an infected ear, and teaching a gorilla to willingly hold out an arm for an insulin shot.

Pet owners use these techniques as well. They work on birds, horses, dogs … and even cats. While there is a lot of science related to canine behavior, you primarily need to understand classical and operant conditioning to train your dog.

Classical Conditioning

Classical conditioning is the process of associating a neutral stimulus with an involuntary response until the stimulus triggers the response. A neutral stimulus is something that doesn't mean anything. The dog does not associate anything with it. An involuntary response is something that an animal does naturally, without thinking. For example, if a dog sees food, he will start to salivate. This is an involuntary response. The dog doesn't think about salivating, he just does it.

Ivan Pavlov, a Russian physiologist, was the first to note the phenomenon of classical conditioning. He was studying digestion in dogs when he discovered that the dogs would start to salivate when his assistant entered the room. The dogs hadn't been given food at that point, but they were still salivating. He theorized that salivation had become a learned response rather than an involuntary one. The dogs were salivating when they saw the assistant, with whom they had come to be associate food.

Pavlov then experimented with other neutral stimuli. He would activate a metronome right before presenting food to the dogs. The metronome meant nothing to the dogs, but after several repetitions of sounding the metronome right before the dogs received food, the dogs began to salivate at the sound of the metronome. The dogs had learned that the sound of the metronome meant that food was coming. The stimulus was no longer neutral; it became what's called a "conditioned stimulus." The conditioned stimulus now produced a "conditioned response"—the salivation.

You've probably done a lot of classical conditioning without even realizing it. The first time your dog saw a leash, it didn't mean anything to him. He may have sniffed it or been curious about it, but he was just investigating it. It was a neutral stimulus. Separately, your dog would get excited when you took him outside for a walk. His excitement was an involuntary response.

Many marine-animal trainers use positive training methods.

After you took him out on his leash several times, the association with that leash changed. After time, when he saw the leash, he may have bounced with excitement or started barking. He came to associate the leash with walks. The leash was now a conditioned stimulus, and his excitement was now a conditioned response to seeing the leash. The leash meant walks!

Operant Conditioning

Operant conditioning is the process of changing an animal's response to a certain stimulus by manipulating the consequences that follow right after the response. Behavior is either rewarded or punished. Behavior that is rewarded increases in frequency. Behavior that is punished decreases in frequency.

There are four main quadrants of operant conditioning: positive reinforcement, positive punishment, negative reinforcement, and negative punishment. As these are scientific terms, there are specific meanings to the words "positive" and "negative." In this case, they don't mean "good" and "bad." Instead, "positive" means "to add" and "negative" means "to take away."

- **Positive Reinforcement**—Something favorable is added after a behavior, which causes the behavior to increase. If you call your dog to come to you, and you give him a treat when he does, he's likely to come to you again when you call him. An example with people would be that if you finish a project at work, and your boss gives you a bonus, you're likely to finish more projects.

- **Positive Punishment**—Something unpleasant is added after a behavior, which causes the behavior to decrease. If you call your dog to you and, when he comes, you yell at him or plunk him in the bathtub when he hates baths, he is less likely to come to you when you call again. Likewise, if you stay late to finish a project at work, and your boss yells at you for incurring overtime, you are less likely to stay late to work on projects in the future.

- **Negative Reinforcement**—Something unpleasant is removed after a behavior, which makes the behavior increase. If your dog has a thorn in his paw, and you call him to come to you and then remove the thorn, making his paw less painful, he is more likely to come to you when you call again. If your boss constantly yells at you until you finish a project, you are more likely to finish projects quickly in the future.

- **Negative Punishment**—Something pleasant is removed after a behavior, and the behavior decreases. If your dog is happily chewing on a bone, and you call him to come to you and then take the bone away, he is less likely to come to you when you call again. If you are late turning in a project at work, and your boss docks your pay, you are less likely to be late with your project next time.

Reinforcement, whether it's added or taken away (positive or negative), always *increases* behavior. Punishment, whether it's added or taken away (positive or negative), always *decreases* behavior.

Positive training generally makes the most use of two of these four quadrants—positive reinforcement and negative punishment. If a dog performs a behavior you like, and you want it to increase in frequency, you reward it—positive reinforcement. For example, every time your dog sits, you pet him, so he starts to sit more often. You've given him attention for sitting, which is rewarding to him.

If the dog does something you don't like, and you want it decrease in frequency, you can take away a reward and the behavior will decrease—negative punishment. For example, if your dog jumps on you and you ignore him completely, giving him absolutely no attention, he stops jumping on you. You've taken away your attention, so the behavior is no longer rewarding to him.

Training Behaviors Step-by-Step

A cue is the word or physical signal you will use in order to ask the dog to perform the behavior. To get a dog to perform a behavior when you cue him, you first have to teach the behavior. There are certain general steps to follow when getting a dog to perform a behavior reliably.

Step 1: Get the Behavior

There are many positive ways to get a dog to perform a behavior, including luring/targeting, shaping, capturing, and modeling.

Luring/Targeting

Luring and targeting are hands-off methods of guiding a dog through a behavior. For example, you may use a treat in your hand to lure a dog to lie down. As you lower the treat, he lowers his nose to follow it, and then his body follows. Or, you may teach a dog to touch his nose to your hand, making your hand a target. You can then teach your dog to come to you, get on and off the furniture, and get in and out of the car by following your hand target.

You can use a treat in your hand to lure a dog to lie down.

Luring and targeting are probably the most frequently used techniques to get behavior. They can also be the fastest, depending on the behavior and the dog. They work very well for most dogs.

In order for luring to work, the lure has to be very interesting to the dog. If you use a boring lure, the dog won't follow it. So if you try luring your dog during a training session, and he keeps giving up after a few sniffs or ignores you altogether, it's time to find a more tempting lure.

In lure training, it's important to lose the lure very quickly, or you and your dog can become dependent on the lure. For example, after you successfully lure your dog with a treat to lie down three times, you will try it without holding a treat in your hand. You'll hold your hand in the same manner as you did before, as if you were still holding a treat. Pretend that you still have the treat in your hand and use your empty hand to lure the dog the same way you did before. Your dog should follow your empty hand into the down position. Once the dog lies down, you will "mark" the behavior (with a click or verbal marker, which are discussed later in this chapter) and *then* give him a treat. This treat is his reward for performing the behavior. You'll lose the lure long before you wean your dog off of rewards.

This isn't a tactic to fool your dog. Dogs have an incredible sense of smell. Your dog knows that there's no treat in your hand. What he is learning is your hand signal. By moving your hand downward, you're actually teaching your dog a hand signal.

If you keep a treat in your hand every single time you ask your dog to Down, he will learn that he should lie down only when you have a treat in your hand. Some owners stay dependent on luring with treats because they are concerned that their dogs won't pay attention to them unless they have treats in their hands. If you keep a treat in your hand too long with luring, this concern could come true! Be sure to lose the treat quickly when luring.

Shaping

Shaping involves building behavior by reinforcing progressive parts of the behavior. For example, if you were shaping the cue Settle on your dog's bed, you would first reinforce the dog for looking at his bed, then for moving toward his bed, then for sniffing his bed, then for putting one paw on the bed, then for putting two paws on the bed, then for putting three or four paws on the bed, and finally for lying down on the bed. The goal behavior is for the dog to move toward the bed and lie down on it. In shaping, you reinforce all of the little parts of that behavior that build up to your goal behavior.

You can use shaping to teach your dog the Settle cue.

Shaping has many benefits. It teaches a dog to really pay attention to your marker (a click or verbal marker) so he knows what behavior you are rewarding. Dogs also seem to retain shaped behaviors longer, maybe because they have to figure out the process. For example, have you ever had someone drive

THE TEN RULES OF SHAPING

Karen Pryor, one of the founders of clicker training, offers ten rules of shaping in her book *Don't Shoot the Dog.*

1. Raise criteria in increments small enough so that the subject always has a realistic chance of reinforcement.

2. Train one aspect of any particular behavior at a time. Don't try to shape for two criteria simultaneously.

3. During shaping, put the current level of response on a variable-ratio schedule of reinforcement (meaning that you don't offer a reward every time) before adding to or raising the criteria.

4. When introducing a new criterion or aspect of the behavioral skill, temporarily relax the old ones.

5. Stay ahead of your subject: plan your shaping program completely so that if the subject makes sudden progress, you are aware of what to reinforce next.

6. Don't change trainers in midstream. You can have several trainers per trainee, but stick to one shaper per behavior.

7. If one shaping procedure is not eliciting progress, find another. There are as many ways to get behavior as there are trainers to think them up.

8. Don't interrupt a training session gratuitously; that constitutes a punishment.

9. If behavior deteriorates, "go back to kindergarten." Quickly review the whole shaping process with a series of easily earned reinforcers.

10. End each session on a high note, if possible, but in any case quit while you're ahead.

you somewhere and then expect you to know the way when you drive there yourself? You may hesitate at a couple of turns or get confused on a few streets before you find your destination. But when you drive to places yourself, you remember the way better. You had to do it yourself to really learn how to get there.

Shaping is very good for a dog that may be too fearful to get near you for luring. You could have a delicious meatball in your hand to lure your dog to perform a behavior, but if the dog is terrified of you, that meatball may not be enough. Shaping allows you to work with a dog that doesn't feel comfortable being near you. In turn, this will help build a strong relationship, as he will get many rewards during your training sessions. Your training sessions will be positive experiences for him.

Shaping is also an excellent training method to teach behaviors that a dog would not normally do. A dog may readily pick up a tennis ball, but what about your car keys? You could shape your dog to bring you your keys, the remote control, laundry items, or other objects.

Shaping is a great technique for teaching service-dog behaviors, such as turning on and off lights, opening and closing doors, and even helping make the bed.

Capturing

Capturing is a method of marking and reinforcing behavior that a dog performs on his own, without lures. For example, when your dog lies down, he sometimes crosses his front paws, and you think that it's adorable and want to put it on cue. You would mark and reward the behavior every time he did it on his own. Behavior that is reinforced increases, so your dog will begin lying down and crossing his paws more frequently. Once the behavior is reliable, you can then put it on cue so that he does it when you cue him. Capturing is a great method for getting unusual, specific behaviors that your dog does and that would be difficult to lure. For example, you could capture a dog shaking himself off after a bath, or tilting his head, or stretching.

Modeling

Modeling is a method that uses physical manipulation to get a dog to perform a behavior. This is a method that we don't normally use. It isn't necessary because you can get behaviors using other, easier methods. Why push your dog's rear down to sit when you can easily get him to do it himself?

Modeling can also be difficult for many people. Imagine a petite woman getting a fully grown Mastiff to sit by pushing his rear down! It also doesn't engage the dog—you are doing all of the work for him. It is not an ideal training method for shy or fearful dogs because they can be further frightened by your physically manipulating their bodies into position.

Step 2: Mark the Behavior and Reward It

Marker training is an extremely effective method of positive training. You mark the instant that the dog performs the behavior you want, usually with a clicker. A clicker is a box-shaped tool that emits a "click" sound when you press it on one side. The brief sound is distinct and therefore easy for a dog to hear and recognize. You follow every mark with a reward, so a click is a promise of a reward. When your dog learns that every time he hears a marker he gets a reward, he learns to work to "earn" the marker noise.

You can also use a verbal marker, but it has to be a very short word to be precise. It should be a word that you don't use often in casual conversation, so you don't confuse your dog.

A clicker is a box-shaped tool that emits a "click" when pressed.

THE CLICK IS STRONGER THAN WORDS

Research has shown that a mechanical clicker is more effective than a verbal marker. According to the study titled Clicker Bridging Stimulus Efficacy by Lindsay Wood, MA, CTC: "The clicker-trained dogs achieved behavior acquisition in significantly ($p < .05$) fewer minutes and required significantly fewer primary reinforcements than verbally conditioned dogs. ... It appears that use of the clicker, by providing a more precise marker than a verbal bridging stimulus, is responsible for superior acquisition of complex behaviors such as that studied here. ... The potential of the clicker stimulus to improve animal learning throughout the entire process of a behavior may not only increase the rate of behavior acquisition but also reduce animal frustration and further enhance the relationship between trainer and animal."

Something like "good dog" is too long to be an effective marker. Think of all of the behaviors your dog could do by the time you start the "Good" and end with "dog." A lot!

Also, praise is not the same as a marker. You use a marker to indicate to a dog that he did something that you like. You use praise as a reward *after* the dog performs the behavior.

There are many good reasons to use a marker.

- **The communication is very clear and precise.** It marks the exact instant the dog performs the behavior you want.
- **Clickers are distinct.** They don't sound the same as other noises, so your dog can easily distinguish when you click.
- **It's consistent.** Especially if you use a clicker, the sound is the same every time.
- **It's non-judgmental.** It's a neutral sound.
- **It's transferrable.** Once the dog learns the sound of the marker means he did something you like, anyone can use it to tell the dog the same thing. This is extremely convenient if you have more than one person in your family who wants the dog to work for him or her.

In order to effectively use a marker, you need good timing. If you've never trained a dog before, or if this is the first time that you've used this type of training, be patient with yourself! You are learning a new skill. As with any other new skill, it will take time to learn to do well. Your timing may be too slow at first, or even too fast, but you will get better with practice.

Another wonderful thing about marker training is that even if you are a rookie, you won't make mistakes that will set back your training very much or hurt your dog. With punishment-based training, punishing your dog at the wrong moment can have unintended consequences. Not the case with marker training! You may mark a bit early or late and not get the exact behavior that you wanted, but you will be able to fix that easily in a few more clicks. No harm done.

Here are some tips on using a clicker correctly.

- Don't point it at your dog. It's not a remote control!
- Click only once per behavior. It's a marker, so you are marking a specific behavior only once. If your dog does something really well, you still click only once, but you can give him a better reward or several rewards if you like.
- Use the clicker only to mark behavior, not for other things. After a dog learns that a click means that a reward is coming, he can get very excited at the sound of the click. It can be tempting, then, to use the clicker to get your dog's attention or to use the sound to have him come running to you if you don't know where he is in the house or yard. If you do this, you've just damaged the power of the click as a marker.
- Always give a treat after clicking. Even if you make a mistake and click at the wrong time, you need to give your dog a reward. It's not your dog's fault that you made a mistake. If you skip the reward because you clicked in error, you will lessen the power of the click. Do it often enough, and your dog could stop paying attention to the click altogether.
- Because the click marks the behavior, it ends the behavior. For example, when working on the Down cue, if your dog lies down, you click, and your dog then gets up, it's OK. You already marked the Down, so it's OK if he gets up to get his treat.

Step 3: Add a Cue

Once a behavior is reliable, which means that the dog is regularly performing the behavior, it's time to add the cue (the word or physical signal you will use in order to ask the dog to perform the behavior).

Why don't we add the cue first? Why don't we say "Down" and then lure a dog into the down position? Because it's not as easy for dogs to learn that way. Remember, they don't speak English. Saying "Down" means nothing to them. Repeating it over and over isn't helpful, either. If someone says something to you in a foreign language that you don't know, does it help you understand it if they repeat it

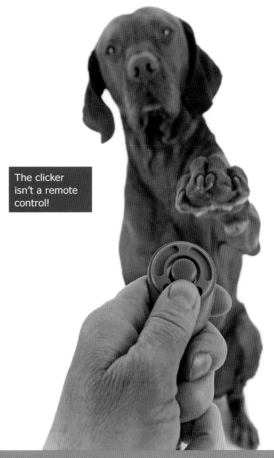

The clicker isn't a remote control!

over and over? If they yell it at you? Of course not. It won't help your dog, either. This is why we teach the behavior first and then label it with a cue.

For stationary behaviors, such as Sit, Down, and Settle, it's helpful to teach a release cue. This is an indication to your dog that it's OK to get up. Otherwise, should he stay seated forever? Or just get up whenever he wants? By teaching a release cue, you'll help him hold a longer, more consistent Stay. You can use the same release cue for each exercise because it will always signify the same behavior—your dog no longer has to hold the position. Choose a word that you don't often use in casual conversation, such as "Ok!" or "free" or "release." The actual word doesn't matter, as long as you are consistent with its use.

Step 4: Train to Fluency

Once you have a behavior on cue, it's time to train it to fluency. This means that you will need to train it so that your dog will perform it with distractions, in different environments, and under different conditions. It doesn't really do you much good if your dog only performs for you in your living room. If that's the only place you train, however, then that's likely the only place in which your dog will reliably perform the behavior.

For example, you teach your dog to Sit-Stay at home. You take him to the park and cue him: "Sit, Stay." He sits but then bounces right up and takes off after a squirrel. This may be annoying, but it's not unusual at all. You never taught your dog to Sit-Stay outside, with all of its scents and distractions, let alone squirrels.

You need to train your dog to perform cues despite distractions.

This can also happen with house-training. Just because you teach your dog not to eliminate in your own home doesn't mean that he learns not to eliminate in other people's homes. So, when you take your dog to a relative's house over the holidays, he may pee on the carpet even though he hasn't done that in your house in some time. While his peeing could be due to stress or excitement, it also could be due to lack of training in different locations.

In order to train a behavior to fluency, you work gradually. Start with just a few distractions and then gradually add more and more. Remember to keep your training sessions short. If you find your dog struggling, you're probably going too fast in your training. Back up to the last step at which your dog was successful, practice more at that level, and then try making it harder again.

It's easy to add distractions to your training. When you first start working on a behavior, you will start with very few distractions. Train in a quiet place that your dog is familiar with, such as your family room. When a behavior is reliable, add a few distractions to your training sessions. Depending on the behavior you're working on, it may be you moving around, getting farther from your dog, changing your training location, dropping items, having other people walk nearby, having other dogs nearby, and the like. Just add the distractions gradually. For example, if you're working on Sit-Stay, you will move one pace away and ensure that your dog holds the position, then two paces, then three. You wouldn't go from being right next to your dog to being across the room. This would likely be too much for your dog, and he would break position.

Depending on your dog's age and disposition, training to fluency can take time. This is normal! Rushing him won't be helpful. You want him to practice being successful rather than practice being unsuccessful. Young puppies have no attention spans, so they will be easily distracted. Something as small as a ladybug could prove a distraction for a puppy as compared to an older dog. Some breeds, such as bouncy Boxers or leaping Labradors, are busy by nature. Stock up on your patience and go only as fast as your dog can progress. Your training will be worth your efforts! By gradually increasing distractions and introducing new environments, you'll have a dog that will perform for you in just about any situation.

Some dogs, like Labradoodles, are busy by nature, so you'll need a little extra patience when training.

Think of therapy dogs that have to be reliable in busy environments, such as hospitals, or emotionally charged environments, such as with hospice bereavement groups. Search and rescue dogs have to perform under sometimes treacherous conditions, experiencing loud noises and sharp smells. Police dogs have to perform in a variety of environments, from schools to alleys. This level of performance doesn't happen automatically or overnight. It takes training behaviors to fluency so the dog learns to be consistent under a variety of conditions.

Reward-Based Training

If someone were to offer you chocolate-chip cookies, ice cream, or tiramisu, would you have a preference? Maybe your teeth are sensitive to cold, so you wouldn't find the ice cream appealing. Maybe you don't like the taste of coffee, so the tiramisu holds little appeal. Or maybe you just don't like chocolate, in which case the chocolate-chip cookies wouldn't hold your interest. Everyone has different preferences when it comes to things that they like. Dogs are similar.

Not every dog loves being petted. Some dogs are OK with it, but they really don't love it. Other dogs would do anything to snuggle with you. Some dogs are crazy about balls. They will play fetch for hours at a time. Other dogs just look at you when you toss a ball and never make an attempt to go after it. Some dogs will eat anything you put in front of them, while others are quite picky.

In using reward-based training, it's very important to determine exactly what your dog finds rewarding. The items you use as rewards must be appealing in the eyes of your individual dog.

So, what does your dog find appealing? Make a list, in order of your dog's preference. This will help you train, especially when it comes to adding distractions or teaching challenging behaviors for your dog. For example, some dogs have trouble with Down. If using a regular food treat as a lure doesn't help him lie down, you may need to go to a higher-ranked reward on your list.

Some dogs are ball-crazy and will play fetch for hours at a time.

One of the most common questions about using rewards in training is "When do you stop using them?" When you are building behavior, you will use rewards. Once a behavior is trained to fluency, it's a good idea to keep the rewards for a while and then gradually wean your dog off of them. This means that when your dog will reliably perform a behavior despite distractions and in different environments, you can start weaning him off of rewards. Most people try to remove the rewards too soon, and they find that the dog's behavior suffers as a result.

There is a big difference between a reward and a bribe. A reward is offered after a behavior. A bribe is offered to get a behavior. You don't want to bribe your dog! If you do, he will become dependent on that bribe, and you definitely don't want that. For example, you want your dog to get off the couch. You give him the cue "Off!" and he gets off the couch. You give him a treat. Thus, you gave him a cue, he performed the correct behavior, and he got a reward.

Take the same scenario, except this time you go get a treat and show it to him, tempting him with it so he gets off the couch. Then you give him the treat. This is a bribe. Do this often enough, and your dog won't get off the couch unless you tempt him with a treat. You don't want to have to carry treats around with you all the time just to get your dog to do what you want. You can train your dog to respond by using rewards, not bribes.

Attention and Affection

Most dogs love attention, although not all of them love petting and other physically affectionate gestures. Many dogs, for example, do not like being petted on top of the head. This is a pretty assertive gesture when translated by dogs, so many will duck out of the way or avoid your hand. Some dogs don't mind at all.

Pay attention to your dog and take note if he is not enjoying being petted.

When physically interacting with your dog, what does his resulting body language tell you? Does he go stiff? Do his ears lay flat, do his eyes have a worried expression? Does he lean away from you? Does he struggle? All of these are signs that he is not enjoying your interaction. On the other hand, does he lean into you? Does his body feel relaxed? Do his eyes get squinty? These are signs that he is enjoying the interaction.

If you love to snuggle with your dog, but your dog doesn't like to snuggle with you, please respect your dog's wishes. If you force him to endure it, he may feel the need to escalate the way in which he communicates to you that he doesn't like it. He may start growling or even snap or bite. This can happen easily with children who don't recognize when a dog is uncomfortable, but it can also happen with adults. Pay attention to your dog. He will tell you if he likes your petting.

If you have a dog that loves physical interaction, learn what he likes best. Does he like a good ear scratch? Belly rub? Chest rub? Find his favorites to use as rewards.

Verbal Praise

While verbal praise is often handy if you don't have a higher value reward with you, it's generally not as appreciated by dogs as it is by humans. If you tell a friend how wonderful she is, she's likely to be pleased. Your dog will be pleased as well, but if given a choice between verbal praise and a treat, the dog will likely choose the treat every time.

Please don't take it personally. It doesn't mean that your dog doesn't love you, and it doesn't mean that you are a bad pet owner. If your dog would rather have a cookie than hear you talk to him, this is actually quite normal. It's humbling, but it's normal.

Food is generally a high-value treat for any dog.

In general, if verbal praise is going to be effective, it should be enthusiastic and effusive. Make a big deal out of it! Watch your dog. Is he giving you positive body language in return? Then you are doing it right.

Food Rewards

Food is generally a high-value treat for any dog. It can be the fastest reward for teaching behaviors. When using food, pieces should be small and easy to swallow. You just need a tiny bite per behavior. Hard treats, such as baked treats, that take a while to chew, are not optimal for training because they will lengthen your training sessions and add too much time in between repetitions of a behavior.

Treats that have strong odors are more appealing to dogs. When training at home, with few distractions, you can use your dog's regular kibble to train if he will work for it. This is a great way to regulate the amount of food you feed him each day and avoid obesity issues. Make him work for his meals! Just measure out what you would normally feed him and use part or all of it in your training sessions during the day. You will not use it all at once because training sessions should be very short.

For example, let's say you feed your dog 2 cups (453.6 g) of kibble a day. You are currently working on confinement training, the Recall, and Settle. You could use 1 cup (226.8 g) of the kibble throughout the day for Recall training, ½ cup (113.4 g) stuffed in a toy for the confinement training to keep him occupied and happy in his crate, and the last ½ cup (113.4 g) also stuffed in a toy for a long Stay when he settles on his bed or mat.

When you start training in other areas and adding distractions, you may have to up the ante with the food. Plain kibble can work for some dogs, but for others it will take a treat that smells stronger. For example, if you take your dog to a training class, it's likely you will need some more tempting treats than your dog's regular kibble. There will be many of distractions, including other dogs and people, so your dog's kibble may not be as rewarding to him in that situation as it is at home.

If you use dog treats, choose ones that are healthy. Treats that you find in the grocery store, for example, are often full of dyes

Try This!

HEALTHY PEOPLE FOOD AS A REWARD

You can use people food to train your dog. You don't want to feed your dog people food all the time because it can cause pancreatitis and other health issues. But for the purposes of training, healthy people food can be a great option. Here are some suggestions:

- Hot dogs (choose low-sodium hot dogs for dogs less than 15 pounds [6.8 kg])
- Cheese, including string cheese
- Deli turkey or roast beef
- Roasted chicken
- Steak
- Oat cereal
- Carrots

Don't free-feed your dog; it will cause food to lose its power as a reward.

and sugars. These are not necessary for training, and they aren't a healthy choice for your dog. Choose a treat with all-natural ingredients.

The food rewards you use may also depend on the behavior you are training and the location. For example, if Sit is an easy behavior for your dog to learn, you can use a lower-value treat as a reward. If you are teaching a more challenging behavior, such as Heel, you may need a higher-value food treat.

If you are training in the quiet of your own living room, you may be able to use kibble successfully. If you are in the middle of a busy park, you may have to bring out higher value rewards in order to keep your dog's attention.

What food does your dog enjoy? Some dogs will easily work for their daily kibble, while others are choosier. Some dogs get excited over lettuce; others would ignore it altogether. Every dog has his own preferences, so it will depend on your dog. It is a myth that some dogs won't work for food at all.

All dogs need to eat. There is a food that is rewarding for every dog. Some just take some more detective work than others! One reason why a dog may seem unmotivated by food is that if food is left out all day for him (called free feeding), then food is always available to him and it doesn't have much power as a reward. This can affect your training potential. Leaving food out all day can also lead to obesity in dogs if they don't self-regulate effectively.

When you train with food, you'll also need something convenient in which to hold the food. You can purchase a bait bag, specially made to hold treats while training. You can also use a fanny pack or a carpenter's apron. A shirt with big pockets can also work. You just need to be able to get to the treats quickly, without having to dig for them.

If using toys as a reward, make sure they are safe and sized properly for your dog.

Toys

Toys can be fun rewards. Some dogs adore toys, while others are not as interested. Some dogs love only fetch toys, while others prefer tug toys. Some dogs will do anything for a ball.

If you're going to use toys as rewards, just keep in mind that training sessions will take longer because you have to allow playtime with the toy as the reward. This may not be practical for some behaviors or early in the training process, when quick repetitions will help your dog learn a behavior faster.

Always pick safe toys for your dog. A chew toy that a dog can fit entirely in his mouth is not safe. He could swallow it whole, and it could get stuck in his throat or digestive tract. Tennis balls are safe for many dogs, but not dogs that will chew on them because the tennis balls' coating will damage their tooth enamel. If your dog wants to chase the tennis ball, that is fine, but he should not settle down with it and chew it like a bone.

Play

While you can use toys to play with your dog, you don't always have to have a toy to play. Games, including chase, hide-and-seek, and recall, can be fun rewards for some dogs, and they provide a nice way to break up a training session if your dog is getting frustrated. If you play chase, encourage your dog to chase you, instead of the other way around. You don't want him to practice running away from you, but playing a fun game in which he's running toward you can help you teach him a fast Come.

Recall games can be great for energetic dogs that like to move. If you have more than one person available to play, each of you can call your dog to "Come." As the dog runs away from a person, that person takes a step backward. Eventually, you can be in different rooms of your house, or spread out in a fenced yard, with your dog running in between. Not only is this a game, it's also training! You can also modify this game into hide-and-seek, with different people hiding and calling your dog to come find them.

As with toys, playing games will extend your training sessions, but short bursts of play during your training sessions as rewards can be very powerful motivators.

Life Rewards

Life rewards are activities dogs enjoy that you can use as rewards. Does your dog love to use his nose? Use the opportunity to sniff as a reward. Does your dog go nuts for a car ride? Give him a ride as a reward! Does he enjoy swimming? Train near a lake and let him swim as a reward. Life rewards can be extremely powerful. If your dog performs a behavior, and you reward him with a life reward, it can be a strong motivator for your dog to repeat the behavior. You generally don't use these rewards all of the time because you wouldn't get much training done, but if used once in a while, life rewards can make a big impression on your dog.

Short bursts of play as rewards can be powerful motivators.

Introducing the Clicker

Dogs don't automatically understand that the click sound from the clicker means that they did something that you like. You need to teach them the meaning of the sound. You need to classically condition the clicker to mean that a treat is coming.

This is the very first exercise to teach your dog before you start training the basics. You'll be using the clicker for all of the exercises, so teach your dog that the click sound means a treat is coming first.

1. Get five small, tasty treats. Be near to your dog. If he is across the yard, you're not ready for this exercise, so make sure that he is close to you. Don't ask your dog to sit or to do anything else. This exercise is just about teaching him that the sound of the click means that a treat is coming, so you don't want to clutter it with anything else.

2. Click once. Immediately follow the click with a treat. Repeat this five times.

3. Do this exercise twice a day for two days.

It won't take long before your dog's ears perk up at the sound of the click. You may see his tail wagging. Now that the clicker is "charged up," it's time to use it to start training!

Introducing a Target

Targeting is an extremely useful training skill to teach your dog. There are two main types of targets—nose targets and paw targets. By teaching your dog to touch his nose or paw to a target, you can teach a variety of behaviors. A nose target to your hand can turn into a Recall, your dog can follow your hand to get on and off furniture, and more. A paw target can teach your dog to go to his kennel or his bed or to stay outside the kitchen while you're preparing dinner. Your first step will be to introduce targets to your dog.

The easiest nose target to start with is your hand.

Introducing a Nose Target

The easiest nose target to start with is your hand. Here are the steps to teaching a nose target:

Goal: Your dog will touch his nose to your hand.

What You'll Need: Clicker, treats.

1. Hold the clicker in one hand. Hold your other, empty, hand with the palm toward your dog and the fingers downward. Hold it 1 inch (2.5 cm) from your dog's nose.

2. Most dogs will reach forward to sniff or lick your hand. The second that your dog's nose touches your palm, click and pull your hand away. Give him a treat. Remove your hand so he won't touch it again before you are ready to click and treat him again.

3. Present your hand again, 1 inch (2.5 cm) in front of your dog's nose. When he touches it, click, pull your hand away, and treat.

4. Repeat for a total of ten repetitions. End your training session.

Tip: *If your dog doesn't touch your hand, you will need to gradually shape the behavior. When you first present your hand, your dog is likely to at least look at it. Click, remove your hand, and treat him for looking. Repeat several times. Your dog will begin to look at your hand more frequently. When he's looking at it consistently, hold off on clicking. Wait to see if he nudges your hand. Be patient—let him think this through. When he moves forward to touch your hand, click and treat!*

When your dog is consistently touching your hand, it's time to move your hand.

1. Hold your palm 1 inch (2.5 cm) to the left of your dog's nose. When he noses it, click and treat. Then hold your palm 1 inch (2.5 cm) to the right of your dog's nose. When he noses it, click and treat.

2. Gradually start moving your hand farther away from your dog, switching between the left and right side. Click and treat for every correct response when his nose touches your palm.

3. Now it's time to get your dog to follow your hand. Start with your hand close to your dog's nose. When he moves to nose it, move it slowly away from him in a straight line so he follows it. Go only a couple of feet (about a meter) before you let him touch it. Click and treat.

4. Gradually work up to your dog following your hand for farther distances.

5. Repeat for a total of ten repetitions. End your training session.

Try This!

INTRODUCING A CLICKER TO A FEARFUL DOG

If your dog is scared of noises or very fearful, you need to introduce the clicker a little differently. If your dog is very sensitive, you may not want to use a clicker at first. Instead, a clickable ballpoint pen serves as a very soft sound that often works well. You introduce it the same way as the regular clicker. You can also muffle the regular clicker by tucking it into a pocket when you click it or wrapping a towel around it. You just want to create a softer noise so that your dog doesn't startle.

When your dog is reliably touching your palm with his nose, no matter where you present it, it's time to add the cue.

1. Just before you present your hand, say the cue "Touch" in a friendly voice. When your dog touches your hand, click and treat.
2. Repeat for a total of ten repetitions. End your training session.

Introducing a Paw Target

Choose a target that your dog will be able to touch with his paw. Keep in mind that some dogs are enthusiastic with their paws, so your target should be durable. For example, try a drink coaster, or a lid from a margarine tub. Here are the steps to teaching a paw target:

Goal: Your dog will touch his paw to a target.

What You'll Need: Clicker, treats, paw target.

1. Place the target on the ground near your dog. If your dog reaches out with a paw to touch the target, click, remove the target, and treat. This is not common, though. Most dogs explore with their noses first. So, if your dog noses the target, click, remove the target, and treat. You remove your target so he won't touch it again before you are ready to click and treat him again.

   Why is it OK to click the nosing of the target instead of the pawing? Because for dogs, nosing and pawing are closely connected behaviors. If your dog starts with his nose, don't worry. He will soon switch to pawing.

2. If your dog started by pawing the target, repeat about ten times and then end your training session.

3. If your dog started by nosing the target, repeat until he is nosing the target reliably, about ten times. Then, present the target and wait. Don't click for him nosing the target. Just wait. He will soon get frustrated when nosing no longer works, and he will try something else, likely a paw. The second he touches the target with his paw, click, remove the target, and treat. Repeat ten more times. End your training session.

Tip: *Some dogs like to use their paws more than others do and will pick this up quickly. Others take a while. Training a paw target may take just one session, or it may take several. Just proceed as far as your dog can succeed. Also, some dogs are mouthier than others. You may*

Try a drink coaster as a paw target.

find your sporting-breed dog trying to pick up the target. If that's the case, just anchor the target with your foot so he can't pick it up. This exercise is not a retrieve. If you let your dog pick up the target, it will be harder to teach him to paw it.

When your dog is consistently pawing, it's time to move the target.

1. Start placing the target in different locations, but within a couple of feet (about a meter) of your dog. Click and treat every time he touches a paw to the target.

2. Hold the target in the palm of your hand, against the ground. Click and treat for every correct response.

3. Gradually start moving the target a little higher, but still at a comfortable height for your dog. Click and treat for every correct response.

4. Repeat for a total of ten repetitions. End your training session.

When your dog is reliably touching the target with his paw, no matter where you present it, it's time to add the cue.

1. Just before you present your hand, say the cue "Paw" once, in a friendly voice. When your dog paws the target, click and treat.

2. Repeat for a total of ten repetitions. End your training session.

Some breeds are mouthier than others and may try to pick up the target.

PART II

PUPPY
TRAINING

CHAPTER 5

EARLY
TRAINING

Puppyhood is a wonderful, adorable, messy, frustrating, critical time in a dog's life. You bring your little, cute puppy home, and you have all sorts of dreams about how he will grow up. He will be a good family companion. He will be your best friend. He will love and protect your children. He will do everything you ask of him without complaint or defiance. He will be an obedience, Rally, or agility star. He will be a therapy dog. He will never eat your shoes, poop on the carpet, or growl at you. He will be perfect!

How your dog achieves those goals depends on the dog that you brought home and, most importantly, on you and the people who interact with him.

You'll start bonding with your puppy the minute you meet him. You should start training him as soon as you bring him home, which should be at about eight weeks of age at the youngest. Puppies need to stay with their mothers and littermates for approximately the first eight weeks to learn valuable social lessons that will help them grow up into stable, social adult dogs. Be wary of any breeder who tries to send a puppy home with you earlier.

Young puppies are sponges for training, but they have very short attention spans. This means that training sessions should be very short, only a couple of minutes at a time. While you're training your puppy, you'll be doing far more than just teaching behaviors. As your hand delivers treats, you'll be teaching him that hands moving toward him are good. This will help you in overall handling, grooming, and even picking him up. You'll also be teaching him that you are fun to be around because each training session will make your bond stronger. You'll be building lots of positive associations with you and with training in general, which will build a solid foundation of trust between you and your puppy.

Your dog's ID tag should list your dog's name and your contact number.

DON'T BE TEMPTED BY THAT PUPPY IN THE WINDOW

Would you pay twice as much for a car that risks breaking down frequently and can leave you stranded? One that will cost you even more money to fix on a regular basis? Of course not. But turn that lemon into a cute, fluffy puppy, and the temptation is harder to resist.

Puppy mills are mass-production farms that breed female dogs at every heat cycle to produce puppies. They often have more than fifty—sometimes hundreds— of dogs, often of different breeds, for breeding purposes. The puppies are not raised in homes but in cages. They are taken from their mothers early so that they will still be very small when they reach stores across the country, and therefore more appealing to sell. The mother dogs often die young, as the toll of frequent breeding is too great on their bodies.

The puppies often have behavioral and developmental issues. Because they never leave their cages, they get used to living in their urine and feces, so they learn that it's OK to stay in their messes. This makes them extremely challenging to house-train, which is often a top complaint among people who purchase these dogs.

People often have good intentions when they visit these mass-production farms. They see sad dogs and want to save them, so they buy one and bring him home. But this just perpetuates the issue, making room for more puppies to be produced.

Puppy mills supply pet stores, so even though the presentation is more attractive, it's still an extension of horrific conditions endured by the dogs back at the farm. Pet stores will dress up the puppies as "designer dogs" or "rare purebreds," charging a lot more money than you would have to pay if you just bought a quality puppy from reputable breeder or adopted a mix from your local shelter or rescue group.

Help put puppy mills out of business. If you are concerned that a pet store is selling puppy-mill puppies, check the ASPCA's website tool to discover the source: http://nopetstorepuppies.com/buy-a-puppy. The site also is a great resource for educational information on puppy mills and why they mean bad news for our canine friends.

Equipment You'll Need

There are many things that you can buy for your puppy, and you may be tempted as you go through the pet-supply store to buy half the store! But here are items that you will specifically need for training.

Leash

Get a 4-to-6-foot (1-m) leash made of nylon, cotton, or leather. Avoid the retractable leashes. Retractable leashes are fine for exercising your dog or to help train some advanced distance exercises, but in general they are not ideal for walking or training your puppy. Even in the locked position, they don't offer you much flexibility or control. Plus, if you drop it and your puppy bolts, the plastic handle will "chase" him and could terrify him.

Be sure to get a size that's appropriate for your puppy. For example, if you have a toy-breed dog, you'll want a ¼-inch-thick (1.5-cm-thick) leash with a small clasp. Some leashes are thin but still have heavy clasps, which could weigh down your little pup. If you have a hefty puppy, then a ¾-inch-thick (2-cm-thick) or 1-inch-thick (2.5-cm-thick) leash is a better choice.

Collar

Get a collar that's an appropriate size for your puppy. You should just be able to get two fingers in between your puppy's neck and the collar, laying your fingers flat against his neck. Any larger, and your puppy could catch his jaw or a paw inside the collar, causing him to panic and hurt himself. Either quick-snap or buckle collars are fine choices. Avoid choke chain, prong, or electric collars.

You should also get an ID tag for your puppy's collar. Choose one that won't tarnish and leave marks on his coat. Get an appropriate size for your puppy so the tag doesn't dangle down too far on his chest. Alternately, you can get a collar that's engraved with your contact information if you prefer, instead of a tag. Just be sure that there is some sort of identification on the collar. It should feature your dog's name and the best way to contact you, such as your cell phone number.

When your puppy leaves the house, he should always wear a collar with identification, even

Because of the shape of the breed's face, Frenchies often do better with a harness.

if you are using a harness to attach your leash. You hope that your puppy will never get away from you, but accidents happen! If your puppy ever gets loose or slips out of the fence, the best chance he has of finding his way home is through identification.

Harness

Some dogs do better with harnesses. If you have a brachycephalic ("smoosh-faced") dog, such as a Pug, Japanese Chin, or Bulldog, then a harness is a better choice for your dog than a collar and leash for walking. These breeds have breathing challenges, especially in hot weather or with strenuous exercise, so you don't want to restrict their airways when they pull against a collar.

Even if you don't have a brachycephalic dog, harnesses can be great for walking your dog.

There are many harnesses on the market, but they attach to a leash in basically two ways. Some have the leash clip on the back, near the shoulders of the dog. Others clip in the front, on the dog's chest.

Harnesses with the leash clip in the back are humane tools to use with your puppy. Keep in mind, though, that these types of harnesses will not help keep your puppy from pulling while walking on leash. The leash attaches to the back of harness, which distributes the dog's body weight effectively.

A harness with the leash clip in the front can help prevent your puppy from pulling while walking on leash by slowing down your puppy's forward motion. This type of harness can be a great tool for a puppy who likes to pull, especially until you are able to teach him to walk nicely on leash.

It's important to have a proper fit with these harnesses. An incorrect fit can cause chafing under the front legs or chest. If the harness sags in the puppy's chest area, he can get his paw or jaw caught and panic, injuring himself. So if you choose a front-clip harness, make sure that you carefully follow the instructions that come with it or consult a professional who knows how to fit the harness properly.

When choosing a harness, try to find one that your puppy can't easily step out of. Puppies can be wiggly! If a harness is very easy to slip onto your puppy, keep in mind that it will be just as easy for your puppy to wiggle out of and escape from.

Head Halter

If you have a really strong puppy, or if you are a petite person with a giant-breed puppy, then you may be interested in trying a head halter. This is also a good tool for a puppy who likes to jump on people. You can train a puppy not to jump, but a head halter can be a nice management tool in the meantime.

A head halter is much more humane than a choke chain or prong collar, which put pressure on the trachea and require yanking in order to "correct" a dog. A head halter simply controls the head of your puppy. If a horse trainer can control a large horse with a head halter, you can control a puppy!

Positive Solutions

EFFECTIVE MANAGEMENT TOOLS

You may find that with a really rambunctious puppy, a head halter works best initially. As you begin training him, you may gradually switch to a front-clip harness, and then eventually you will be able to walk him with just a collar and leash. There is nothing wrong with using effective management tools while you train. Some owners choose to keep using the tools, which is also just fine. It's up to you—all of these tools are humane choices.

There are different head halters on the market. Whichever type you choose, make sure that it is fitted properly. Your puppy should be able to breathe and take treats easily. The nose loop should not chafe his muzzle or push up against his eyes so he ends up squinting. Be sure to follow the instructions that come with the head halter or consult a professional with experience in fitting head halters properly.

Clicker

Clickers are available at most pet-supply stores and online. The most common kind of clicker is a little rectangular box. This type offers the loudest click, so if you will be working with your dog in a class or outside, the sound will travel nicely. There are also some versions that have a softer click, which are fine when you are training in a quiet location. These are also easier to click, which you may prefer if you have arthritis in your fingers or another condition that makes using your fingers difficult. It's also helpful to purchase a wrist coil to attach your box clicker. This allows you to drop the clicker but still have it attached to you. Some clickers have a loop that slips over your finger for convenience.

Once you start clicker training, you'll quickly discover that you and your dog enjoy it! So get several clickers to keep handy throughout the house.

Crate

Crates are important tools for puppy training. A crate will help you house-train your puppy and help keep him safe from chewing inappropriate items. For the purposes of house-training, a crate should be just big enough for a puppy to stand up, stretch out, and turn around in. The goal is to confine the puppy enough so he will learn to hold his bladder and bowels. Most puppies won't soil their "dens."

A crate used for house-training should be just big enough for a puppy to stand up in, stretch out, and turn around.

There are a variety of crates on the market. Get a sturdy one that will withstand puppy chewing. Save the cute canvas travel carriers for when your puppy is out of his chewing stage. In general, a plastic or wire crate is a good, sturdy choice.

A typical plastic crate consists of a top and a bottom that you put together with nuts and bolts. You don't need any tools; you can hand-twist the bolts into place.

Puppies make messes, so being able to take the top off of the crate to clean out the bottom is very handy. Some plastic crates are also approved for use on airlines. If you are interested in taking your puppy on an airplane, always check ahead of time with your individual airline, as they each have their own specific rules.

Wire crates come in a variety of styles. Choose epoxy-coated wire to help prevent rust. You can get a crate that folds down "suitcase-style" and comes with a handle for easy carrying and storage. A wire crate usually has a plastic tray in the bottom that you can remove for cleaning. If you choose a wire crate, be sure that the holes in the grate are not large enough that your puppy can get a paw through. It could get stuck, and he could get hurt.

If you have a large-breed puppy, consider getting a wire crate that includes a divider. The divider allows you to gradually increase the size of the puppy's allocated space in the crate without having to purchase different crates as your puppy grows.

You can also find very nice designer crates. Some are made of rich woods and can also function as tables in the home. These are usually more expensive than plastic or wire crates. When it comes to training a puppy, choose function over form. Spending several hundred dollars on a designer crate that your puppy considers a chew toy is going to be a frustrating experience!

Toys

Toys are important to puppy development. Puppies love to chew, and the desire to chew grows even stronger when they are teething. Giving your puppy appropriate toys to chew on will give him a healthy, acceptable alternative to chewing on things you may not like him to chew, such as your furniture or your shoes.

There are so many toys to choose from that it can be a bit bewildering. What will make toy selection even more challenging is that different puppies prefer different toys. You won't know what your puppy likes until you try a few different kinds. There are some puppies who don't seem to like any toys, but you can teach your puppy to enjoy playing with toys instead of chewing on off-limits items.

Give your puppy appropriate toys to chew on.

Chew Toys

When selecting chew toys, choose durable ones that are larger than your puppy's mouth. If your puppy gnaws a toy into pieces that are small enough to fit entirely in his mouth, you need to throw the toy away. He could easily swallow it and choke, or it could get lodged in his digestive tract and require surgery to remove.

The life span of a toy will depend on your puppy's chewing style. Some puppies are gentle with their toys and keep them into adulthood. Others act as if they could chew through tires! Choose toys that are appropriate for your puppy's chewing style. It's always best to err on the side of caution and choose a more durable toy if you're not sure. Some chew options include deer or elk antlers, beef marrow bones, plastic toys, and rubber toys.

Interactive Toys

Interactive toys are great for keeping puppies entertained and focused. Fill a durable interactive toy with your puppy's regular kibble and some treats. As he works to empty the toy, the toy provides mental enrichment. Some toys are meant for long-lasting chew time, while others are more like puzzle games for dogs. The long-lasting ones are great for crate time or for occupying your puppy when you are unable to supervise him as closely as necessary.

Tug toys are also fun interactive toys. Tug is a perfectly safe game for most puppies, although you'll find that, when your puppy is teething, he may lose some teeth in the tug toy.

Balls

Balls are another type of toy that may amuse your puppy. Be sure to use a ball that is not too small for your puppy's mouth. If you use tennis balls, also be sure that your puppy doesn't use it as a chew toy because its rough coating could damage his enamel.

Flirt Pole

If you have a very energetic puppy, or perhaps a herding breed or mix who likes to chase things, a flirt pole can be a fun toy that offers great exercise. A flirt pole is a long stick that has a long cord attached to it. At the end of the cord is usually a toy. It looks like a fishing pole, except you normally can't retract the cord. By flicking the pole, you can get the toy to bounce in different directions for your puppy to chase. This is also a good toy for limited space. If you have a cleared space indoors where you can play with the flirt pole, it can offer great exercise for your puppy on a rainy day when you can't take him outdoors to play.

Did You Know?

EDIBLE CHEWS

If you buy chew bones that are edible, make sure that they were made in a country with strict regulations (such as the United States). There have been canine deaths due to ingredients in treats and chews made in other countries.

Squeaky and Stuffed Toys

Other toys include those that make sounds and stuffed toys; sometimes they are a combination of both. Some puppies go nuts for squeaky toys. Just make sure that your pup doesn't remove and eat the squeaker or the stuffing. Stuffed animals should be those made especially for dogs, not leftover children's toys. And, remember, if you do have children in your life who have beloved stuffed animals, giving your puppy a stuffed animal to chew on is just going to confuse him. He will not know the difference between his stuffed animal and your child's, and it won't be fair to yell at him or punish him for chewing on the wrong stuffed animal.

Expert Tip

ROTATE THOSE TOYS!

Even if you buy your puppy a hundred toys, he will still, on occasion, attempt to chew something that he shouldn't. You can help prevent this by rotating his toys on a regular, frequent basis so that they seem new to him. If you leave the same toys out all the time, he'll easily get bored with them and could go looking for something else to chew on ... probably something you won't approve of.

Puppy Games

By playing with your puppy with his toys, you teach him what you *want* him to chew on. You also teach him to share his toys with you rather than hoarding them to himself. Take turns playing with him with his toys and then letting him play with them by himself. You also want your puppy to learn how to amuse himself. It's a healthy part of his development to not become overly dependent on you.

Getting your puppy to come to you should be easy at first, so make the most of it! Crouch down, clap your hands, and make kissy noises to your puppy. When he comes to you, praise him! Play with him, give him a treat—anything he finds rewarding. Coming to you should always be a positive experience for your puppy. If you ever call him to punish him or yell at him, you'll teach him that he should stay *away* from you. That is not the goal!

Make sure that your puppy can't remove and eat the squeaker in a stuffed toy.

You can also play hide-and-seek with your puppy. Make it easy at first. Hide around a corner and call your puppy to come find you. When he does, make a big deal about it! This will also build a positive association with coming to you in your puppy's mind.

A Good Workout Makes for a Good Dog

Puppies are full of energy one minute and suddenly napping the next. As your puppy gets older, those naps will come fewer and farther between. You may wonder at times if there are batteries in your puppy because he never seems to slow down or rest!

Exercise will be an important part of your puppy's health development, and it will also significantly help you during training. If your puppy is not getting enough exercise, it will show in your training sessions. You may find that your puppy can't focus, is overly excited, or is completely ignoring you. While this sometimes is an indication that your training session is too long, more often it's a sign that your puppy hasn't had enough exercise. Exercising your puppy before training sessions can "take the edge" off and help him better focus on learning.

How much exercise your puppy will need will depend on his age and breed (or breed combination). Obviously, at eight weeks of age, puppies will need less exercise than at twenty-two weeks. A sporting breed such as a Weimaraner will need more exercise than the companion Maltese.

Think about what your dog was originally bred to do—was it an energetic activity? If so, that puppy is going to need exercise to the same level, even if you choose not to do that activity. Your puppy's DNA is still programmed for his breed's intended function. For example, Dalmatians were used to run in front of firehouse carriages, clearing the way for the horses to get through. This required an athletic, energetic dog. If you don't want to run daily with your Dalmatian, you'll need to find another way for him to expend that energy.

How much exercise your puppy will need will depend on his age and breed.

Walking with you may be enough exercise for a young puppy, but as he reaches adolescence, it won't be enough. You just don't walk fast enough or far enough to get his heart rate up consistently for a good workout. Plus, you normally want your puppy to walk nicely by your side, which slows him down. This is why it's common to hear people complain that they walk their dogs "miles (km) a day" and he still has energy to burn.

This doesn't mean that you should run marathons with your puppy. He's too young for this. When you exercise your puppy, do so safely. Your puppy's brain and heart may be telling him to run around like a wild thing, but his body may not be ready. He's a puppy—not known for good judgment! You are responsible for ensuring that your puppy's exercise doesn't do more harm than good. Make sure that you are not putting too much strain on your young puppy's body.

If you are a jogger, you didn't run a marathon your first day out. You trained gradually. If you want to run with your puppy, you will need to train him gradually as well. He should not be your running partner until he reaches physical maturity.

Discourage strenuous jumping until your puppy is full grown because his growth plates aren't yet closed and could sustain damage. For larger puppies, jumping on and off furniture is usually OK (if you want to allow it), but you shouldn't allow them to practice jumping for agility competition until they are older. Small puppies can hurt themselves even jumping off the couch.

Exercise and the Weather

The weather will play a role in determining if your puppy can exercise or play outdoors. Some puppies will be picky and not want to go outside when it rains, but other pups love to splash in puddles. Some puppies love to play in the snow, while others are convinced that it will kill them. You will need to decide if the temperature outside is too extreme for your puppy and monitor him while he is outside to make sure he remains OK.

If you live in an area that is very hot, make sure that your puppy doesn't overheat. Signs of heatstroke in dogs include:

- Excessive panting
- Drooling, with thick, sticky saliva
- A bright red tongue
- Vomiting
- Diarrhea
- Dizziness

If your dog has these symptoms, remove him from the heat immediately and call your veterinarian or emergency clinic.

If you live in an area that gets very cold, be careful with outdoor activities.

Another heat-related danger is to your puppy's paws. Puppies don't wear shoes, so walking on hot asphalt can cause burns on your puppy's pawpads. If your area has sidewalks or grass for him to walk on, it will help in the heat, but some neighborhoods don't have sidewalks, so people have to walk their dogs in the street. The asphalt can get very hot. If your puppy starts "dancing" on the ground and acting distressed, check his paws. He may be getting heat blisters.

Conversely, if you live in an area that gets very cold, you also have to be careful with outdoor activities. Did you know that dogs can get hypothermia and even frostbite? Toy breeds, dogs with short coats, and puppies are especially susceptible to hypothermia, meaning that the body temperature drops too low. Here are the signs of hypothermia:

- Lethargy
- Violent shivering
- Weak pulse
- Coma

If you think that your puppy has hypothermia, wrap him in a blanket and bring him inside where it's warm. Call your veterinarian or emergency clinic immediately.

Frostbite, in which part of the body freezes, usually accompanies hypothermia. Common targets are the tail, ear tips, and pawpads. If your puppy has frostbite, the skin in the affected areas will be pale white or blue. As circulation returns to the area, the skin will appear bright red and may start peeling. Days later, it will eventually turn black. The areas will be very painful. If you suspect that your dog has frostbite, apply warm—not hot—water to the affected areas and contact your veterinarian or emergency clinic.

The Key to Successful Puppy Training: You

You play the most important role in your puppy's training and future. It's a lot of responsibility! Be patient—with both your puppy and yourself. Training is work, and you are bound to make a few mistakes along the way, especially if this type of canine training is new to you. But you can do it. Your puppy is going to try your patience from time to time, but remember that he is just a baby. You need to teach him what you want, in terms that he can understand.

Do not use harsh tones with your puppy when training. When you were in school, if your teacher yelled out all of her instructions to you, school would have been pretty stressful. You don't need to yell at your puppy to train him to do what you want. Save your harsher tone of voice for when he's doing

Expert Tip

CHECK THOSE PAWPADS!
Frequently check your puppy's pawpads for signs of cuts, scrapes, or other injuries. This will help you keep track of any problems and also help your puppy learn to accept handling of his paws.

something awful. (Better yet, teach him not to do those things.)

Use a friendly voice when communicating with and training your puppy. You especially don't want to use his name or the Recall cue in a negative manner. Yelling "FIDO! COME HERE!" when you are angry with your puppy will just teach him to avoid you when you call his name or tell him to come to you. That's not something you want him to learn!

Set boundaries for what you will allow and what you won't, and be sure that your family sticks to the same rules. For example, if you don't want a dog to sleep on your bed, don't let your new puppy sleep on the bed just because he is a bit stressed during his first few days in a new home. It will be too confusing, and stressful, for your puppy to get accustomed to sleeping with you on the bed, only to be booted off when he gets bigger.

If you don't want your grown dog jumping on you, don't encourage jumping in your puppy. It's very tempting to let your cute little puppy jump up to kiss your chin, but this is rewarding the jumping behavior. If you continue to reward this behavior, it will become a habit that will be harder to fix. It's confusing to your puppy if you allow jumping for a while and then later don't want him jumping on you.

It's better to start with restrictions and lessen them as your puppy goes through training so that he learns control and to follow your cues. For example, if you don't mind a dog that jumps on you, that's fine. But you may have other people in your life, such as senior citizens or small children, who could be injured by a dog jumping on them. Teach your puppy not to jump up on people right from the start when you bring him home. As he gets older and you train him to respond to your cues, you can then teach him a cue for jumping up. You can teach him to jump up only when he gets the cue. This will better control who he does and doesn't jump up on.

It's the same with allowing a puppy on the furniture. Perhaps you don't mind if your grown dog snuggles with you on the couch, but a puppy launching himself at you while you're on the couch, eating a snack, could cause a mess or even hurt you. Teach your puppy not to get up on the furniture right from the start. As he gets older and you train him, you can teach him a cue to indicate that he's allowed up on the furniture. This means that *you* get to decide when he gets up on the couch.

Set boundaries for what you will and won't allow.

CHAPTER 6

HOUSE-TRAINING

House-training is often frustrating for puppy owners. It's never fun to clean up messes. There may be times when you think that your puppy deliberately pees in the house just to annoy you, but that is never the case. Puppies don't pee or poop out of spite. Elimination is a natural behavior. Your puppy just doesn't understand that you don't want him to eliminate on your carpet. Even if you think you've been very clear in indicating to him where you want him to eliminate, this may not be the case.

House-training takes consistency, patience, and clear communication. It also takes keeping an eagle-eye watch on your puppy. The phrase "supervise your puppy" really means that you need to be like an FBI witness protection unit, watching your puppy every minute to prevent accidents. Puppies can pee really quickly! If you turn your back for just a few minutes, you'll turn around to find a new puddle on the floor.

You puppy only eliminates in inappropriate places because you let him. He either has too much freedom or not enough supervision, or you didn't take him to his elimination spot often enough. Every time he does eliminate in the inappropriate place, he's practicing the incorrect behavior. Your goal is to manage your puppy so that he has very little opportunity to eliminate where you don't want him to and every opportunity to eliminate where you prefer.

Puppies only eliminate in inappropriate places because you let them.

Your first decision in house-training will be where you want your puppy to eliminate: indoors or outdoors? Please choose *one* option. If you want your puppy to eliminate indoors sometimes but outdoors at other times, it will be just too confusing for your puppy. Keep things simple.

Outdoor elimination means that your puppy will not pee or poop inside the house. Indoor elimination means that your puppy will eliminate on pee pads or in a litterbox. So, for example, if you choose to teach your puppy outdoor elimination, you wouldn't put pee pads inside the house and encourage him to eliminate on them, too.

Once you decide where you want your puppy to eliminate, it's time to start confinement training. For this, a crate is the best tool.

Crate Training

A crate is an enclosure for your puppy that you can use to greatly speed up house-training. Used properly, it will help teach your puppy to hold his bowels and bladder because most puppies do not want to soil their dens. In addition to house-training, there are many benefits to crate training for puppies.

- Crates keep your puppy safe from eating or chewing things that can hurt him, such as electrical cords or small items that he could swallow.
- Crates keep your puppy from destructively chewing on items you would prefer he leave alone, such as your furniture, shoes, your children's toys, the carpet, and more, which in turn keeps you from getting angry at your puppy for inappropriate chewing!
- Crates help teach your puppy how to be by himself. You can't be with your puppy all of the time, so it's healthy for him to learn how to be by himself and be OK with it.
- Crates help keep a puppy still when recovering from illness, injury, or surgery. For example, when your puppy is spayed or neutered, he will need to rest for some time afterward. Once the anesthesia wears off, your puppy will likely be ready to zoom around long before he should! A crate will prevent him from getting too much activity. Also, puppies can sometimes zig when they should zag and end up pulling a muscle or sustaining a soft-tissue injury. Your veterinarian may recommend several days or weeks of crate rest. How do you keep a wiggly puppy still? Use a crate.
- Crates are excellent for travel. If your car is big enough to accommodate your puppy's crate, he should ride in the crate for safety reasons. Dogs should never be loose in your car while driving. If you were in a car accident, your puppy would become a projectile. (If your car isn't big enough for the crate, you can get a canine safety belt.) If you take your puppy on your travels, the crate will be a familiar den to provide some comfort for him and keep him from getting into trouble. It's going to be embarrassing if

Did You Know?

VERY YOUNG PUPPIES NEED LONGER POTTY BREAKS

You take your puppy out, he pees and poops, and you head back inside, only for him to immediately pee and poop again. This is very common. Very young puppies, usually less than twelve weeks old, often have to eliminate twice or more per potty break. Give your young puppy enough time to get everything out during his potty break, and you will have fewer accidents indoors.

your puppy pees all over your grandmother's fancy rug, so bring your puppy's crate along for the trip.

Crates are more effective for house-training than simply confining your puppy to a room, such as the kitchen, laundry room, or bathroom. If your puppy has that much room, he can pee or poop in a corner and simply move away to a clean area. He will not learn to hold his bladder and bowels as effectively in a room as he will in a crate of the proper size. Plus, some puppies have been known to chew through wooden doors or jump over baby gates and escape from rooms.

Introduced properly, a crate can be your puppy's safe harbor. He'll have a comforting den to take breaks in when he's stressed or overtired. You may find that he willingly goes into his crate for naps. To achieve this, you need to crate-train your puppy so he learns to love his new den.

Crate Location

Where do you put your puppy's crate? Preferably, put it in an area where you commonly hang out, such as the family room or living room. It's perfectly fine if you want to move the crate into your bedroom at night. In fact, it may help your puppy acclimate to your home faster because he may feel more secure being near you.

Try not to put the crate off by itself, such as in a laundry room or another room where you don't spend much time. Your puppy wants to be part of your family, and if you want him to bond with you, you should keep his crate close by. He won't be in the crate all the time, but when he's very young, he will spend a good deal of time in his crate when you can't supervise him closely—so you want him nearby.

Place the crate in a room where the family spends a lot of time.

Crate Accessories

Puppies should have access to water in their crates. Avoid plastic bowls that your puppy can chew. You can get stainless steel bowls or "coop cups" that affix to the crate's door. If you find that your puppy frequently splashes his water and makes a mess, then you may not be able to keep water in his crate. In this case, make sure that he has plenty of access to water when he is outside his crate.

You can try to put a crate mat or blanket in the crate, but don't be surprised if your puppy chews it. Puppies love to chew. If your puppy doesn't chew the blanket, it's fine to leave it in the crate. But if you see any sign of chewing, take the blanket out of the crate. If he were to shred up pieces and ingest them, they could get stuck in his intestines, requiring surgical removal. Your puppy will be fine in the crate without a blanket or bed. You can try putting one in there again once he grows up a bit and gets out of his chewing phase.

You can also find an attractive crate cover made of fabric to drape over your puppy's crate for some privacy and a more den-like environment. Crate covers work for some puppies, but others will find a way to pull the fabric into the crate and chew on it. If your puppy is a chewer, then leave the crate uncovered.

Do not put pee pads in your puppy's crate. You may think that it's a good idea to put them down to absorb urine in case he pees, but this is not a good idea. Some pee pads are treated with a scent to encourage puppies to eliminate, which could teach your puppy to eliminate in his crate. Even if the pads are not scented, if your puppy pees on them and the urine is absorbed, it will teach him that it's OK to eliminate in the crate. Crate training is supposed to help teach your puppy to hold his bladder, not eliminate in his den. If you want to use pee pads to teach your puppy to eliminate indoors, that's fine—just don't put them in your puppy's crate.

Introducing the Crate

The crate should always be a positive experience for your puppy. Never use the crate for punishment. Following are the steps to introduce your puppy to the crate. Keep in mind that all of these steps may not happen in one session. Keep your sessions very short—just a few minutes at a time—with breaks in between.

Goal: Your puppy will learn to go into his crate on cue and remain there.

What You'll Need: Clicker, treats, crate.

1. Take your puppy to where you've set up the crate. Click and treat for any interest in the crate, even if he just looks at it. Don't lure him into the crate with the treats. It will be better if he explores it on his own and then gets a treat for a reward. Some puppies are so focused on treats that they could go right into the crate for the treat but then become distressed to find out where they are because they really weren't paying attention. So use the treats as rewards, not bribes.

2. Your puppy should start moving toward the crate or even sniffing it. Click and treat for any interaction.

3. Gradually work to where your puppy puts one paw inside the crate. Click and treat.

4. Once your puppy will put one paw in the crate reliably, wait to click. He should try something new, such as putting two paws inside the crate, to get a reward. Click and treat!

5. Work to where your puppy will go all the way into the crate. Click and treat all correct responses.

Now that your puppy is happily going into his crate, it's time to add the cue.

1. Just before your puppy goes into the crate, give the cue "Kennel up!" or "Go to kennel!" or "Crate up!" in a friendly voice. When he goes in, click and treat.

2. Now it's time to shut the door. Cue "Kennel up," let your puppy walk into the crate, shut the crate door, and click and feed him a treat through the door. Immediately open the door and let him come out if he chooses. If he chooses to stay in the crate, give him another couple of treats.

3. When your puppy will go into his crate and you can shut the door for a second, start gradually increasing the amount of time that you keep the door closed. Cue "Kennel up," let your puppy go into the crate, shut the door, wait a few seconds, and then click and pass a treat through the crate door. If he remains quiet, wait another couple of seconds and then give him another treat through the crate door. Open the door and let him out if he chooses. Repeat several times.

4. Gradually increase the amount of time that you leave your puppy in the crate with the door closed. Let him out only if he is quiet. If he starts pawing at the crate door or whining or barking, do not let him out. Keep waiting for him to settle down and be quiet before you let him out. In the next repetition, decrease the amount of time so that your puppy can be successful.

Keep your crate-training sessions short, with breaks in between.

Up until now, you've stayed with your puppy near his crate. Now it's time to teach him to enjoy his crate without you nearby.

1. Cue "Kennel up," let your puppy into the crate, shut the door, click and treat. Walk across the room and then immediately walk right back. Feed another treat through the crate door and then open the door and let your puppy out if he chooses (as long as he is quiet). Repeat several times.

2. Gradually work to where you can leave the room for longer periods of time.

Return several times and feed your puppy a treat through the crate door, as long as your puppy remains quiet.

3. When you reach five minutes, start leaving your puppy a food-stuffed rubber toy or a chew bone for him to enjoy while you are gone. This will make his time in the crate more rewarding.

Tips: *Do not let your puppy out of his crate if he cries, whines, or barks. You will just be teaching him that crying, whining, or barking means that you will let him out. Just wait him out. If you don't, you will regret it later because it will be harder to teach him to stay in his crate. Your puppy will need confinement for some time, so be consistent with your training now. Keep making the crate rewarding, working in short steps, and he will soon learn to love his crate.*

This training may take several sessions over several days, but you will need to crate your puppy overnight on the first night you have him home. So what do you do if you haven't finished your crate training yet? It's OK. Just put your puppy in his crate, give him several treats and a toy, and leave him there overnight. For the first few nights that you crate your puppy, if you haven't finished your training and if his previous home never crate-trained him, he may protest. Check on him. Is he caught on anything? Is he hurt? If not, then do not let him out of the crate. Sometimes it helps, if the crate is in your bedroom, to put your fingers in the crate door so he can sniff them and feel comforted that you are near. But don't let him out if he's making a ruckus. Be strong! When you complete your crate–training, he'll love his crate, and you'll be able to get peaceful nights of sleep.

Remember, if you have a very young (around eight weeks old) puppy, he may not be able to go the entire night without a potty break. In this case, just take him out for his potty break and return him to his crate immediately with a treat. During the early days of crate-training, you should always give him a treat when he goes into his crate to help build a positive association with it.

When you are home with your puppy, you should have him out of the crate as much as possible, as long as you can supervise him appropriately. Make sure that you crate him on occasion while you are at home, however, so he doesn't always associate your leaving with crate time. For example, you could crate him with a food-stuffed rubber toy while you are fixing and eating dinner.

When you are home with your puppy, you should have him out of the crate, under your supervision, as much as possible.

Setting Schedules

Determine your puppy's feeding schedule and potty schedule. In general, free feeding puppy is not recommended. If he is eating all day, he'll have to eliminate all day, which makes it harder to house-train him.

Puppies of less than six months of age should get three meals a day. Simply put the food down for about fifteen minutes. Take the food bowl away after fifteen minutes, even if there is food left. If you feed your puppy on schedule regularly, he will soon learn when it's time to eat. He may end up reminding you!

Try to space out his feedings evenly. You don't want to make the last feeding too late in the evening because then your puppy will have to eliminate in the middle of the night. It is also OK to take away your puppy's water about an hour before bedtime to help reduce his need to pee during the night. Just be sure that he has had plenty of opportunity to have water during the day.

If your schedule is different on the weekends, your puppy's schedule should *not* be. Puppies do best and learn faster with consistency, so keep to his feeding and potty schedule as closely as possible every day of the week.

Your puppy's potty schedule will greatly depend upon the age of your puppy and, to an extent, his breed or breed combination. Very young puppies (around eight to sixteen weeks of age) will need more frequent potty breaks than six-month-old puppies. Toy and small breeds also seem to need more frequent potty breaks.

In general, puppies need to eliminate when they wake up (even from naps), after they eat, after playing, and after baths. You will be pretty safe in taking your puppy for a potty break at these times as well as every couple of hours. As your puppy gets older, he will need less frequent potty breaks.

If you consistently take your puppy to his elimination spot and he doesn't eliminate, then start decreasing the number of potty breaks you give him. With the sample schedule outlined here, there are eight potty breaks per day. The average adult dog needs about four potty breaks a day. So as your puppy ages, you'll gradually go from about eight potty breaks a day to four. Each dog is an individual, and may need more or fewer potty breaks. As your dog ages into a senior citizen, he will need more frequent potty breaks again.

Positive Solutions

GETTING ATTACHED WITH TETHERING

When you are home and slightly busy, but you don't want to crate your puppy, you still need to supervise him closely, or he may have potty accidents in your home. These are the times when tethering can be a good solution. Simply put your puppy on leash and attach the leash to your belt or tie it around your waist. This will keep your puppy close to you and give you the opportunity to watch him to prevent accidents.

Sample Schedule for a Young Puppy

This schedule is set up for a typical workday if no one is home.

7:00 a.m.	Take your puppy to his elimination spot the minute he wakes up.
7:15 a.m.	Breakfast (leave food bowl down no more than 15 minutes).
7:30 a.m. (or immediately after he completes breakfast)	Potty break.
Noon	Potty break.
12:15 p.m.	Lunch (leave food bowl down no more than 15 minutes).
12:30 p.m.	Potty break.
5:30 p.m.	Take your puppy out as soon as you return home.
6:30 p.m.	Dinner (leave food bowl down no more than 15 minutes).
6:45 p.m.	Potty break.
8:45 p.m.	Potty break and take up water.
10:45 p.m.	Last potty break call before bedtime.

Schedules help you stay consistent and help you train more efficiently, but puppies don't always memorize your schedules! So learn the signs that your puppy has to eliminate. Note that very young puppies may not give you much notice at all. They have very little control, and they have not yet learned to recognize the sensation that tells them that they have to eliminate. As your puppy gets older, he'll offer you more signals. He may whine. He may start sniffing the ground, going in circles. If you see these signs, play it safe and take him to his elimination spot.

Training Your Puppy to Potty Outside

If you do not have a yard for your puppy to eliminate in, but you want him to eliminate outside, you'll need to teach him to eliminate during your walks outside. Or maybe you have a yard, but you want to eventually travel with your dog and thus want to teach him to eliminate on different surfaces (also called "substrates"), such as grass, pine straw, rocky areas, and the like. Some dogs can develop specific preferences if they haven't been taught to eliminate in different environments. For example, if your puppy eliminates only on grass and you travel to a location with mainly rocky terrain, your dog might "hold it" for hours rather than go on an unfamiliar surface. So save yourself future hours of persuasion under the duress of travel. Teach your puppy that different outside locations are OK for elimination.

Simply putting your puppy outside according to a potty schedule will not teach him to eliminate outside. Puppies are easily distracted. Your puppy has no idea that you want him to eliminate outside. He may think that you took him outside to check out the neighbors or dig up bugs. You need to keep him focused on the task you want. To do this, you should always take your puppy out on leash.

When you are attached to your puppy, you can limit the amount of environmental interference that he will experience. A fenced yard isn't enough to keep distractions to a minimum for the average puppy. While you hold the leash, you can gently guide him to an elimination spot of your choosing, whether in your yard or on the curbside as you walk, and prevent him from running off to explore. Leashing your puppy will help make potty breaks more efficient because you won't be chasing your puppy all over the yard while he gets distracted by every scent and sight. He will learn to eliminate quickly, which is extremely convenient if you have a busy schedule, are traveling, or need to monitor his elimination for health reasons.

Leashing your puppy will also help you encourage your puppy to eliminate during bad weather. Yes, it means that you have to go outside, too! To effectively house-train your puppy, you have to go outside with him. You have to be there at the second that he eliminates so that you can reward him. Once your puppy is fully house-trained, you will not have to always go outside with him.

Goal: Your puppy will eliminate outside.

Always take your puppy out on a leash when you start house-training.

What You'll Need: Treats, plastic bags for cleanup, leash.

1. Hide the treats from your puppy. Some puppies will be so focused on the treats that they may be too distracted to eliminate.

2. Leash your puppy. Take him outside to his elimination spot. If you want to teach your puppy to eliminate while on a walk, don't walk too far before choosing an elimination spot. You get to decide where your puppy eliminates. If you consistently choose a spot early in your walk, he'll develop the habit of eliminating first and then enjoying the rest of the walk. If you choose a spot close to

home, you can then also go back and dispose of the poop bag so you won't have to carry it all along your walk.

3. As soon as he starts to eliminate, say "Go potty" in a friendly voice. If you're outside for ten minutes and your puppy does not eliminate, bring him back inside and confine him or closely supervise him for about fifteen minutes and then repeat this step.

4. As soon as your puppy finishes eliminating, praise him and give him a treat.

5. Play or walk with your puppy for a few minutes outside. You can unleash him if you prefer (as long as you have a fenced yard). You don't want to immediately take him inside, or you could be teaching him that elimination means that outside time is over.

6. Repeat Steps 1–5 for each potty break.

Tip: *Keep in mind that this is a gradual process. Your puppy won't be able to anticipate when he has to eliminate until he is at least four months old. If your puppy goes one week without any accidents, don't be fooled into thinking he's completely trained. Every accident that he has indoors will set you back a bit. So be vigilant, manage your puppy, and follow the training program. Stick with the program consistently until you have months, not days, of success.*

Once your puppy is regularly going outside on leash with you and eliminating on cue, it's time to start weaning off the leash if you prefer. These steps assume that you have a securely fenced yard where you want your puppy to eliminate. Your puppy should never be allowed off leash in an unfenced yard or when out on a walk. These steps will let you send your puppy out into the yard to eliminate while you remain by the door.

If you want to wean your puppy off the leash for house-training, you must have a securely fenced yard where you want your puppy to eliminate.

1. Take your puppy outside to eliminate, following the previously outlined house-training program, but this time letting the puppy drag the leash. Follow him closely. Be sure that the leash does not get tangled on anything. When he eliminates, praise and treat. Repeat until he is reliably eliminating with you following him.

2. Take your puppy outside to eliminate, following the house-training program, but this time without a leash. Follow him closely.

CHOOSING YOUR CUE

Some people prefer to have one cue for elimination, such as Go Potty or Do Your Business. Others prefer to have separate cues for peeing and pooping, such as Go Pee and Go Poop. It's up to you. Just be consistent. Make sure your family is also consistent. If you have a neighbor helping you, or if you hire a petsitter to help you offer a mid-day break for your puppy, be sure you give them the proper cues to use.

When he eliminates, praise and treat. If your puppy continues to eliminate quickly without being on leash, move on to Step 3. If he decides to run about and play, then go back to holding the leash for a week and then try Step 1 again.

3. Take your puppy outside to eliminate, following the house-training program, but gradually stay farther away from your puppy. Always praise him when he eliminates and, when he returns to you, give him a treat. If at any time your puppy gets too distracted, decrease the distance between you and then gradually work back up to more distance. (Some puppies will have formed the habit of eliminating quickly by this point, but some will still be easily distracted. Both responses are normal. Just go at your puppy's pace.) Your goal is to work to the point at which you can stay by the doorway while you send your puppy out into the yard to eliminate.

Tips: *Please don't be discouraged if things go great for a while, and then you experience a setback. The outdoors has many more smells and distractions for your puppy than inside your home does. You may have several weeks of success, and then, one day, your adolescent puppy goes outside and gets obsessed with one corner of the yard, completely ignoring your cue to eliminate. It may be that a rabbit recently paid your yard a visit, or a neighborhood cat used your yard as an elimination spot. Remember, puppies and adolescent dogs have terrible attention spans. So, if you have a frustrating house-training experience, that's actually typical. Just stick with the program, be consistent, and wait out your puppy's lack of focus. If necessary, go back several steps to a point in your training where your puppy is successful so that you can stay on track. You don't want a momentary distraction to become a new habit for your puppy.*

Training Your Puppy to Eliminate Indoors

Training your puppy to eliminate indoors can be convenient if you live in a high-rise apartment or have a tiny or small dog. Puppies normally have to eliminate as soon as they wake, so rushing a puppy down fifteen flights to get outside is problematic. Some people cannot make it home for a midday break or may live in an area that isn't conducive to outdoor elimination. This is when litterbox or paper-training can be very convenient.

Indoor elimination can be both convenient and inconvenient for travel. If you are in a hotel room, it can be easy to set up your puppy's elimination area, and you won't have to worry about taking him outside. If you are taking him to visit friends or relatives, however, they may not appreciate or allow you to have an indoor elimination station.

First, choose whether you want to train your puppy to eliminate in a litterbox or on paper or pee pads. Litterboxes come in a variety of styles. Some require litter, and others use sod or artificial turf. Note that litter for dogs is different than litter for cats! Do not use kitty litter in your puppy's litterbox; it may not be healthy for him. Sod or turf is a good choice if you eventually want to teach your puppy to also eliminate outdoors.

Goal: Your puppy will eliminate indoors in a specific location.

What You'll Need: Elimination station, treats.

1. Hide your treats from your puppy. Some puppies will be so focused on the treats that they may be too distracted to eliminate.
2. Take your puppy to his elimination spot. As soon as he starts to eliminate, give your cue (such as "Go potty") in a friendly voice. As soon as your puppy finishes, praise him and give him a treat.
3. If you wait ten minutes, and your puppy does not eliminate, confine him or closely supervise him for about fifteen minutes and then try Step 2 again.
4. Repeat Steps 1–3 for each potty break.

Once your puppy is regularly eliminating on cue, it's time to start teaching him to move toward the elimination spot on his own, without your having to go with him.

1. Take your puppy to his elimination spot, but stop about one step away from the location. Let your puppy continue the rest of the way by himself. Follow the previously outlined house-training program. Don't forget to praise him and give him a treat when he eliminates. When your puppy regularly continues to the elimination spot by himself, you're ready for the next step.

Did something "scary" block your puppy's path to his elimination spot?

2. Gradually move farther away from the elimination spot, one step at a time, each time your puppy eliminates. Follow the house-training program. Your goal is to eventually be able to send your puppy to his elimination spot from a different room.

Tips: *If at any time your puppy misses the litterbox or pee pad, go back to the last point at which he was successful. Stay at that point for a week and then try moving farther away again.*

With consistency and practice, your puppy should start going on his own to the elimination spot when he has to eliminate. It will take some time before he is consistent, and he first must be old enough to understand the sensation that signals that he has to eliminate. Continue to monitor your puppy. If you find messes outside the elimination spot, first check to make sure that the path to the elimination spot was not blocked. For example, if the spot is in your bathroom, was someone in there with the door shut? Or was something potentially scary, such as a parked vacuum cleaner, in the puppy's way? If you don't find anything impeding the path to the elimination spot, back up in your training. Go back to supervising your puppy more closely for a few weeks, and then gradually move farther away again. Don't be discouraged! It's very common to have house-training accidents on occasion. Just stick with the program consistently and be patient.

Only introduce a dog door if your puppy has done well in his house-training for several months.

Future Training

Once your puppy understands that you want him to eliminate in a certain area, you can consider some advanced training if you like.

Dog Doors

Some people believe that if they have a dog door, their puppy will automatically learn to eliminate outside the house. It's true that some puppies are innately wired to go outside to eliminate, but not all puppies are, and you shouldn't depend on a door to do your work for you in house-training. Plus, if you ever travel with your puppy to a place that doesn't have a dog door, he could be confused.

Another drawback to using dog doors with puppies without supervision is that your puppy could bring things indoors from outside that you may not appreciate! Dogs have been known to bring items ranging from sticks to live animals indoors. Puppies are naturally curious, so the possibility of your puppy's carrying something into your home is high. He might also carry your nice things outside and leave them there.

If you bring home a new puppy and you already have another older dog or dogs in your home that regularly use a dog door, don't completely depend on them to house-train your puppy. For example, puppies sometimes learn to follow other dogs outside to eliminate. Then, when the other dogs pass away and are no longer around to lead them, they start eliminating in the house. Be sure that *you* are the one teaching your puppy what you want.

Once your puppy has done well in his house-training for several months, it should be OK to introduce him to the dog door.

Goal: Your puppy will go through a dog door.

What You'll Need: Clicker and treats.

1. Sit near the dog door with your puppy. Click for any interest in the dog door, even if he just looks at it.

2. After a few clicks for showing interest, your puppy should start moving toward the dog door or nosing it. Click and treat. Gradually work to where your puppy will open the door with his nose. Click and treat.

3. If your puppy seems confused or a bit hesitant about the door, open it yourself and hold it open. Don't let it slam shut, or it could startle him. Click and treat for every exploratory action.

4. Gradually work to where your puppy will go through the dog door. Click and treat for every correct response.

5. Go outside the dog door and repeat the steps. Just because your puppy learns to go through the door one way doesn't mean that he will understand that he can come back through!

Tip: *This may take one session or several, depending on your puppy. Some puppies will boldly charge right through the door right away, while others are more hesitant. Each reaction is normal, so just go as fast as your puppy is comfortable with and can succeed.*

Did You Know?

BIRDS OF PREY CAN ATTACK SMALL DOGS

If you have birds of prey in your area, do not use a dog door for your toy breed or small puppy. Birds of prey, such as hawks and owls, have been known to snatch little dogs. If you think about it, a tiny puppy isn't much bigger than a rabbit. So do not allow your puppy to be outside without you to protect him from birds of prey. If you have a dog door, you won't know when your puppy goes outside. If your puppy will grow up to be a larger dog, then wait until he is older and larger to introduce him to the dog door. By then, he will be safer from attacks from the sky!

Teaching Your Puppy to Ring a Bell

As your house-training progresses, you can teach your puppy to give you a signal that he needs to eliminate. This behavior is for a puppy who is trained to eliminate outdoors only.

Goal: Your puppy will ring a bell to go outside.

What You'll Need: Bell attached to a long ribbon tied to the door leading outside, clicker, treats, leash. To determine what length of ribbon to use, position the bell so that it will hang no higher than your puppy's shoulder. You want your puppy to be able to easily paw the bell. Attach the bell to the door that you use to take your puppy in and out for elimination. For training purposes, you will use only this door.

1. Sit near the bell attached to the door. Click and treat for any interest your puppy shows in the bell, even if he just looks at it. He should then begin to show increased interest and start to nose the bell. Click and treat. Alternately, if you have already taught him his target cue, you can cue him to "Touch" the bell. Click and treat for all correct responses.

Attach a bell to the door that you use to take your puppy in and out.

2. When your puppy is regularly ringing the bell, it's time to teach your puppy that ringing the bell means that you will open the door and take him outside. For this phase, you will need to leash him. When it's time for a potty break, leash your puppy and wait by the door. Just be still and wait for him to ring the bell. When he does, click, treat, and immediately open the door to take him outside. Give him his cue to eliminate and then give him a treat for doing so. Repeat for each potty break.

3. With repetition, your puppy will learn that when he rings the bell, you open the door. One day, you will not be near the door, but you will hear the bell ring. This is your puppy experimenting! Immediately stop what you are doing, go to your puppy, leash him, and open the door. At this point, you no longer need to click because he has learned the behavior of ringing the bell.

4. Give him ten minutes to eliminate. If he does, praise and treat him. If he doesn't,

simply bring him back inside. At this point, your puppy probably hasn't learned that ringing the bell is only for when he wants to eliminate. He has learned that ringing the bell means he gets to go outside. By leashing your puppy, you will quickly determine if he really needs to eliminate or just wants to play, and you can easily bring him in if he thinks it's playtime.

5. Repeat Steps 3 and 4 each time you hear your puppy ring the bell. You may find that your puppy rings it a lot at first! This is typical.

Tips: *If you suspect that your puppy just wants to go outside and play, and you don't open the door, you will teach him that ringing the bell doesn't mean anything. This will set back your training. You may also find that he eliminates indoors because you didn't let him out. So even if you think that your puppy's playing, go and open the door. As long as you leash him so he can't run and play outside, you will soon teach him that ringing the bell is only for when he needs to eliminate.*

Cleaning Up Messes

Despite your best intentions, there are bound to be times when your puppy eliminates somewhere that you don't want him to—this is typical. Your goal in house-training will be to minimize the amount of times that this happens, but when it does, don't overreact.

If you catch your puppy in the act of elimination, use a stern "No!" and immediately take him to his elimination spot (leashing him if you are training him to eliminate outside). If he finishes at his elimination spot, praise him enthusiastically. You need to make it clear that you are not happy when he eliminates in an inappropriate place, but you love it when he eliminates in his specific spot.

You do not have to, and you shouldn't, use harsh punishment, or you could cause significant problems. Just use a stern voice. Never use your hands for punishment, and never roll up a newspaper to hit your puppy. This will not teach him to stop eliminating in the house at all. Instead, it will just teach him to be afraid of you or to hide from you to eliminate. This is how you create a puppy that hides in closets or under tables to eliminate. Not what you want to teach!

If you do not catch your puppy eliminating, you can't punish him. He's long forgotten what you are yelling about. Just be more vigilant in your supervision to prevent it from happening again.

Try This!

CLEANING UP

When you clean up urine or feces, use an enzymatic cleaner to be thorough. If you use other types of products, or white vinegar, you may not eliminate all of the particles, which your puppy can still smell. This may encourage him to return to the spot and eliminate again. Enzymatic cleaners are available at pet-supply stores.

CHAPTER 7

EVERYDAY MANNERS AND LIFE SKILLS

As a puppy owner, you have a responsibility to ensure that your puppy behaves appropriately when out in public. Puppies are babies, and they don't understand manners. You'll be teaching your puppy manners, but in the meantime, you'll need to manage his behavior to prevent him from become a nuisance or accidentally hurting someone or another animal.

Great Expectations

There are certain expectations for canine good manners in public. Mannerly puppies and dogs:

- **Are leashed in public wherever it is required.** They do not run loose in neighborhoods. Puppies that run loose can easily be hurt by cars, by unfriendly loose dogs, or even by people who don't appreciate strange dogs getting into their yards.

- **Are not permitted to run up to another dog without the owner of that dog's permission.** While it is great if your puppy is social, infringing on another dog's space without permission is rude. Puppies often greet overenthusiastically, which is not always appreciated by other dogs. It could result in your puppy getting bit if he gets in the face of a dog that doesn't like his greeting. It could also frighten a dog that is already shy or fearful, which isn't fair to that dog.

- **Are not permitted to jump up on people.** A jumping puppy is usually being friendly! But that doesn't mean that everyone appreciates a puppy jumping on them. And depending on the size of your puppy, he could accidentally hurt someone.

- **Always have their poop picked up by responsible owners.** If your puppy eliminates while off of your property, you should pick it up and dispose of it. It's just part of being a dog owner.

You can achieve most manners just by leashing your puppy when you're out in public or when you have guests over. That way, you can stop him from getting into most trouble. As you train him, you won't have to manage him so closely.

Lifeline: Your Puppy's Collar and Leash

Puppies are not born liking their collars or being controlled by leashes. It's common for a puppy to scratch at his neck, trying to dislodge a collar, or put on the brakes and refuse to move when first leashed. You will need to teach your puppy to love his collar and leash. He will soon realize that they are associated with walks, exploration, and fun.

Goal: Your puppy will learn to wear a collar (or harness).

What You'll Need: Collar, treats, toys.

1. Allow your puppy to sniff the collar. Give him a treat. Repeat.

2. Put the collar on your puppy. Immediately give him three treats in a row. Remove the collar, but only if he is not pawing at it. Repeat several times.

3. Put the collar on your puppy. Give him three treats. Let him wear it for a couple of seconds and then remove it. Do not remove it if he is pawing at it. Repeat, gradually working up to a minute of wearing the collar.

4. Put the collar on your puppy. Give him a treat and then play with him. Engage him with his toys, give him lots of praise, and tell him how handsome he is. After several minutes, remove the collar, and be quiet, withdrawing your attention. Repeat, making a huge fuss over him while he wears the collar and being quiet when you take it off.

Never yank your puppy's leash.

Tips: *If your puppy is pawing at his collar or fussing with it, do not remove it. Instead, distract him with a toy. If you remove it while he's pawing at it, you'll teach him that his behavior will work in getting you to take the collar off. Always make sure that the collar fits properly so he can't catch his jaw or paw in it. Remember to check it frequently, because puppies grow quickly. A collar that fits fine one day could be too tight the next.*

Once you get your puppy used to wearing a collar, it's time to attach the leash. Here are the steps.

Goal: Your puppy will learn to wear a leash attached to his collar (or harness).

What You'll Need: Leash, collar, treats.

1. Have treats ready. Put on your puppy's collar and attach the leash. Give your puppy three treats.

2. Let your puppy drag the leash in a safe area where it won't get tangled. Supervise him closely to be safe. Randomly give your puppy treats as long as he is not chewing on his leash.

3. Gently take up the leash and just hold it. Give your puppy a few treats.

4. Start walking and encourage your puppy to come with you. If he puts on the brakes, don't say anything. Just wait him out. Only exert enough pressure to slightly tighten the leash; never yank it. When he does start walking with you, give him a lot of praise and a couple of treats.

5. Repeat until your puppy readily allows you to maneuver him with the leash. Only use gentle pressure if necessary. Never use the leash to yank your puppy's neck.

Mannerly dogs are leashed whenever required in public.

Teaching Self Control: Settle Down

There are times when you just want your puppy to be calm and quiet, to settle down. This can be a very hard thing for a puppy to do!

Goal: Your puppy will settle and be calm.

What You'll Need: Clicker, treats.

1. Jump, pat your legs, use a high-pitched voice, or run around to get your puppy really excited and bouncy. After he's all riled up for a few seconds, stand perfectly still. Don't say anything. If he's leaping for your hands, cross your

arms so they are out of his reach. Just be quiet. Wait for him to be quiet and, when he is, click and treat.

2. Repeat nine times. End your training session.

3. Now it's time to add the cue. Jump up and get your puppy excited. Just before you are still, give the cue "Calm," "Settle," or "Easy"—or whatever you want, just be consistent. Use a friendly voice. When he settles, click and treat.

4. After ten successful repetitions, you no longer have to click. Continue to treat another dozen times. Then treat every other time, then every third time, and then randomly as you wean off the treats.

Bite Inhibition

Puppies have little needlelike teeth, and they like to put those teeth into everything, including you! Your puppy is not trying to hurt you or assert himself as "alpha." Chewing on everything is a very normal puppy behavior. Some puppies enjoy it more than others. For example, if you have a retriever, you may have a very mouthy puppy. Retrievers are bred to put things in their mouths. This trait has been accentuated with many years of selective breeding.

Puppies chew because they are exploring their worlds. It doesn't seem like a very effective testing method—putting an item in your mouth to figure out what it is—but it's the puppy way. Puppies also chew on things because, at about four months of age, they are teething. They lose their baby teeth as the adult teeth push through the gums. This can be very uncomfortable, so they chew to relieve the pain in their gums. Puppies also chew because it's fun. They like to chew things, and their teeth are built for the task. Puppies also chew in play with other dogs. When two dogs play and wrestle, they often chew on each other quite happily.

Puppies can also chew when they are stressed. For example, dogs that experience separation anxiety and sometimes fear of thunder will often chew doorways and windowsills in their stress to escape. This isn't spite; it's stress.

One of the main complaints of new puppy owners is that their puppies love to chew on them. Those little needlelike teeth can be quite painful. Teaching your puppy bite inhibition is extremely important during his younger months. After he reaches adolescence, it will be harder to teach.

Goal: Your puppy will learn bite inhibition.

What You'll Need: Toys.

1. When your puppy's teeth touch your skin, give a pathetic, whiny

Puppies chew because they are exploring their worlds.

"owwwww" as if you are gravely injured. Don't sound sharp or angry, or your puppy will probably just bite harder, thinking that you are playing back. Act really sad about it.

2. Withdraw all attention from your puppy. Your puppy does not want to hurt you; he wants to play with you. When faced with an indication that he has injured you, your puppy is likely to immediately stop mouthing you. He may start kissing you instead. At this point, praise him for the kisses.

3. Grab a toy that he is allowed to chew on and offer it to him. Praise him! You want to teach him that chewing on you is painful and hurts you, but you love it when he chews on his toys.

4. Repeat this every single time your puppy's teeth touch your skin. You will have to do it frequently, as puppies have very short memories.

Be consistent. If you start trying other techniques, you will have less success and just confuse your puppy.

Another thing that you can do to reduce your puppy's mouthy behavior is avoid roughhousing with him. If you, or your family or friends, wrestle with your puppy and think it's funny when he gnaws on you, then you are teaching him bad habits. You can't allow it in some instances and not in others—that's just too confusing for a young puppy. There are many games that you can play with your puppy instead of roughhousing. Now, if your puppy isn't very mouthy, then roughhousing may be perfectly fine. It depends on your puppy.

If your puppy is mouthing you, withdraw your attention and give him a toy that he is allowed to chew on.

When your puppy mouths you, it definitely can be frustrating. Do not yell at him, pop him in the nose, push your fingers down his throat, scruff shake him, or use any other physical punishment. This will just make the situation worse. Remember, your puppy is just trying to play with you. You need to teach him that he should not play with his teeth.

If you push back, a boisterous puppy may think that you've caught onto the game and will bite down harder. Or, if you scare him, he may no longer chew on you, but he is very likely to continue chewing on other people. You will not have taught him that chewing on you is painful; instead, you will have taught him you, specifically, are scary. So he'll go chomp on the children or your grandmother.

Every single time your puppy's teeth touch your skin, give the pained "owwww," withdraw your attention, and then, when he stops chewing, give him a toy that he is allowed to chew on and heap praise on him for that action. With consistency and repetition, your puppy will start heading to the toy first, rather than your skin!

Trade

Resource guarding occurs when a dog tries to prevent a person or other animal from taking something he perceives as his. He may block access to the item, or tense, growl, snarl or even bite. One way to prevent resource guarding in puppies is to teach them to give up their toys when you ask. Even if your puppy shows no sign of guarding items, this is a good prevention exercise.

Goal: Your puppy will give up an item when you cue him.

What You'll Need: Two items that your puppy is likely to take into his mouth.

1. Give your puppy one item, such as a toy. Let him settle down with it and chew on it for a few minutes.
2. Offer him the other item. When he goes to take it, praise him and give it to him. Pick the original item up.
3. Repeat Steps 1 and 2 three times. End your training session.

Tip: *Vary the items you use during your sessions.*

Handling

You should be able to touch your puppy all over his body without his getting squirmy and nipping at you, and without his flinching in fear. This is one of the most important things that you can teach your puppy. He should enjoy your touching him. Throughout his life, you will have to handle him, whether it's to check for fleas, administer medicine to his ears, clip his nails, groom him, or treat an injury.

Teach your puppy to accept handling.

Goal: Your puppy will enjoy handling.

What You'll Need: Treats.

1. Lightly touch your puppy's ear. Immediately give him a treat. Lightly touch his other ear. Give him a treat.
2. Lightly touch your puppy's paw. Immediately give him a treat. Repeat for all paws.
3. Gently open your puppy's mouth. Treat.

4. Lightly touch your puppy's tail. Treat.

5. Repeat all steps five times. End your training session.

6. In future training sessions, as your puppy grows more comfortable with handling, start to gently massage your puppy's ears, paws, mouth, and tail. If at any time your puppy gets squirmy or fearful, slow down. Give lots of treats. Work up to where you can touch your puppy all over while you praise him and give him occasional treats.

Tips: *Some puppies have certain areas in which they really don't like being touched. For example, some puppies really dislike having their mouths opened. If your puppy is especially balking at this exercise, tire him out beforehand by playing with him. Use high-value treats and go slower with your handling. For example, instead of touching him with your hand, use just one finger. Be gradual. The time you take with this exercise will pay off throughout your puppy's lifetime.*

Nail Clipping

Once your puppy has gotten used to your handling him all over, you can take it further by teaching him to enjoy having his nails clipped and his feet trimmed, if necessary. First, learn how to properly cut your puppy's nails. If you don't know how, you can ask your groomer or veterinarian to show you how.

Goal: Your puppy will enjoy nail clipping.

What You'll Need: Nail clippers, treats. Have some styptic powder or gel on hand in case you nick a nail and it bleeds.

1. Show your puppy the clippers and immediately give him a treat.

2. Repeat nine times. End your training session.

3. Repeat Steps 1–2 for one week.

4. Show your puppy the clippers and touch one nail—but do not cut! Immediately give a treat. Repeat for a few nails and then end your session. Gradually work up to where your puppy is comfortable with your touching all of his nails. Only go as fast as your puppy is comfortable with.

5. When your puppy doesn't mind your touching his nails, it's time to cut one nail. Cut one nail, give your puppy three treats, and stop your session.

6. Repeat Step 2, adding no more than two nails per day until you can cut all of his nails. Do not rush the process; doing so could set you back in your training, which could be difficult to fix.

Try This!

SETTLING THE EXUBERANT PUPPY

Some puppies find the Settle exercise very challenging. If your puppy has a tendency to get so riled up that it's hard for him to settle down, play with him before you practice this exercise to take the "edge" off of his exuberance.

Tip: *You can use this same technique to introduce your puppy to a brush, comb, or scissors if you have to trim the fur between his paws. Just go slow and make each part of the training a positive experience for your puppy.*

Happy Veterinarian Visits

It's easy for puppies to be frightened of the veterinary office. To take care of your puppy, your veterinarian and the veterinary technicians will need to do things that are uncomfortable for him, such as inserting a thermometer or giving him shots. These actions can make a puppy dread visiting the veterinarian. There are also animals that are sick, in pain, and on medication, which your puppy can hear and smell. This can be very frightening.

It doesn't have to be that way, though. You should teach your puppy to love visiting the vet, because he will need to do so for his entire life.

Goal: Your puppy will enjoy veterinary visits.

What You'll Need: Clicker, treats.

1. Take your puppy to the veterinary office for a visit when he doesn't have an appointment. Click and treat for all signs of outgoing behavior. Any time he reaches forward to sniff something in curiosity, click and treat. Any time he happily lets someone pet him, click and treat.

2. Explain to the staff you are socializing your puppy to their office and ask them to give him treats. Most veterinary staff will be happy to participate in this training because they want your puppy to be comfortable visiting them, but please be respectful that they are busy.

3. Repeat, preferably at least twice a week, until your puppy is eager to go inside the veterinary office.

Tip: *Do not allow your puppy to go up to other animals in the veterinary clinic when you visit. This is not polite, and it's also not wise because they could be there because they are sick. If your puppy shows any signs of being fearful or shy, proceed very slowly. Use extremely high-value treats.*

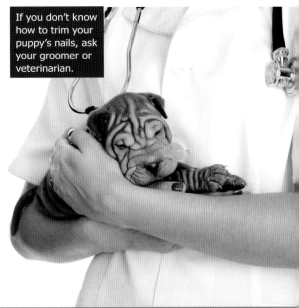

If you don't know how to trim your puppy's nails, ask your groomer or veterinarian.

Getting your puppy to love the veterinary office will depend on how outgoing and confident your puppy is naturally and how often you will be able to make these successful training visits. If you are only able to make one, especially during your puppy's critical socialization period before about sixteen weeks, then your puppy could continue to be afraid of the veterinary office.

CHAPTER 8

SOCIALIZATION

There is some debate about the exact age when the socialization window for puppies closes—generally between twelve and eighteen weeks of age. What isn't debated is the importance of the socialization period. During this time, puppies learn about the world around them, forming opinions that follow them into adulthood.

If during this time, a puppy doesn't have positive exposure to a wide variety of people, animals, environments, surfaces, sounds, and other experiences, then he or she could become frightened of them later. For example, if a puppy doesn't have a lot of exposure to children, and he meets a toddler when he's a year old, he could growl at the child. Toddlers move and act differently than adults—they shriek unexpectedly, make jerky movements as they learn to walk, and like to grab things tightly. This can be very startling to a dog that is not used to toddlers, and a growl is a signal that the dog is afraid. Conversely, if a puppy is exposed in a positive manner to children before he is eighteen weeks old, he is more likely to be comfortable around children as an adult.

When people adopt a rescue dog that proves to be fearful of men, or children, or certain situations, they often think it's because the dog had previously been abused. While that's certainly possible, if it were the case in every situation of a fearful dog, there would be a tremendous amount of abuse going on. The more likely scenario is that the dog was not properly socialized during his critical socialization period.

If a puppy spends most of his time in a backyard with other dogs, he is likely to be wary of people.

For example, if a puppy is mainly raised in a backyard with other dogs, with very limited experience with people, he is very likely to love other dogs but be very wary of people. He was never around people during the critical socialization period to bond with them and learn that people can be trusted. This is why some rescue dogs get along quickly with other dogs but not people—they were more socialized with other dogs as puppies than they were people.

The socialization period is the most important time in your puppy's life, and you have a tremendous responsibility to get it right! Skimping on properly socializing your puppy can cause major behavioral problems later. Get a calendar and chart the amount of time you have until his socialization window closes. Commit to a number of visits each week, during which you will take your puppy to different places to meet different people and animals, making it your puppy's social calendar. Having set appointments can help you plan and stick to a schedule better.

Socialization, however, is not just taking your puppy everywhere. You must make sure that each new experience is a positive one for your puppy, watching him for any signs of fear or stress. If he has bad experiences, they will linger with him and could cause the fear or aggression you're trying to avoid.

Recognizing Signs of Fear and Helping Your Puppy Cope

Throughout your socialization training, watch your puppy for signs of stress. Many people don't even realize when their puppy is afraid. Learn the signs so that you can recognize them. Signs of stress include:

- Licking lips
- Yawning
- Turning away
- Tucking his tail
- Trying to avoid the situation
- Refusing treats

If your puppy demonstrates any of these symptoms, assess the situation. What is he concerned about? See if you can get some distance between him and what he is afraid of, or you can try to make the situation less scary for him and start clicking and treating for brave behavior.

Vet Tip

PUPPY SOCIALIZATION

Mary Fluke, DVM, a veterinarian at Mallard Creek Animal Hospital in Charlotte, North Carolina, warns that puppies that do not get socialized within the critical socialization period are at risk for behavior problems. "We need to immunize puppies against disease with vaccines, but we also have to immunize them against 'the world' with proper socialization," Dr. Fluke says.

"I suggest a focused program of socialization to people early in the critical period by inviting people to the home for the first few weeks, then taking the puppy out into the world in the latter part of the first three months. Start vaccines by six to eight weeks and follow your vet's advice for how often and how many doses are needed. Once the puppy has had at least two vaccinations and is ten weeks old, it's OK to start puppy classes—with other well-cared for, healthy puppies!"

Dr. Fluke also recommends having your puppy play with older dogs more than other puppies. She explains, "When puppies play together, they can learn some very bad habits. When they interact with grown-up dogs, they learn to be polite to other dogs."

She also agrees that your puppy's socialization experiences should be fun for your puppy. "If you think things are getting out of hand," she says, "bail out!"

For example, your puppy shows that he is afraid of your friend, a very tall man wearing a hat. Ask your friend to sit down so that he doesn't appear so tall. Take your puppy farther from your friend and then click and treat him for any look or movement toward the man. Your friend should avoid eye contact and not pet your puppy if he is afraid. As your puppy gets more confident and begins to approach your friend, he can start dropping treats for your puppy and eventually hand him treats. Just take it slow, realizing that it may take more than one session for some puppies to gain confidence.

If you find that you are not making progress, remove your puppy from the situation. It's better to limit a scary experience than push your puppy. Never force a puppy to confront his fear. For example, allowing your tall male friend to pick up your frightened puppy would be a terrible idea. Your puppy will trust you less for allowing the scary man to pick him up, and it could backfire and cause the puppy to become even more frightened of tall men, or even men in general.

Some people will try this and see their puppy frantically licking the man's face, thinking, "He likes him! It worked!"—but this is actually an appeasement behavior. Your puppy is pleading, not showing affection. Puppy kisses aren't always the sign of a happy puppy—you need to view them in context with the rest of his body language and demeanor.

Even the most confident puppy can find something that startles him. A bold, rambunctious puppy could be scared of the vacuum cleaner or an umbrella. As long as you are prepared and watch your puppy for signs of distress, you can help turn scary situations into better ones for socialization success.

If your puppy hasn't had all of his vaccinations yet, take him only to places where you can carry him.

Be Social but Safe

While your puppy needs as many positive social experiences as possible before his critical socialization window closes, remember that he has not had all of his shots yet. He won't complete his puppy series of vaccinations, including the rabies vaccine, until the end of the socialization window. This means that it's not safe for him to walk on surfaces where sick dogs might have been, including pet stores, public parks, and your neighborhood. Dogs that are infected with distemper, parvovirus, or other diseases spread the diseases through bodily fluids. Stray dogs can carry disease because they do not get regular health care and vaccinations. So if a sick dog pees in your neighborhood and your puppy walks in that spot, he could contract the disease.

In order to keep your puppy safe, don't take him to those places unless you are able to carry him. For a small puppy, this is relatively easy for most. Larger puppies could prove harder! You can successfully socialize your puppy safely. You just have to get creative.

Instead of taking your puppy places, bring experiences to your puppy. Have people and safe dogs come visit you. If you take your puppy to a store that allows dogs, have him ride in the cart. (Don't forget to make the cart ride a positive experience, too!) If you have friends who have enclosed yards that have never had exposure to contagious diseases, such as parvovirus, you can take your puppy there. Note that parvovirus can survive in the environment for up to about seven months.

If your puppy does need to have paws on the ground in an area you suspect may not be disease-free, carry baby wipes with you and wipe his paws once you get him in the car or another "safe zone."

When people meet your puppy, have them wash their hands first. If they've been walking in places that are suspect, have them remove their shoes when they come into your house so they don't track in disease.

As long as you take the proper precautions, the benefits of properly socializing your puppy will greatly outweigh the chances of your puppy contracting disease. You will be preventing serious behavioral problems, such as fear and aggression, as your puppy grows up.

Meeting People

Dr. Ian Dunbar, veterinarian, behaviorist, and the founder of the Association of Professional Dog Trainers (APDT), recommends that puppies meet more than one hundred people during their socialization periods. Choose a variety of people to meet your puppy—people of different genders, ethnicities, and ages. Make sure that everyone you choose is comfortable and confident with puppies. If someone is afraid of your puppy and acts nervous, jerks his hands away, and only tentatively pets the puppy, the puppy will pick up on this, and it could frighten him, too.

Trainer Tip

EXPLORING DIFFERENT ENVIRONMENTS

Whenever you take your puppy to a new place, bring your clicker and treats. Click and treat for exploratory behavior. Try to vary the surfaces that your puppy explores, from carpet to slick floors. Keeping in mind safety precautions, take your puppy to different homes, stores that allow pets, the veterinary office, the groomer, and more.

Give people treats to give your puppy. Have a person present the treat in an open hand to prevent those sharp puppy teeth from chomping down on his fingers.

When you introduce your puppy to all of these different people, monitor him closely. Does he seem to be more hesitant around some types of people than others? Try giving those people extra special treats to give your puppy.

Meeting Children

Make sure that you choose children to meet your puppy who can follow your directions and who will be gentle with your puppy. Do not let him meet kids who are afraid of dogs because this could frighten the puppy, too. If you have an exuberant or large puppy, keep him on leash so you can better control him from jumping on the children and potentially hurting them.

If your puppy is in the teething stage and especially nippy, have the children drop treats on the floor for the puppy instead of handing them to him. Children have fragile skin, and you don't want the puppy to accidentally nip fingers.

Children often love to pick up puppies, but that doesn't mean it's a good socialization experience. Only allow children to pick up your puppy if they are able to do so correctly, picking him up slowly and supporting his rear. Do not allow children to pick your puppy up under his front legs or tote him around like a doll. Your puppy will not feel supported and could become frightened.

Choose children who can follow directions and will be gentle socializing your puppy.

Meeting Other Dogs

Before you allow your puppy to meet another dog, you must be absolutely certain that dog is good with puppies. Not every dog likes other dogs. Even some dogs that enjoy the company of other adult dogs may not like puppies. You don't want to find this out too late, after your puppy has been bitten or injured!

Also, some dogs like puppies but may be too exuberant to safely play with your puppy, depending on the size difference. Always check with the dog's owner first. Ask what interactions that dog has had specifically with puppies. If you have any concerns, do not allow a greeting. Your puppy could get hurt and develop a fear of other dogs.

If you are confident that the interaction will be safe, and the dogs are enclosed in a fenced yard, it's often best to let them meet off leash. Leash tension can increase aggression in some dogs. Stay close to the dogs and be ready to intervene if necessary.

If you need to introduce the dogs on leash, try to keep the leashes loose enough to reduce leash tension but without so much slack that the dogs could get tangled. Give the dogs room to circle each other. On leash, three-second interactions are ideal. Allow the dogs to interact for three seconds and then call them away. Assess the situation. Are the dogs eager to return to each other? Friendly? Allow another three-second introduction. Repeat several times until you are sure that they will get along, and then you can allow longer interactions.

In appropriate dog–dog play, each dog enjoys the interaction. It's normal for one dog to be "on top" for a bit, and then for dogs to switch positions. Chasing, body slamming, jaw sparring (when the dogs have open mouths and make lots of noise clashing their muzzles together but aren't doing any damage), tug-of-war, and chewing on each other are all typical canine games.

Different breeds have different play styles. Herding breeds generally love to chase, while sporting breeds can play pretty

Did You Know?

DOG PARKS ARE *NOT* FOR PUPPIES

Dog parks can be good places for adolescent and adult dogs to socialize, but they are terrible for puppy socialization. One bullying experience at a dog park (e.g., several dogs gang up on your puppy) can cause your puppy to be fearful toward other dogs for years, or even for life. Fearful puppies often grow up to be aggressive dogs. While some dog parks are designed well and attended by people who supervise their dogs and only bring appropriate dogs to the park, this is not the case with every park. Some people bring reactive dogs to dog parks. Others are busy on their cell phones and don't even notice when their dogs bully other dogs. Others are not educated in canine behavior, so if their dog is a bully, they just say that it's how he "plays." You can't control the environment at a dog park, so don't expose your puppy and risk a bad experience. When your puppy grows up to be a teenager, do your research. If there is a quality dog park nearby, then you can visit without a socialization risk.

rough wrestle/tackle games. Some dogs do not do well with dogs that have play styles different from their own. Always watch canine play closely to ensure that everyone is having a good time. Praise them for good behavior!

If your puppy's tail is tucked and he tries to get away from the other dog, hides under a chair or in a corner, or runs to you for safety and acts distressed, your puppy is not enjoying being with the other dog. Conversely, some puppies are too much for older dogs. If the older dog is looking distressed, take your puppy away. The older dog may not appreciate a boisterous puppy with needle teeth chomping on him!

If you already have dogs and have brought home a new puppy, the techniques for introductions still apply. You will just need to watch the dogs for extended periods of time to ensure that everyone is getting along consistently. You may find that older dogs need occasional breaks from your puppy or that your puppy needs breaks from an overattentive older dog.

Even if you do have dogs at home for your puppy to meet, don't check off that socialization box just yet, especially if all dogs are the same breed. Make sure that your puppy gets to meet other dogs outside the home so that he learns to get along with a variety of canines.

Socialization Games

Getting your puppy socialized is going to be hard work, but that doesn't mean it can't be fun! Socialization games will keep the task enjoyable for you, your puppy, and your friends. Here are some games to try.

For handling games, choose people who are comfortable with puppies.

Handling Games

You can ask people to participate in the handling training exercise—the same one that you will be doing with your puppy. Choose people who are comfortable with puppies and can handle yours appropriately. No grabbing! Only gentle touches. It's good for your puppy to learn to be handled by others because your veterinarian and perhaps a groomer will need to handle him. The game will go better if you tire your puppy out a bit beforehand. Play with him, let him run in your yard, or do another activity to settle him down a bit before your friends help you with this game. Take one meal's worth of your puppy's kibble and divide it into separate baggies, one for each person who will participate. To each bag, add a few extra tasty treats. As each person touches the puppy on various places—his paws, ears, mouth, and tail—he or she will give the puppy a treat.

Tip: *If your puppy gets too squirmy or starts biting your friends' hands, then he may need a break. The game may be too much for him. Try to tire him out some more and then try again.*

Scavenger Hunts

Come up with a scavenger hunt to complete your socialization exercises. Your puppy will get lots of treats during the hunt, but you should also reward yourself for completing it! For example, on one weekend outing, plan to:

1. Meet a stranger wearing a hat or hoodie.
2. Meet a small group of children.
3. Meet a man with a beard.
4. Meet two people wearing sunglasses.
5. Meet a person using a cane or crutches.
6. Meet a child on a skateboard.
7. See a balloon.
8. Experience a sudden noise.
9. Watch a sprinkler when it is turned on.
10. See a big truck drive by.

Bring your clicker and treats. Click and treat for brave, confident behavior. If you are actually greeting a person, he or she can give your puppy treats. If you are just watching the person go by, you can give the treats to your puppy.

Note what your puppy likes and what things concern him. For the things that make him worried or afraid, try them again on your next scavenger hunt so you can make them more positive associations for your puppy.

Circle of Friends

This game also involves other people, preferably enough to form a large circle when sitting on the

Try This!

GOING TO KINDERGARTEN

Consider taking your puppy to a puppy kindergarten class. A good puppy kindergarten class may teach obedience exercises such as Sit, Down, and Come, but the main focus should be on socialization and handling, with education on house-training and bite inhibition. Check the curriculum before you register to make sure that it's not just an obedience class for puppies. You can teach obedience at any age, but you can only seriously impact socialization during your puppy's socialization period. Make sure the trainer has experience with teaching puppies and uses only positive methods.

ground. Divide up your puppy's kibble into a baggie for each person. Add some tasty treats to each bag. Each person should also have a clicker.

Each person should take turns calling the puppy's name in a friendly voice, encouraging the puppy to come to him or her. When the puppy arrives, click and treat. Take turns randomly going around the circle.

This game builds positive associations for the action of approaching people. Vary the people in the circle each time you play it so that your puppy learns to happily approach a variety of people.

Doggy Daycare: A Tired Puppy Isn't Always a Good Puppy

Doggy daycare has a lot of appeal. Your puppy will get to play with other dogs, won't have to be completely alone during the day, and comes home tired. While some doggy daycares are run by professionals in canine behavior who closely supervise all interactions, many are not. Some are just as detrimental to your puppy as dog parks.

Some doggy daycares let all of the puppies just run loose together, with little supervision or understanding of how the interactions can affect young puppies. If a group of other puppies or dogs gang up on your puppy, it could cause him to become fearful around other dogs. Or your puppy could be one that learns that picking on other puppies is fun and become a bully himself.

If you are interested in taking your puppy to a doggy daycare, do your research. Interview each staff member responsible for supervising your puppy and ask about their background in canine behavior. "I've had puppies all my life" is not an acceptable answer! Ask them to

Show your puppy a balloon on one of your weekend scavenger hunts.

describe the signs that a puppy is stressed, how they determine when to separate dogs, and what they do when puppies act inappropriately. Do they use positive methods?

Observe the daycare on random days and times to see what the place is like. Is it clean? Do they separate large and small dogs for interaction?

If you try a daycare, observe your puppy, knowing that signs of problems may not show up right away. Your puppy may be very tired and sleep when he gets home, which you'll probably like because it will give you a break! Just know that he could be sleeping because he had a stressful day rather than a fun day of exercise.

Do you notice your puppy shying away from other dogs or lunging at them, perhaps growling? These are signs that his dog interactions at daycare may not be healthy ones for proper socialization. He could be learning bad things instead of good things. A doggy daycare may be better for your puppy after he has completed his socialization period and already has established positive associations with other dogs.

When the Window Closes, Open the Door

Cramming so much socialization into your puppy's early weeks can be a challenge, but one you can definitely accomplish. Just because that window closes, however, doesn't mean that you can stop socializing your puppy. You definitely need to continue the process, but you don't have to be on such an intensive schedule.

People who socialize their puppies very well early on but then stop once their puppies hit adolescence often find that their dogs develop problems in adulthood. They may end up fearful of certain types of people, or the veterinarian's office, or other dogs. So don't quit while you're ahead! Keep up the scavenger hunts, meeting new people, and other socialization activities so that your puppy grows up to be a confident, social adult dog. It will actually be easier for you once your puppy has had all of his vaccinations. You will be able to take him more places safely.

Doggy daycares can be stressful for puppies. Your pup may be sleeping because he had a stressful day, not because he had a fun day full of exercise.

CHAPTER 9

GOING
TO SCHOOL

Y ou can learn a lot from training books and DVDs, but you might also want to consider taking your dog to a training class. Just as with any profession, there are good trainers and bad ones. There are good classes and bad ones. Take your time and look for a class that will be of excellent quality for you and your puppy. Observe a class before enrolling your puppy. A good instructor will happily allow that.

What to Look for in a Trainer

Some things to look for in a trainer include their methods, experience, and certifications.

Positive Methods

The trainer uses positive methods. A website or brochure may tout "positive methods," but that doesn't mean that they truly are. Look for a trainer who uses clicker training or lure and

Your dog's trainer should have experience and an education in canine behavior.

reward training. Avoid trainers who use those methods at first but then "correct" a dog after he "should know what he's doing." This is another term for a collar yank or other physical punishment, which are not necessary when training behaviors. Avoid trainers who use choke chains, prong/pinch collars, or electric collars.

Experience and Education

The teacher has experience and an education in canine behavior. Unfortunately, anyone can call him- or herself a dog trainer. There is no certification or license required. Ask what specific education the trainer has had. "I've had dogs all my life" doesn't qualify.

Earning titles on dogs doesn't necessarily mean that the trainer has the experience that you need or the ability to train others. If you are interested in pursuing competitive events with your dog, however, look for a trainer who has titles on his or her dogs and has successful experience training others to achieve titles on their dogs. If you are not interested in competition, then this should not be a deciding factor. You need a trainer who has experience and education in teaching family manners.

What education should you look for? If the trainer states a specific school or academy, look it up and find out what training methods the school instructs. Ask if the trainer pursues continuing education, either by attending conferences or workshops or with webinars. A quality trainer always pursues current continuing education. If a trainer says, "I've been training for X years and my methods have always been successful," this is not a good answer. Dog training has evolved tremendously in recent years, and it's important that trainers keep up with current methods and information. There are many educational opportunities available for trainers these days, and there's no excuse not to learn.

Certifications

Ask if the trainer has any certifications. There is currently only one certifying body, independent of any specific school, which offers credentialed testing for dog trainers. It is the Certification Council for Professional Dog Trainers (CCPDT). The CCPDT offers several different designations for trainers. All require a minimum amount of hours teaching as a lead instructor, plus recommendations

Did You Know?

CCPDT DESIGNATIONS
CCPDT designations include:

Certified Professional Dog Trainer— Knowledge Assessed (CPDT-KA)

Certified Professional Dog Trainer— Knowledge and Skills Assessed (CPDT-KSA)

Certified Behavior Consultant Canine— Knowledge Assessed (CBCC-KA)

Certified Behavior Consultant Canine— Knowledge and Skills Assessed (CBCC-KSA)

from fellow canine professionals and clients and a passing grade on a proctored examination. The designations that include skills assessment require video proof of training skills. In order to keep their designations, trainers must pursue requirements in continuing education.

Independent schools and other training programs also offer credentials to their graduates. These can at least demonstrate that a trainer has been dedicated in completing an academic program or has successfully passed a knowledge assessment. Just keep in mind that the credential only reflects that of the particular training school, so research the school to ensure that it covers modern, positive methods. It should also require continuing education in order to keep the designation.

Just because a trainer doesn't have a certification doesn't mean that he or she is not a good trainer or can't help you with training your dog. Ask if the trainer is interested in pursuing credentials. It may be cost-prohibitive for him or her.

Professional Association

The trainer belongs to a professional association, such as the Association of Professional Dog Trainers (APDT) or the International Association of Animal Behavior Consultants (IAABC). Membership in professional associations does not guarantee that a trainer is qualified or uses positive methods, but it does show a commitment to the profession. Ask if the trainer is involved in the association—does he or she attend meetings or conferences? Keep up with the association's publications? Look for an interest in continuing education and an emphasis on professionalism.

Make sure that the overall tone of the trainer's class is upbeat and positive.

Assess the Class

When you visit the class, look for the following:

- The trainers and assistants treat dogs and people with respect. No one is made to feel put on the spot or bullied.
- The overall tone of the class is upbeat and positive.
- The trainer offers time to answer questions, either in class or by email or phone.
- There is a good instructor-to-student-ratio, such as one trainer per eight students. If there is one trainer for twenty students, this is not ideal unless there are qualified assistants helping with the class.
- The dogs and owners are clearly enjoying the class.

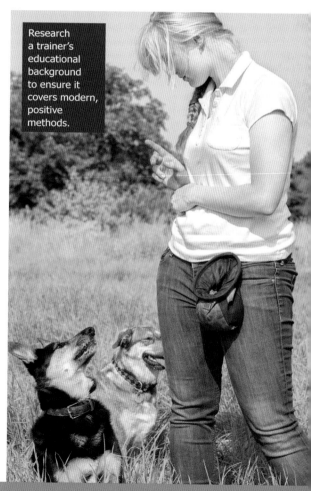

Expert Tip

ASK AROUND

In trying to find a quality class for you and your puppy, ask for recommendations from your veterinarian and friends. Keep in mind that their criteria for a good trainer may not match yours, so still do your research.

Safety

The class appears to be safe, with plenty of room for each dog. The trainer quickly responds to any dog showing reactivity. This doesn't mean that the trainer punishes the dog. Most dogs that growl or lunge in a group class are actually afraid, and yelling at that dog will not help the situation. Instead, if the reactivity is mild, the trainer should either put up a barrier around that dog to prevent it from seeing the other dogs and people or, if the dog is acting very aggressively, remove that dog from the class.

Research a trainer's educational background to ensure it covers modern, positive methods.

No Guarantees

The trainer does *not* offer guarantees. This may seem strange at first, as most everything comes with a guarantee these days! You are not purchasing an appliance, however. It is against the codes of ethics of several noted dog-trainer associations and organizations for trainers to offer guarantees for your dog's behavior. This is because the trainer won't be living with you, can't make you do the homework necessary for success, and cannot control your home environment. It is unethical for a trainer to guarantee training results because much of your puppy's success will be up to you.

Also, the trainer should have business liability insurance.

Training Clubs

Training clubs are another place where you can find group classes for your puppy. These are clubs sanctioned by organizations such as the American Kennel Club (AKC). Their focus is on holding trials in which dogs compete to earn ribbons and titles in agility, Rally, and obedience. If you would like to pursue these activities, training clubs can be good places to learn from those who already compete.

Keep in mind that many of the instructors in training clubs are volunteers, and they may not meet the criteria you are looking for in a trainer. Keep your standards high and make sure that they use modern, scientific methods. You may want to enlist a professional trainer to help you and your puppy get started and then take additional classes at a training club that focus more on your competitive goals.

Choosing Private Lessons

There are many reasons why some prefer private lessons to group classes. It may be that your schedule doesn't match that of a class, or the location of the class is inconvenient for you. You may just personally prefer private instruction over a group class. If your dog is very shy, a group class may be overwhelming. Certainly, if your dog is reactive toward other dogs, he should not be in a group class. You should instead pursue private lessons to address his reactivity.

In choosing a trainer for private lessons, apply the same criteria as you would for a trainer who teaches group classes. The main difference is that you can't observe a private lesson as you would a group class. It would not be appropriate for a trainer to allow you to accompany him or her to someone's home.

Trainers who offer private lessons should offer professional contracts that clearly outline his or her responsibilities and yours. Always review contracts before signing, and keep a copy for your records.

Daytraining and Board & Train Options

If you prefer that a trainer does most of the work in training your dog, there are also daytraining and board & train options. Many people make the mistake, however, of thinking that the trainer does *all* of the work, and that when your dog is turned over to you, he will be completely trained without your having to do a thing. Not true! If a trainer trains your dog, you will need to attend transfer sessions so that the trainer can teach you how to work with your dog, and so your dog learns to listen and respond when you give the cues. Otherwise, your dog will learn to listen to just the trainer. There are usually several transfer sessions after a daytraining or board & train program—you will not be able to accomplish everything in just one session.

In daytraining, a trainer comes to your home and works with your dog. In board & train options, you send your dog to the trainer for training, normally for a few weeks.

Apply the same criteria to choosing a trainer. This is especially important for board & train programs, as you will not be there to supervise how your dog is treated. Be wary of trainers who promise "boot camps." Ask specific questions about what techniques the trainer will use to ensure that the trainer is not resorting to shock collars or other punitive methods. Ask how many dogs the trainer works with at one time, and what living arrangement your puppy will have. For example, will he live in a house with the trainer or in a kennel? How many hours a day will he be kenneled? Ask for references and check them.

With board & train, you send your dog to the trainer for a few weeks.

PART III

THE
TRAINING
PROGRAM

CHAPTER 10

BASIC CUES

Basic cues should be foundation behaviors for any pet dog. Teaching them to your dog will help you live together better. They make for nice manners. A dog that understands Sit can learn not to jump on people upon greeting them. A dog that knows how to Walk Nicely on Leash won't drag you down the street. A dog that can hold a Down-Stay can lie quietly on his bed while you have guests over.

These basic cues can also keep your dog safe. A dog that understands Come will return to you, instead of running off, when you cue him. One that understands Leave It will leave something alone when you tell him to, which could save his life if it's something dangerous.

The basic cues are also the foundation for more advanced behaviors. For example, you start with your dog on leash when teaching him to Come and then work up to an off-leash Recall.

Have a Plan

If you don't have a specific goal in mind, you can't train it, so have a plan before you start training. Here are some things to consider:

- What are you specifically going to teach? Get a picture in your mind of what you want the behavior to look like.
- What do you want to accomplish during this particular session? Some behaviors can be taught in one session, but many will take several sessions. What are your goals for this particular training session?
- What will you do if you don't reach your goal? If your dog isn't keeping up? How will you adjust the training session so it ends on a positive note?
- What will you do if your dog does better than expected? Are you ready for the next step? Always plan ahead at least one step. If your dog has a breakthrough, you want to be able to keep up!

Before you start a training session, have all of your tools and items ready. Starting to train a behavior only to find that you forgot your clicker or treats is just going to confuse and frustrate your dog.

Training sessions should be very short—just a few minutes at a time. It is always better to stop a training session a bit early, while your dog is succeeding, than to push the situation and have your dog get frustrated. Your goal should be to end the training session with your dog wanting more. He will then look forward to the next lesson!

There are a couple ways to remember to keep training sessions short. For example, while you're watching your favorite TV shows, you can train during commercials. By the time your program comes back on, it's time to stop training. You can also count out ten to twenty training treats. By the time you finish using them, it's time to stop.

Tracking Your Progress

Ideally, you will keep track of how your dog progresses for each session. Yes, keeping charts and notes can be tedious, but it doesn't have to be complicated. You can create a nice chart on your computer and complete it each time you train, but jotting down a couple of simple notes will do just fine. Keeping notes can really help you see what you've accomplished and remind you of any issues that you noticed. Charting your progress is especially helpful if you are working through some particularly challenging behaviors for your dog, and if you have more than one person who is helping you train your dog.

If you take notes about what you achieve during each training session, you will see where you are making progress and where you aren't. If you are teaching a behavior that is hard for your dog, or an alternate behavior to one that you don't like, it can be easy to focus on what he's doing wrong rather than on any progress you're actually making.

For example, you are training your dog not to jump up on people. This is very frustrating for your family because they don't like your dog leaping on them all the time. So you train him to Sit instead when people approach. During your first training session, he jumps up on people six out of ten times. During your second training session, he jumps four out of ten times. The next day, he jumps on your spouse, and he or she complains. But you can see from your notes that your dog is actually making progress in his training. So rather than getting frustrated and upset, you know that you just need to keep up your training to see further success.

If you see that the behavior is getting worse rather than better, it tells you that something needs adjusting. It could be your training—perhaps you are adding distractions too early. Or it could indicate something is up with your dog. For example, you notice that your dog isn't as enthusiastic during one training session as he was during the last one. He is yawning in stress and tries to walk away from you a few times. You mark this in

Have a plan before you start training.

your notes, and then you notice the same issues during the next training session. This tells you that something is wrong. You could be progressing too fast for him to keep up, and he is getting frustrated. You may need to lower your criteria, go back to an earlier step that was successful, and then work your way back from that point. Or your dog could be ill or injured. Some dogs are very stoic, and it's only by paying careful attention to changes in his behavior that you can tell when he's actually sick or hurt. If you keep notes about your training sessions, you can help pinpoint exactly when you noticed a change in his behavior. If your dog is actually sick, this information can help your veterinarian.

Practice Makes Perfect

The more you practice, the better success you will see. Just remember to keep those training sessions short. Good practice in dog training is not thirty minutes of repetitive training. This is just going to bore you and your dog! Practice at least fifteen minutes a day, but not all at once. Break it up into multiple training sessions per day. If you have a very young puppy, the shorter, the better! Adult dogs will have longer attention spans and can usually go for longer periods of time. Of course, if you want to train more than fifteen minutes a day, that's great! Just add more short training sessions each day. Dogs, just like people, take a certain amount of repetition before they can perform behaviors reliably.

When you hold your training sessions can depend on what behavior you are teaching. If you work away from home and return to find an exuberant dog that's bouncing to greet you, this is a great time to work on Come, but not a great time to work on Sit-Stay.

Look for signs of stress during your training sessions.

Especially at first, when your dog is just learning a new behavior, set your dog up to succeed. Work on stationary behaviors—Sit, Down, Settle—when your dog has had some exercise and is a little tired. If you have a dog that already pulls on the leash when walking, also tire him out a bit before you work on Walking Nicely on Leash.

Teaching the Basic Lessons

Every dog is different. If you have a young, bouncy adolescent dog, it may be more challenging to train him the stationary behaviors, such as Sit-Stay or Down-Stay, than if you have an older dog. On the other hand, it may be easier to teach your young dog a lightning-fast Recall!

Some breeds and breed mixes are more active as well. For example, it may be harder to teach an active Golden Retriever to Down-Stay than it will a Mastiff.

Just know that you need to progress as far as your individual dog can succeed. All dogs can learn, no matter their age or breed. It is never too late to teach an older dog new behaviors. And it's a complete myth that some breeds can't learn a thing.

This chapter outlines specific training sessions, all very short in duration. It is completely normal for you to have to repeat a session several times before moving onto the next step. There are indicators to help you recognize when you will be ready for the next step.

Watch Me

This behavior helps you get and keep your dog's attention. If your dog is looking at you, he won't be staring at something else that could engage his attention, such as another dog or a squirrel. You can also use this cue to preface another one, such as getting your dog to look at you to help him focus on you before you start walking him on leash.

Goal: Your dog will make eye contact with you when you call his name.

What You'll Need: Clicker, treats. Optional: leash. If your dog is very busy and easily distracted, despite being in a quiet area, you can put him on leash to limit his room to explore and lose focus.

Preparation: Train this behavior in a quiet room with very few distractions. Put away your dog's toys so that they don't distract him.

Teach your dog to make eye contact with you when you call his name.

Try This!

TEACHING EYE CONTACT TO A SHY DOG

If you have a very shy dog, teaching him to have eye contact with you can be challenging for him. Direct eye contact is a confident behavior, which is going to be harder for a shy dog. It may help if you sit down to make yourself appear smaller and less potentially threatening. Don't ask for prolonged eye contact until your dog grows more confident with the behavior.

1. Stand quietly, with your feet planted. Wait for your dog to look you in the eye.
2. The second that he makes eye contact, click and treat. Make sure that he is not looking at your hand or the treats. Wait for him to look you in the eye.
3. Repeat for a total of ten repetitions. End your training session.
4. Repeat Steps 1–3 until your dog is reliably giving you eye contact.

Tip: *Be patient! This exercise can be challenging for young puppies because they are easily distracted by many things. Even a spot of dirt on the floor is fascinating to a puppy. Just stand quietly and wait. When the eye contact happens, it will likely be very quick, so be ready!*

When your dog is reliably giving you eye contact, it's time to add the cue.

1. Say your dog's name, once, in a friendly voice. Wait for him to make eye contact.
2. The second that your dog makes eye contact, click and treat.
3. Repeat for a total of ten repetitions. End your training session.
4. Repeat Steps 1–3 until your dog is reliably responding to his name by giving you eye contact in areas with few distractions.

Walking Nicely on Leash is one of the most important behaviors for pet dog owners.

Walking Nicely on Leash

Polite behavior on leash is one of the most frequently requested behaviors from dog-training clients. No one likes to take a dog for a walk if he or she is going to be dragged down the street or pulled off his or her feet. It's not fun, and it can be dangerous if you fall and hurt yourself. It's also embarrassing to be seen trying to walk your dog while he wheezes and strains at his collar.

Dogs don't pull you because they are being dominant or trying to establish themselves as "alpha." They simply want to *go*! Dogs can walk and run very fast, and it can be boring for them to walk at a slow pace. Dogs follow their noses and are eager to explore new scents. They want to go faster, usually much faster than is comfortable for you on a walk.

Your dog can also become really good at pulling on leash because you've rewarded him for doing so. Every time he pulls you

WHEN IS YOUR DOG'S BEHAVIOR REALLY A PHYSICAL PROBLEM?

Sometimes, what you think is a training issue is really caused by a medical problem. Greg Brown, DVM, and Mark Foy, DVM, partners in Sunset Animal Clinic in West Columbia, South Carolina, offer tips on some common physical issues that masquerade as training problems.

"Probably the most common thing we see that people think is a behavior issue is actually due to urinary problems," Dr. Foy explains. If your dog is eliminating in the house, it may not be a house-training problem. "Get your dog's urine checked," Dr. Foy advises. Dr. Brown adds, "There are also diseases that cause a dog to have increased thirst, which can cause him to have accidents, like Cushing's and diabetes."

If your dog is having orthopedic issues that cause him pain, he may balk at walks or refuse to go up steps or jump in the car. Hip dysplasia, juvenile bone growth issues, and other bone and joint issues can all contribute to a dog appearing stubborn or non-compliant. "Some breeds, such as Dachshunds, are also prone to back problems," says Dr. Foy.

"Another thing to consider is cardiac problems," Dr. Brown explains. "The dog loses his breath, has reluctance to exercise, can no longer walk to the mailbox—all of these things could be related to a cardiac problem."

Loss of senses can be another source of problems. Dr. Brown says, "Blindness or vision problems can cause dogs to act differently. You associate this with senior dogs, but it's not always the case." Dr. Foy adds, "We had a puppy in here the other day because the owner thought something wasn't right. What he didn't realize was that his puppy was deaf." A deaf puppy could bark louder, seem to "refuse" cues, and not pay close attention to people. These can appear to be training problems until you discover the real cause.

If your dog ever experiences a sudden change in behavior, or if your training program isn't going as expected, please consult your veterinarian. It's better to rule out physical issues first.

and gets to explore something new, you've rewarded him. Every time he drags you so he can smell an enticing spot, you've rewarded him. If you drop a treat that rolls away, and he pulls you so he can reach the treat, you're rewarding him for pulling. If you keep doing this, he'll keep pulling. Behavior that is reinforced gets stronger. Keep this in mind when you are working with your dog on leash. Are you accidentally paying him for pulling?

If your dog has been dragging you for some time, this behavior will be harder to fix, but it's not impossible! But you will have a more entrenched habit that you are trying to change. For some dogs, pulling is very rewarding, so you will need to work hard to change their minds. **Goal:** While on leash, your dog will walk next to you without pulling. He will stay on one side of you, not cutting in front of you or cutting behind you.

What You'll Need: Clicker, treats, leash. Optional: front-clip harness or head halter.

Preparation: Decide which side of your body you want your dog to walk on. It will be easier for him to learn if you are consistent. If you would like to enter formal competitions with your dog, choose the left side; otherwise, it's your preference. Be sure that everyone in your family works on the same side for consistency.

You also need to decide how you want to hold the treats, leash, and clicker. One suggestion is, if your dog is on your left, to let the leash cross your body and hold it in your right hand along with the clicker. In your left hand, you will hold a handful of treats so that you don't have to dig around for them in your bait bag when you need them. Or, it may be more comfortable for you to hold the leash in the hand nearest your dog and the clicker in your other hand, reaching into your bait bag for treats. Just be sure that you can get to the treats quickly. It may take you a few training sessions to be comfortable and find a way that works best for you, and that's OK. Experiment with different configurations until you find one that fits you best.

Choose a quiet area for this training with few distractions. Your home is ideal, but you can also use your yard if necessary. You will need a long stretch of space. At this stage of training, your dog is not ready for training in the neighborhood or park, as those places hold too many distractions.

1. Put your dog on leash and stand next to him, with both of you facing the same direction.
2. Take two steps. Just before you stop, click and then treat. Hold your treat next to your side, by your leg on the side you want your dog to be, so that your dog must be at your side in order to eat the treat. At this point, don't worry about his position. If he's turned around or if his rear is off to the side, it's OK.
3. Repeat Step 2 nineteen times. End your training session.
4. Repeat Steps 1–3 until your dog is staying closely by your side for the entire duration.

Tip: *This exercise teaches your dog that it is better for him to be by your side rather than lunging in front of you. This is why you only go two steps at a time at first. You need to really reinforce that he must be next to you rather than enjoying the fun of forging ahead.*

If you walk your dog for exercise, you will need to continue to do that while you work on this exercise separately. At this stage, it will be too distracting for your dog to try and walk nicely

Try This!

ALTERNATIVE METHODS FOR SMALL DOGS

When working on Walking Nicely on Leash with a very small dog, it can be awkward to reach down and give him a treat. There are a couple of things that you can do to make this exercise easier on your back.

Use a squeeze-tube treat. You can find them in most pet-supply stores. You'll be able to extend the tube with your hand and squeeze out a small amount each time as a reward.

Dip a long rubber spatula in peanut butter and deliver a lick as the reward.

by your side during walks for exercise in environments with many distractions. There may also be times when you don't mind if your dog wanders at the end of the leash, exploring. It is healthy to let him just be a dog! This doesn't mean that he should drag you, though. After you've worked on this exercise and your dog is under more control, you can have a cue for walking nicely and a separate cue for wandering and exploring.

When your dog is doing well at two paces, it's time to proceed to the next step.

1. Put your dog on leash and stand next to him, with both of you facing the same direction.
2. Take two steps. Just before you stop, click and then treat. Hold your treat next to your side, by your leg on the side you want your dog to be, so that your dog must be at your side in order to eat the treat.
3. Repeat Step 2.
4. Take three steps. Just before you stop, click and then treat.
5. Repeat Step 4.
6. Take four steps. Just before you stop, click and then treat.
7. Repeat Step 6 nineteen times. End your training session.

Tip: *Continue to feed your dog at your side. If he still gets ahead of you, he will need to come back to your side to eat the treat. If you feed him in front of you, you are teaching him to walk ahead of you and to cut in front of you.*

When your dog is reliably staying by your side during your session, it's time to add the cue.

Once your dog is doing well, venture outside the area you have been working in.

1. Just before you start walking, cue "Let's go" or "Let's walk" and begin walking.
2. Take two steps. Just before you stop, click and then treat. Hold your treat next to your side, by your leg on the side you want your dog to be, so that your dog must be at your side in order to eat the treat.
3. Repeat Steps 1–2 nineteen times, gradually increasing the number of steps you take before you click and treat. End your training session.

When your dog is doing well at this stage, it's time to make things a bit more challenging.

1. Warm up by cueing "Let's go" and taking two steps, clicking just before you stop and then treating.
2. Repeat a few times to get your dog in the mind-set that you are working on this behavior.
3. Gradually increase the amount of steps you take before you click and treat.
4. Venture outside the area that you have been working in, which will increase the distractions. For example, if you've worked only in your backyard, continue the exercise by walking around your house. Or, if you've been working only inside, continue the exercise by walking outdoors into your yard.
5. If your dog is very distracted, click and treat more often while he is still in position. Gradually work up to fewer clicks and treats as he grows accustomed to the new area.
6. Repeat Steps 4–5 nineteen times. End your training session.

Tip: *Your goal is to click before your dog pulls. As you start venturing outside your familiar area, it will become more distracting for your dog. Don't wait for him to pull. Click while he is still in the right position, before he pulls. If you find that you end up in an area that offers too many distractions for your dog, try higher value treats as a better reward.*

Try This!

SITTING FOR STOPPING

If you would like to polish Walking Nicely on Leash by getting your dog to sit every time you stop walking, here's how. If you want to enter formal competition with your dog, he will need to know this behavior. You'll need to teach Walking Nicely on Leash and Sit separately before you can combine them.

1. Warm up by cueing "Let's go" and taking a few steps, clicking just before you stop and then treating.

2. Cue "Let's go." Take a few steps. Stop and cue "Sit." When your dog sits, click and treat.

3. Repeat nineteen times, varying the number of steps you take before you stop. End your training session.

Sit

This is such a simple behavior, but it can solve many problem behaviors. A dog that understands Sit won't bolt out the door or jump up on you. A dog can't chase the kids and sit at the same time.

Goal: Your dog will place his rear on the ground so that he is in a sitting position.

What You'll Need: Clicker, treats.

1. Hold a treat in your hand, just above your dog's nose. Slowly move it up over his head, toward his shoulders. Your dog's nose should move to follow the treat. If you lose his attention, start again or try a treat with a higher value. If he jumps up, you are holding the treat too high. Keep it low.

2. As your dog's nose rises to follow the treat, he should lower his rear. The second that his rear touches the ground and he sits, click. Toss the treat a couple of feet away so he will get up to get it. This will reset him for the next repetition.

3. Repeat Steps 1–2 two more times.

4. Hold your empty hand as if you still had a treat in it. Use the same motion with your hand, starting at your dog's nose and moving up over his head, toward his shoulders.

5. When your dog sits, click and toss a treat.

6. Repeat Steps 4–5 five times. End your training session.

Tip: *You only use treats in your hand for the first three successful repetitions. After that, you follow the same hand motion, but without a treat in your hand. This is called "losing the lure." If you were to continue holding a treat in your hand for every repetition, your dog could become dependent on treats. And so will you! You don't want a dog that only works for you when you are holding a treat. By using the treat as a lure for only three successful repetitions, you will avoid this trap.*

Your dog knows when there is not a treat in your hand—he can smell that it isn't there. So you are not tricking your dog, you are actually teaching him a hand signal for Sit. You always give a treat after you click.

When your dog is sitting reliably, it's time to add the cue.

1. Cue "Sit" one time, in a friendly voice. Give the same hand motion you've been using, which is your hand signal.

2. When your dog sits, click and toss a treat.

3. Repeat Steps 1–2 for a total of ten repetitions. End your training session.

Down

All dogs lie down to sleep, but if you have a very active dog, you may think that he never does it otherwise! Teaching the Down will teach your dog to settle when you need him to, such as when you have company over.

Goal: Your dog will lie down.

What You'll Need: Clicker, treats.

Preparation: Teach Sit first.

Training Down will teach your dog to settle when he needs to.

1. Cue "Sit."

2. Hold a treat in your hand. Hold it by your dog's nose and then tuck it under his chin toward his chest. *Slowly* move the treat downward, straight down, until you reach the floor. Slowly move the treat between his front paws, away from your dog. Your dog's nose should follow the treat. If your dog raises his rear, just cue him to sit again and start over, this time moving the treat much more slowly.

3. As your dog's nose follows the treat, he should stretch out into a Down. The second that his belly touches the ground, click. Toss the treat a couple of feet away so he will get up to get it. This will reset him for the next repetition.

4. Repeat Steps 1–3 two more times.

5. Hold your empty hand as if you still had a treat in it. Use the same motion with your hand, starting at your dog's nose, tucking under his chin, lowering to the floor, and moving outward.

6. When your dog lies down, click and toss a treat.

7. Repeat Steps 5–6 five times. End your training session.

Tip: *Just as in teaching the Sit, you only use treats in your hand for the first three successful repetitions.*

You always give a treat after you click.

When your dog is lying down reliably, it's time to add the cue.

1. Cue "Down" one time, in a friendly voice. Give the same hand motion you've been using, which is your hand signal.

2. When your dog lies down, click and toss a treat.

3. Repeat Steps 1–2 for a total of ten repetitions. End your training session.

Before teaching Come, warm up with a few Hand Targets.

Come

Coming when called is more than a convenience—it can save your dog's life. Should your dog ever slip out of his collar and get loose while you are out walking, you want him to come right back to you when you call him.

Coming to you must always be a positive experience for your dog. Don't ever call your dog to come to you and then punish him. This will teach him to avoid you! Don't call him to come to you if you ever have to do something that he may find unpleasant, such as forcing him to take a pill or tending an injury. In those situations, it's better to go to your dog, with treats, and make the experience as positive as you can.

Goal: Your dog will come to you and sit when you cue him.

What You'll Need: Clicker, treats, leash.

Preparation: Teach Hand Target first.

1. Have your dog on leash. Warm up by cueing a few Hand Targets (cue "Touch"). Click for all correct responses. Toss the treat behind your dog so that he has to turn away from you to get the treat.

2. As your dog eats the treat, cue "Touch" again. Click and toss the treat.

3. Gradually toss the treat farther and farther behind your dog so that he has to travel farther to come back to you for the next repetition.

4. Repeat Steps 2–3 for a total of ten repetitions. End your session.

When your dog is reliably coming to you to target your hand, it's time to add the Sit.

1. Cue "Touch." When your dog touches his nose to your hand, click. Toss the treat about 6 feet (1.8 m) behind him.

2. As soon as he eats the treat, cue "Touch." Just before he gets to you, cue "Sit." When he sits, click and toss the treat.

3. Repeat for a total of ten repetitions. End your training session.

When your dog is reliably coming to you and sitting, it's time to replace the "Touch" cue with your final cue.

Preparation: Choose a cue that doesn't already have a negative association with it. For example, if you have already used "Come" and punished your dog or done something unpleasant to him, don't use that cue. Or, if your dog thinks "Come" means that you're supposed to chase him, it's not a good cue to use, either. You can choose any word you like, such as "Here!" or "C'mere!"—just be consistent. When introducing a new cue, you say it before the previously taught one.

Coming to you must always be a positive experience for your dog.

1. Cue "Come!" and then "Touch." When your dog touches his nose to your hand, click. Toss the treat about 6 feet (1.8 m) behind him.
2. As soon as he eats the treat, cue "Come!" and then "Touch." At this point, when he sits, click and toss the treat.
3. Repeat eight times.
4. Cue "Come!" Click and treat all correct responses.
5. Repeat five times. End your training session.

Now that you have a complete behavior, it's time to make the recall a bit faster. You want your dog to run to you when you call him.

1. Start walking with your dog. This is not Walking Nicely on Leash—let him wander ahead of you.
2. When your dog is ahead of you, cue "Come!" and start jogging backwards.
3. After about 10 feet (3 m), stop. Let your dog catch up (if he is not already there) and sit. Once he sits, click and toss the treat ahead of you.
4. Repeat Steps 1–3 for a total of ten repetitions. End your training session.

Tip: *Be careful! Don't trip. If you are not able to run, that's fine. Just go as fast as you are able. The goal is to move backward quickly. This encourages your dog to chase you.*

Sit-Stay

There may be times when you want your dog to hold a sit position for longer periods of time. If you ever want to enter formal competitions with your dog, you'll need this behavior. It also comes in handy in your household. For example, it's hard to take a cute picture of your dog while he's zooming about! Teaching him a Sit-Stay will help him pose pretty for the camera.

For extended position behaviors, remember that the click ends the behavior. Once you click, you've marked the behavior, so it doesn't matter if the dog changes position at that time; you've already captured the instant that he did what you wanted.

1. Cue "Sit."
2. Wait three seconds. Click and toss the treat so that your dog has to get up to eat it, resetting him for the next repetition.

Use Sit-Stay when you want your dog to hold the Sit for longer periods of time.

3. Cue "Sit." Wait five seconds. Click and toss the treat.

4. Cue "Sit." Wait eight seconds. Click and toss the treat.

5. Cue "Sit." Wait two seconds. Click and toss the treat.

6. Repeat Steps 1–5 six times, but vary the length of time that you wait. Make some repetitions longer and some very short. Work up to your dog sitting for ten seconds. End your training session.

Tip: *By varying the amount of time for which you ask your dog to hold a sit, it's a bit unpredictable. This will better keep your dog's interest.*

Once your dog is reliably holding his Sit for ten seconds, it's time to extend the Sit longer.

You will be rewarding your dog a bit differently for this exercise when you start extending the time—the reward won't come only at the end. You want your dog to remain in position, so you'll reward him both for staying put and at the end of the exercise.

You build a Sit-Stay with duration and distance. You will extend the amount of time for which your dog remains in a Sit, and you will also increase your distance from him so that you don't have to stand in front of him all the time. You do not work on duration and distance at the same time, however. You work on them separately because that makes it easier for your dog to learn. You won't be increasing the criteria too much at one time.

Here is how to increase the duration of the Sit:

Keep in mind that older dogs with orthopedic issues may find it hard to sit for long periods of time.

1. Cue "Sit."

2. Wait ten seconds. Give your dog a treat.

3. Wait two seconds. Click and toss a treat.

4. Repeat Steps 1–3 two times.

5. Cue "Sit." Wait ten seconds. Give your dog a treat.

6. Wait five seconds. Give your dog a treat.

7. Wait two seconds. Click and toss a treat.

8. Cue "Sit." Wait five seconds. Give your dog a treat.

9. Wait ten seconds. Give your dog a treat.

10. Wait five seconds. Click and toss a treat.

11. Repeat Steps 5–10 five times. End your training session.

In future training sessions, vary the amount of time your dog must wait before receiving a treat and before ending the behavior.

Tips: *If your dog gets up when you give him a treat, it means that he has associated the treat, not necessarily the click, with the end of the exercise. Just cue him to "Sit" again and start over, this time using shorter durations.*

Take note of how long you are asking your dog to sit because it will help you make things easier or more challenging for him, depending on how he is doing. For example, if he gets fidgety at eight seconds, give him a treat at seven seconds. Or, if he does great at twelve seconds, give him a treat at fourteen seconds. Vary your treat delivery to keep it interesting for your dog and keep him engaged in the session.

If you find that your dog lies down, you could be rewarding him too late. Reward him, or click to end the exercise, before he lies down. If your dog persists in lying down, please consider taking him to a veterinarian. Dogs that have orthopedic issues, such as hip pain, find it very uncomfortable to sit for long periods of time. You never want to cause your dog pain while training.

Here is how to add distance to the Sit-Stay:

1. Cue "Sit."
2. Take two steps away from your dog. Immediately return to your dog and give him a treat.
3. Take two steps away from your dog. Click and toss a treat.
4. Cue "Sit." Take three steps away from your dog. Immediately return to your dog and give him a treat.
5. Take three steps away from your dog. Immediately return to your dog and give him a treat.

You build a Sit-Stay with duration and distance.

6. Take three steps away from your dog. Click and toss a treat.
7. Cue "Sit." Take four steps away from your dog. Immediately return to your dog and give him a treat.
8. Take four steps away from your dog. Immediately return to your dog and give him a treat.
9. Take four steps away from your dog. Click and toss a treat.
10. Cue "Sit." Take two steps away from your dog. Immediately return to your dog and give him a treat.
11. Take two steps away from your dog. Immediately return to your dog and give him a treat.

12. Take two steps away from your dog. Click and toss a treat.

13. Repeat Steps 4–12. End your training session.

In future training sessions, vary the amount of steps that you take from your dog. Don't always walk farther away. Vary the distances between near and far to keep it more interesting for your dog.

Tips: *At first, it is easier to move away from your dog in a straight line. You can soon vary this so that you are off to one side and then the other. Vary your location, but don't try to go behind your dog at first because he will be likely to get up to turn and look at you.*

If you find your dog getting fidgety at a certain distance, work at a closer distance for a few repetitions before trying to get to the farther distance again.

Down-Stay

Like the Sit-Stay, the Down-Stay is useful if you'd like your dog to hold the Down for a longer period of time.

Goal: Your dog will hold a Down until you indicate that he can get up.

Preparation: Teach Down first.

1. Cue "Down."

2. Wait three seconds. Click and toss the treat so your dog has to get up to eat it, resetting him for the next repetition.

3. Cue "Down." Wait five seconds. Click and toss the treat.

4. Cue "Down." Wait eight seconds. Click and toss the treat.

5. Cue "Down." Wait two seconds. Click and toss the treat.

6. Repeat Steps 1–5 six times, but vary the length of time that you wait. Make some repetitions longer and some very short. Work up to your dog lying down for ten seconds. End your training session.

Varying the amount of time for which you ask your dog to hold the Down position will keep his interest.

Tip: *By varying the amount of time you ask your dog to hold the Down, it's a bit unpredictable. This will better keep your dog's interest.*

Once your dog is reliably holding the Down position for ten seconds, it's time to extend it longer.

You build a Down-Stay with duration and distance. You will extend the amount of time that your dog remains in a Down, and you will also increase your distance from him so that you don't have to stand in front of him all the time. Do not work on duration and distance at the same time.

Here is how to increase the duration of the Down:

1. Cue "Down."
2. Wait ten seconds. Give your dog a treat.
3. Wait two seconds. Click and toss a treat.
4. Repeat Steps 1–3 two times.
5. Cue "Down." Wait ten seconds. Give your dog a treat.
6. Wait five seconds. Give your dog a treat.
7. Wait two seconds. Click and toss a treat.
8. Cue "Down." Wait five seconds. Give your dog a treat.
9. Wait ten seconds. Give your dog a treat.
10. Wait five seconds. Click and toss a treat.
11. Repeat Steps 5–10 five times. End your training session.

At future training sessions, vary the amount of that time your dog must wait before receiving a treat and before ending the behavior.

Tips: *If your dog gets up when you give him a treat, it means that he has associated the treat, not necessarily the click, with the end of the exercise. Just cue "Down" again and start over, this time using shorter durations.*

Don't work on duration and distance at the same time.

Always keep in mind how long you are asking your dog to lie down because it will help you make things easier or more challenging for him, depending on how he is doing. For example, if he gets fidgety at eight seconds, give him a treat at seven seconds. Or if he does great at twelve seconds, give him a treat at fourteen seconds. Vary your treat delivery to keep it interesting for your dog and keep him engaged in the session.

Here is how to add distance to the Down-Stay:

1. Cue "Down."
2. Take two steps away from your dog. Immediately return to your dog and give him a treat.
3. Take two steps away from your dog. Click and toss a treat.
4. Cue "Down." Take three steps away from your dog. Immediately return to your dog and give him a treat.
5. Take three steps away from your dog. Immediately return to your dog and give him a treat.
6. Take three steps away from your dog. Click and toss the treat.
7. Cue "Down." Take four steps away from your dog. Immediately return to your dog and give him a treat.
8. Take four steps away from your dog. Immediately return to your dog and give him a treat.
9. Take four steps away from your dog. Click and toss a treat.
10. Take two steps away from your dog. Immediately return to your dog and give him a treat.
11. Take two steps away from your dog. Immediately return to your dog and give him a treat.
12. Take two steps away from your dog. Click and toss a treat.
13. Repeat Steps 4–12. End your training session.

Build up to adding distance to the Down-Stay.

In future training sessions, vary the amount of steps that you take from your dog. Don't always move farther away. Vary the distances between near and far to keep it more interesting for your dog.

Tips: *At first, it is easier to move away from your dog in a straight line. You can soon vary this so that you are off to one side and then the other. Vary your location, but don't try to go behind your dog at first because he will be likely to get up to turn and look at you.*

If you find your dog getting fidgety at a certain distance, work at a closer distance for a few repetitions before trying to get to the farther distance again.

Leave It/Take It

This behavior is a popular one, and it could save your dog's life. If something falls on the floor, your dog likely thinks it's fair game for him to eat or at least pick up. But what if it's dangerous? It's much better to tell your dog to leave something alone so that he never touches it rather than trying to get it away from him later, after it's already in his mouth or, worse yet, swallowed.

Leave It is used when your dog is headed toward something that you don't want him to touch. If taught correctly, your dog will not touch the item at all. Do not cue "Leave It" after your dog already has something in his mouth. That is something completely different to a dog. How can he leave something alone when he already has it? Only use "Leave It" before your dog has gotten hold of something.

It's much better to tell your dog to leave something alone before he gets a hold of it.

Training this behavior may feel awkward at first because you will need to hold your clicker and treats in the same hand. Be patient with yourself as you learn how to manage—you can do it! You will not have to do it for very long because you will replace the click with a cue rather quickly.

Take It is used to indicate to your dog that it's ok for him to pick something up or eat it. Many dogs automatically assume that if something falls on the floor, it's theirs! This is not a safe practice. Sure, sometimes you drop something and don't mind him having it, but what if you drop something that could hurt him? How is he supposed to know when it's ok to take it and when he isn't? You can train him! By teaching your dog the Take It cue, you will teach him to only take something when you say so. You teach Leave It and Take It at the same time.

Goal: Your dog will leave something alone when you cue him and take something when you cue him.

What You'll Need: Clicker, treats.

1. Hold a bunch of treats in both hands. In one hand, hold the clicker. This will be your delivery hand—the hand with which you will deliver the reward. Put this hand behind your back.

2. Show your dog the treats you have in your other hand. Quickly make a fist so that he cannot get them. Do not pull your hand away from your dog. It should be right under his muzzle.

3. Wait. Your dog will likely poke or lick your hand to get the treats. He may even chew or paw your hand. Just wait.

4. The second your dog moves his head away from your hand, for any reason, click. From your opposite hand, toss a treat in the opposite direction. If you are using your right hand to tempt your dog, you will toss a treat with your left hand, toward the left. If you are using your left hand to tempt your dog, you will toss the treat with your right hand, toward the right.

5. Repeat Steps 1–4 for a total of ten repetitions. End your training session.

Tips: *Do not ask your dog to sit, lie down, or do anything for this exercise. Solely concentrate on the Leave It behavior. Click at the second that your dog's head moves away from your hand. It doesn't matter why he does it because the goal behavior is movement away from the temptation. He may look down at the floor to see if you dropped the treats—you would click this. If he hears a noise and turns away to look, click this. Click for the first movement away from the hand. He will soon learn that moving away from the item is what earns the reward.*

When you toss the treat in the opposite direction, it builds a nice automatic head turn into the behavior. This could be especially handy if your dog is headed for something dangerous. When you cue "Leave It" and he automatically turns away, it will break his focus and give you extra time to get his attention away from the item if necessary.

Keep the hand with the treats and the clicker behind your back so that you don't accidentally distract your dog with it. You want him to leave the other hand alone on his own, not be distracted by the treats you have in another hand. That's a bribe, not a paycheck! If you drop something in your home that you don't want your dog to have, you are unlikely to have treats handy to lure him away. So wait to toss a treat until after you click.

Don't hold up your hand high, away from the dog. Instead, your hand should be right below the dog's muzzle.

When your dog is reliably and quickly moving away from one hand, it's time to proceed to the next step.

1. Repeat the previous steps, except reverse hands. If you were holding the clicker in your left hand, now hold it in your right. If you were holding the clicker in your right hand, now hold it in your left hand.
2. Do ten repetitions and end your training session.

When your dog is reliably leaving the treats alone, no matter which hand you tempt him with, it's time to proceed to the next step.

1. Repeat the previous steps, varying the hand that your dog must leave alone. For example, do three repetitions in one hand then switch hands for two repetitions, and then switch back.
2. Do a total of ten repetitions and end your training session.

Tip: *Practice in different locations, especially in the kitchen and bathroom, where you are likely to drop things that you don't want your dog to have.*

When your dog is reliably and quickly leaving both hands alone in different locations, it's time to add some cues.

1. Have treats in both hands, with one hand also holding the clicker, just as before. Cue "Leave It" one time, in a friendly voice. Don't threaten! Show your dog the treats you have in your other hand.
2. The second your dog leaves the hand alone, click and treat with the opposite hand.
3. Cue "Leave It." Show your dog the treats you have in your other hand.
4. Repeat this training session at least two times.
5. Cue "Leave It." Present your treats-only hand.
6. The second your dog leaves the hand alone, cue "Take It!" Then, click and treat with the opposite hand.
7. Repeat Steps 5–6 for a total of ten repetitions. End your training session.
8. After this time, you no longer need to use the clicker. You have replaced the clicker with the cue "Take It!"

When your dog is reliably responding to the cues "Leave It" and "Take It" with treats in your hand, it's time to make the behavior more challenging.

The closer the treat, the more challenging it is for your dog to Leave It.

1. Have treats in both hands. Place one hand behind your back.

2. Cue "Leave It." With your other hand, place one treat on the floor, about 12 inches (30.4 cm) from your dog. (He will likely move toward it, and that's OK.) Keep your hand very close to the treat because you will likely need to cover it. If he goes to take the treat, simply cover it with your hand and be still.

3. Wait for your dog to leave the covered treat alone. The second he moves away from the treat, cue "Take It" and toss a treat in the opposite direction from your opposite hand.

4. Repeat Steps 1–3 for a total of ten repetitions. End your training session.

In future training sessions, gradually work to where you no longer have to cover the treat with your hand to get your dog to leave it alone. You can also vary how far you place the treat from your dog, keeping in mind that the closer it is, the more challenging it will be.

Tip: *Placing treats on the floor is often more challenging for a dog than having the treats in your hands. That's why we start easy, with treats in hand, first. Your dog may already have a history of grabbing things from the floor, so he may have the assumption that if something lands on the floor, it's his! It's also harder for him because items on the floor are closer to him.*

When your dog leaves the treat you place on the floor alone, it's time to proceed to the next step.

1. Have treats in both hands. Put one hand behind your back.

2. Cue "Leave It." Drop a treat from your hand from about an inch from the ground. Get ready to cover it with your hand if necessary.

3. When your dog leaves the treat alone, cue "Take It" and toss a treat in the opposite direction from your opposite hand.

4. Repeat Steps 1–3 for a total of ten repetitions, varying the height from which you drop the treat. Always keep your hand close to the treat so that you can cover it if necessary. End your training session.

As your dog continues to progress during future training sessions, start dropping the treat from greater and greater heights.

Tip: *At some point, you will not be able to reach the treat with your hand to cover it. Your dog may realize this, too. Simply cover it with your foot, taking care not to kick your dog if he lunges for it.*

Your dog may already assume that anything that lands on the floor is his!

CHAPTER 11

BEYOND
THE BASICS

Once you and your dog have mastered the basic cues, you can continue to polish them, start weaning off of treats and the clicker, and tackle some advanced behaviors. The wonderful part about training your dog is that it's a lifelong process. There's always something new you that you can teach your dog. The more you work together, the closer you two will become.

Adding Distractions

Your dog is likely to sit in the comfort and quiet of your living room, but will he sit in the middle of a busy park? Will he hold the Sit even if you drop a dozen tennis balls around him? To get that steady level of behavior, you need to introduce distractions into your training. Adding distractions is sometimes called "proofing" the behavior.

There are many distractions that you can use. Some will depend on what you want to do with your dog. For example, do you want to enter formal competitions with your dog? If so, then you'll want to add the types of distractions that your dog will experience during a competition trial. This can include the following:

- Lots of people
- Other dogs
- Being crated in a busy environment
- Loud noises
- Ring gating
- Mats
- A person walking near or behind him holding a clipboard
- Booths or tents
- Other dogs getting treats and attention

Perhaps you would love for your dog to be a therapy dog—a dog that visits patients in health-care facilities. He will need to perform with these types of distractions:

- People who move differently than usual, such as bent over or with jerky movements
- People who talk loudly or slur their words

- Crutches, wheelchairs, walkers
- Elevators
- Slick floors
- Floor-length curtains (in hospitals)
- Beeping noises (from monitoring machines)

Think about your ultimate training goals for your dog. Choose distractions to add into your training program whether you want him to perform his behaviors reliably in a show environment, in new places with new people, or at the local park.

Start slow and work gradually. Following is an example of adding distractions to the Down behavior. You can apply this basic concept to just about any behavior.

Goal: Your dog will hold the Down position, despite distractions.

What You'll Need: Clicker, treats, regular leash, long leash (12 to 15 feet [2m]), low-value toys, high-value toys, dog bowl.

Preparation: Teach Down first.

1. With your dog on the regular leash, warm up with a few Down repetitions.
2. Exchange the regular leash for the long one. Perform a few Down repetitions, gradually moving farther from your dog.
3. Cue "Down." Place one low-value toy in the training area. Position it at a distance where you think your dog will ignore it. If he remains in position, click and toss a treat away from the toy.
4. With the toy still in the floor, repeat Step 3 two times, each time working closer to the toy.

If you want to enter a formal competition with your dog, then you should accustom him to the type of distractions you are likely to encounter there.

5. Add a second low-value toy to the training area.
6. Repeat Steps 3–4.
7. Add one high-value toy to the training area.
8. Repeat Steps 3–4, each time working closer to the toys.
9. Add another high-value toy to the training area.
10. Repeat Steps 3–4, gradually working closer to the toys. End your training session.

In future training sessions, start adding treats along the ground, then eventually an empty dog-food bowl, and then a food bowl with some treats in it. Only progress as far as your dog can succeed.

Tips: *The act of switching to a long leash is a distraction unto itself for your dog. He now has a greater distance at which to get distracted. Once he gets used to the additional distance, start adding the toys as distractions that he has to ignore along the way. Then, you will add food.*

Each dog gets to decide what is tempting to him, so learn from your dog which items will be more challenging than others. Add those later in the training program. For the repetitions in which he leaves a very tempting item, be sure to give him a high-value reward.

If you want your dog to perform in different areas, you need to train in different areas. Every time you train in a new area, back up your criteria. Go back to your earlier training steps and work up from there. New areas can be very distracting for dogs, with different scents that they want to explore and different noises that may interest them or make them nervous.

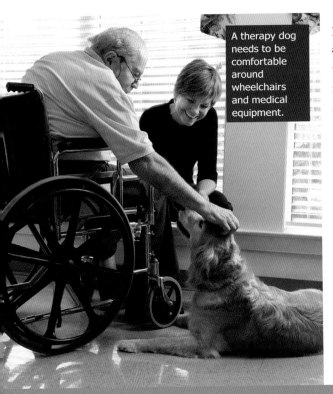

A therapy dog needs to be comfortable around wheelchairs and medical equipment.

For the Come behavior, you can continue proofing your dog in a variety of environments and with added distractions until you achieve the level you want for your dog. Please remember to always leash your dog when you are working in an unfenced area. You don't want a distraction to end in injury if your dog decides to bolt after something and into traffic or another dangerous area.

Working Off Leash

If you would like the reliability of your dog performing off leash, there are several ways to achieve it.

You can apply the following general steps to your basic behaviors, such as Watch Me, Walking Nicely on Leash, Sit-Stay, and Down-Stay.

- Start by practicing the behaviors off leash. Only do this in a securely enclosed area.
- For behaviors to which you want to add distance, such as Down, add a long leash after you've taught the behavior on a regular leash; you can also use a retractable leash for distance work. You can also tether your dog in one location on a long leash while you move farther away. After working successfully on the longer leash, you can transition to off leash.
- For behaviors that you want close to you, such as Walking Nicely on Leash, you can transition to a tab leash. This is a short leash with just a small handle for you to grab just in case. Choose one that extends only partway down your dog's chest; you don't want it so long that your dog's foot can get tangled in it. After working successfully on the shorter leash, you can transition to off leash.

Always be mindful of your area's local laws regarding leashed dogs. If your community has a leash law, be a good pet-owning citizen and keep your dog leashed. Also know that your dog … is a dog. You may train him to be excellent and reliable in most situations, but one day a distraction may come along that you couldn't have predicted or that your dog just finds way too tempting to ignore. Before you disconnect your dog from his leash, always assess the situation and weigh the consequences. It would be terrible if you risked his life!

Practice behaviors off leash in a secure setting.

When to Stop Clicking

You will not have to click forever. A clicker is a building tool. Once you've built a behavior and trained it to fluency, you no longer need the click. Fluency means that you have taught a behavior, added distractions, and trained it in different locations. When you cue your dog no matter what is going on, he's likely to respond correctly.

If you find that the behavior breaks down or that you need to build the behavior in a new environment, pull out your clicker again and rebuild the behavior. For example, at home, your dog always sits when you cue him. You replace the click with a release cue, "OK!," and you no longer use the clicker at home. You take your dog on a vacation to a relative's house. There are lots of adults, children, and other dogs there. You cue your dog to sit, but he doesn't respond. This is because his current environment is very different from the one at home—there are too many distractions for him to concentrate.

Pull out your clicker and back up your training. He will learn to sit in this environment faster than he did initially, but he will still need a refresher course. Once he is reliably sitting in this new environment, you can go back to using your release cue ("OK!") instead of clicking. You've successfully used the clicker to rebuild the behavior.

Another example would be time delays. If you don't work your dog for months and then start training again, he may not necessarily pick up where you left off. You may need to review some steps. If you've already stopped using the clicker for certain behaviors, and a lot of time has gone by between training sessions, you may need to use the clicker again to rebuild those behaviors.

If you need to build a behavior in a new environment, go back to using the clicker.

Replacing the Click with a Release Cue

The click ends the behavior. So if you don't need to use a clicker forever, how do you teach your dog when it's OK to end the behavior? For example, when you cue your dog to sit, how does he know when he can get up? You need to teach a release cue—a cue that indicates that the behavior has ended.

If you don't teach a release cue, you will end up with a dog that may need repeated cues to perform a behavior. Your dog may sit and then get up, so you cue him to sit again, but then he gets up

... and on and on. Teaching him a release cue is better communication. Here's how to replace the clicker with a release cue.

Goal: Your dog will release from position when cued, ending a behavior.

What You'll Need: Clicker, treats.

Preparation: Teach the behavior to fluency first.

1. Choose a release cue that will only mean "the behavior is over," such as "OK!" or "Free!" Be consistent.
2. Just before you click, give the cue "OK!" and then click and treat.
3. After about ten times, you no longer need to use the clicker. Use just the release word instead.

When to Stop Treats

One of the most common training questions from dog owners concerns when to stop giving treats to their dogs. Stopping the treats too soon can cause your dog to lose interest in your training and can teach him that working for you isn't very rewarding. If people work for a living, they get a paycheck. Your dog deserves one, too!

This doesn't mean, however, that you will have to carry treats with you for the rest of your life. You can wean your dog off of the treats. Here's how.

Goal: You will no longer use treats to reward your dog for performing a behavior.

What You'll Need: Clicker, treats.

Preparation: Train the behavior to fluency first. Transition the clicker to a release cue.

You can wean your dog off of the training treats.

1. Start rewarding your dog with a treat for every other repetition of a behavior. For the repetitions on which you don't give a treat, praise your dog instead.
2. Reward your dog for the third repetition of a behavior, then after just one repetition. For every repetition you do not give a treat, praise your dog instead.
3. Continue to vary the number of repetitions in between rewards, sometimes increasing the number and sometimes decreasing the number, to keep your dog interested.
4. After ten repetitions, end your training session.
5. Repeat the training sessions at various times, repeating Step 3 until you no longer are using treats as a reward.

Tip: *If at any time your dog loses interest or you notice the behavior breaking down, reduce the number of repetitions in between treats. You can also try keeping your training sessions shorter.*

Building a Rock-Solid Recall

Come is such an important behavior, so you will want to polish it and make it as rock solid as possible. If your dog is truly distracted, it can be very hard for him to leave the distraction and come to you; this is especially true if he is doing what he was originally bred to do, such as hunting or chasing something. No matter how positive a trainer you've been and what kind of wonderful relationship you have with your dog, chasing a squirrel may trump you as a reward!

You *can* achieve a reliable recall, however. It just takes work. The foundation you've built so far is a great start. Here is how to take Come to the next level.

Goal: Your dog will come when called, despite distractions.

What You'll Need: Clicker, treats, regular leash, long leash (12 to 15 feet [2 m]), low-value toys, high-value toys, dog bowl.

Preparation: Teach Come first.

1. With your dog on the regular leash, warm up with a few Come repetitions.
2. Exchange the regular leash for the long one. Perform a few Come repetitions.
3. Place one low-value toy in the training area. Position the toy at a distance at which you think that your dog will ignore the toy.

To build a solid Recall, you'll need a long leash.

4. Cue "Come!" If your dog goes near the toy, encourage him to come to you instead.(You can also use your Leave It cue.) When he reaches you and sits, click and treat.
5. Repeat two times, each time working closer to the toy.
6. Add a second low-value toy to the training area.
7. Repeat Steps 4–5.
8. Add one high-value toy to the training area.

9. Repeat Steps 4–5, each time working closer to the toys.

10. Add another high-value toy to the training area.

11. Repeat Steps 4–5, gradually working closer to the toys. End your training session.

At future training sessions, start adding treats along the ground, then eventually an empty dog-food bowl, and then a food bowl with some treats in it. Only progress as far as your dog can succeed.

Tips: *If at any time your dog chooses to go to the distraction instead of to you, don't punish him. Just back up your training to the point at which he was last successful. Do some more repetitions at that level and then try making it harder again. The more challenging the distractions, the higher value of reward you should use.*

The Joy of Heeling

You may have achieved your goal of on-leash behavior by teaching your dog the Walk Nicely on Leash cue. If you are interested in fancier footwork, however, you'll want to teach Heel. This will be a necessary skill for your dog if you ever want to compete in obedience or Rally competitions. It's also an integral part of canine freestyle—dancing with your dog.

The Heel behavior means that your dog stays in position on your left side, very close to your leg, with his shoulders even with your leg, his head up, and his eyes looking at you. Every time you stop, he automatically sits straight, facing forward. Watching a heeling team, with a dog glued to his handler's side, matching her steps and happily gazing into her eyes, is a beautiful example of teamwork. It can be challenging to teach, though. There are entire seminars devoted to just this exercise.

Heeling Basics

Heeling is an exercise in which you have to be just as conscious of your body position as you are of your dog's. In most other behaviors, you're only concerned about what your dog is doing. If you ask him to sit, you want his rear on the ground. If you want to be precise about it, you'll want his legs tucked evenly under his body rather than sprawling out to one side. But you can be doing whatever you want—standing, sitting, or lying down. In Heel, your body position makes a difference because it offers cues to your dog às regarding in what direction you are going.

Try This!

RECORD YOURSELF

Your body position is very important when teaching Heel. This is where recording your training sessions can really come in handy. It's hard to be aware of what you're doing and what your dog is doing at the same time, so a video can show you things you need to improve, as well as things that are going right.

When teaching Heel, you will need to be more conscious about your own body position. For example, when you compete, you will be walking straight forward with your shoulders straight, so when you train, you want to assume this same position. If you are turned to your left, looking down at your dog to see if he's in the right place, this is a different position and will teach your dog to be farther back, as he will back up to look at you. When you then face forward with shoulders straight, your dog will look like he is lagging a bit behind your leg, because you inadvertently trained him to be in that position by turning and moving your left side farther back.

Another very important thing to keep in mind when teaching Heel is your dog's physical health. In Heel position, your dog is looking up and to the right, at your face. You don't want to do extended repetitions of this behavior and cause your dog to have neck or joint problems. If you kept your head turned to one side for long periods of time, you'd get a crick in your neck.

Luckily, with clicker training, training sessions are very short. Just remember not to get caught up in your goal of a beautiful Heel and do too many repetitions at one time. Here is how to teach a basic Heel.

Goal: Your dog will walk in Heel position by your left leg, keep pace with you, and keep eye contact.

The Heel means that your dog stays in position on your left side.

What You'll Need: Clicker, treats. You'll also need room to move, preferably a large, closed room or even a fenced yard.

Preparation: Teach Watch Me and Sit first. You can do the Heel exercise on leash or off leash. If you move on to advanced competition, you will eventually have your dog off leash, so it can be convenient to go ahead and train that from the start.

If you choose to train the Heel off leash, you will still need to hold your hand as if you have a leash in it so that your body language will be consistent. You will also need to eventually add the leash because you will need to learn how to hold it so that it doesn't tighten or tangle in your dog's legs. For competition purposes, the leash should be loose. At first, stick with either on leash or off-leash until your dog is reliably holding position, at which point you can gradually incorporate the other.

1. Warm up with a few repetitions of the Watch Me behavior. This will get your dog primed to look up at you.

2. Cue "Sit" at your left side. Have your left elbow bent, with your left hand at your belt buckle. Face forward—you will have to peek downward to your left to ensure that your dog is in the right position. Cue "Watch Me." Start walking.

3. After just two steps, if your dog is in Heel position, with his shoulder right by your leg, click, stop, and give him a treat. If it takes a few more steps, that is OK; it may take a little longer if your dog is off leash. Just walk briskly, with a purpose, which is more likely to get your dog's attention. Most dogs, especially if you've already established a history of fun training sessions, will be trying to earn a click and treat. If you find that your dog is more interested in the yard than in your training, you need to get better treats and make it more interesting for him.

4. After you deliver the treat, start walking again. Click and treat every time your dog gets into Heel position. You will see that your dog finds the Heel position more and more frequently. After about ten clicks, end your training session.

5. Repeat Steps 2–4 until your dog is maintaining Heel position consistently. Only do ten clicks and treats per session. With this exercise especially, it's important to keep it short so your dog does not get bored.

Watch Me will get your dog primed to look at you.

Tips: *For your initial training sessions, it's easier if you just walk in a straight line. You don't have to do that for long, though. Don't try extremely evasive maneuvers, but you can start turning right and left. You can walk in a square pattern or weave in between cones, to better keep your dog's attention. The more often you change directions, the more likely your dog is to pay attention to you because this keeps things interesting for him.*

PLATFORMS

There are many ways to teach the Heel with Straight Sit. Another method you may want to try is platform training. The goal is to teach your dog to sit on a short platform that is just big enough for him so that he learns to sit within the parameters of the platform. Then, you gradually fade out the platform while he still keeps the ideal position. You can purchase ready-made platforms, or you can easily construct your own. Purchase some interlocking foam squares, such as the type often used for children's playroom flooring, from your local home-supply store. Interlock the squares if necessary and cut them until you have a piece that is just the length and width of your dog. Duct-tape several same-size pieces on top of each other so that your platform is a couple of inches (cm) high.

Put the platform by your left side and cue "Sit." Click and treat when your dog sits on the platform. Practice in different rooms and environments and then try removing the platform to see if your dog holds the same position.

If you are interested in canine freestyle, make several platforms because your dog will have to learn to work on both sides of you, and even in front of and behind you. Platforms can help your dog learn exact positions.

Also, you may find that your dog gets in Heel position but doesn't look up at your face. It is harder for a dog to look at you while walking. He wants to see where he is going, or he's interested in the ground smells. If this is the case with your dog, simply click and treat for Heel position at first. You will often find that your dog starts looking up at you as he becomes more interested in the exercise. When that happens, you will start clicking and treating him only when he is watching you in Heel position. You can also continue to practice the Watch Me behavior so that it becomes more ingrained in his routine.

The Straight Sit

One part of Heel is a Straight Sit. When a dog is sitting by your side, he can have a tendency to swing his rear out away from you. It makes sense because this makes it easier for him to see your face. But, in competition, you want your dog to sit straight, facing forward. This polished Sit behavior is taught separately from the walking part of Heel.

Goal: Your dog will sit straight by your side, facing forward.

What You'll Need: Clicker, treats. You'll also need a long wall to work near.

1. With the wall parallel on your left side, stand with just enough room so that your dog fits, sitting, in between you and the wall. Lure your dog to your left side if you need to. Cue "Sit." When he sits right next to your leg and is sitting straight, click and treat.

2. Repeat Step 1 five times.

3. Take a half step away from the wall. Repeat Step 1. If your dog still sits straight, without swinging out toward the wall, click and treat. If he starts to lose his Straight Sit, then move back closer to the wall. Do nine more repetitions and then end your training session.

4. Gradually work to where you can move farther away from the wall with your dog still holding a Straight Sit. If at any time your dog starts to swing out, just move closer to the wall, to the point where he last succeeded, do more repetitions in that location, and then try moving out again.

When your dog is reliably walking beside you in Heel position and looking up at you, and he can do a Straight Sit, it's time to combine the behaviors and add the cue.

Goal: Your dog will walk in Heel position, looking at you, and automatically sit when you stop.

What You'll Need: Clicker, treats.

1. Start with your dog sitting by your left side. Cue "Heel" once, in a friendly voice. Start walking.
2. After just a few steps, stop walking and cue "Sit." When your dog sits, click and treat.
3. Repeat Steps 1–2 five times. End your training session.
4. At your next training session, repeat Steps 1–2, except do not cue "Sit." Instead, wait to see if your dog automatically sits. If he does, click and treat. From this point on, you will click and treat for sitting automatically. If you wait for a minute and he still doesn't sit, then cue "Sit." Repeat Steps 1–2 for another couple of training sessions before trying for an automatic sit again.

Next Steps

Once your dog is keeping the Heel position for at least twenty steps in your current training area, you can take your training sessions to different locations. Keep in mind that for each new

One part of Heel is a Straight Sit.

location you try, you may have to back up your training and work through the steps again. This is normal. If your goal is competition, be sure to practice in environments with mats and ring gating so that your dog gets used to performing in that environment.

Gradually work up to your dog's holding Heel position for longer periods, but remember to keep these training sessions short, with few repetitions. If you want to train your dog to Heel on your left and right, you can teach a different cue for each side. Working on both sides of you will help prevent physical strain on your dog's neck and joints.

If you have not started working off leash at this point, you can start now. Start in quiet areas at first, then work up to areas holding more distractions.

Perfecting Your Steps

Your dog watches your body cues to figure out which way you are going. You can help him, and make your Heel much more polished, by being consistent with your body cues when you make a turn. This will require some practice because you may not be aware of what your feet and shoulders are really doing whenever you're walking along. Have you ever noticed your footprints in the sand on the beach? Do your feet align straight, or do the balls of your feet splay outward from your heels? If you expect your dog to maintain a perfect Heel position and your left foot leans even a fraction left before you turn right, then he could think you mean to turn left instead, which will cause him to lag behind on the turn. If you just want your dog to walk by your side in something more polished than Walking Nicely on Leash, this is no big deal. But in the competition ring, it will cost you points.

In obedience competitions, you will need to walk together as a team.

It's actually best to practice these moves without your dog. Get your body used to consistent movement first, and then you can add your dog. Here are some of the movements that you will need for competition and how you can develop some body cues to help you and your dog walk together as a team. Keep in mind that you need to signal your dog before you actually change direction. To teach change of directions, it can be helpful to use a target stick to help your dog better learn exact positions. (A target stick is a long stick that you teach your dog to touch with his nose. Some are telescopic, which is very convenient. You can start with it very long, then gradually shorten it, then fade it out altogether.)

- **Right Turn**. When you turn right, and your dog is walking on your left, he has to speed up on the outside of the turn in order to maintain Heel position. Signal that you are going to turn by stepping with your right foot slightly swiveled out to the right, then picking your left foot up, and then turning right. You can also drop your right shoulder slightly back.

- **Left Turn**. When you turn left, and your dog is walking on your left, he has to slow down on the inside of the turn in order to maintain Heel position. If he doesn't know that you're going to turn into him, it's easy for you to run into him! Signal that you are going to turn by stepping with your left foot slightly swiveled out to the left, then picking your right foot up, and then turning left. You can also drop your left shoulder slightly back.

- **About Turn**. In an About Turn, you'll turn to your right and circle around to continue in the direction that you came from. It's similar to a Right Turn in that your dog will have to speed up in order to keep in Heel position on the turn. Signal that you are going to turn by stepping with your right foot slightly swiveled out to the right, picking your left foot up and past your right foot, and then completing your turn. You can also drop your right shoulder slightly back.

Your dog watches your body cues to figure out where you will go.

- **Figure Eight**. In obedience competition, you'll need to do a Figure Eight exercise, in which you walk in a pattern that looks like the number 8, around two people who serve as "posts." This will require you to teach more gradual turns, with your dog on both the inside of the turn and outside of the turn. You can help your dog by doing similar footwork as in the Left Turn and Right Turn, except that your turns will be more gradual.

CHAPTER 12

TRICKS TO TEACH YOUR DOG

While some behaviors are necessary to teach your dog to instill family manners, some are just plain fun! Trick training is a great activity to do with your dog. It's a fun way to take breaks from your regular training sessions. Some tricks, such as Fetch and Drop It, are also very practical.

The training process for tricks is the same as training for any other behavior. Here are twenty-five tricks that you can train your dog to perform.

Back Up

Here's how to teach your dog to back away from you.

Goal: Your dog will move away from you, walking backward.

What You'll Need: Clicker, treats. You'll need a narrow area, just wider than your dog's shoulders. For example, you can work alongside a wall, lining up four chairs a couple feet away from the wall to form a narrow "hallway."

The training process for tricks is the same as training for any other behavior.

1. In the narrow training area, stand close to your dog, facing him.
2. Take one small step toward your dog. Look for any indication of your dog's moving backward, even if it's just one paw. When you see it, click and feed him a treat.
3. Repeat. Click and treat for any movement backwards.
4. When you get to the end of the "hallway," take a brief break to get back into position. You can just turn around so that your dog will back through in the opposite direction.
5. Repeat Steps 1–4 two more times.

End your training session.

As your dog starts to move backward regularly, it's time for you to stop moving toward him.

1. In the narrow training area, stand close to your dog, facing him.

2. Take one small step toward your dog. Look for any indication of your dog's moving backward, even if it's just one paw. When you see it, click and feed him a treat.

3. Hold still. Wait for your dog to move backward without your moving towards him. When he starts to move, click and feed him a treat.

4. Repeat Step 3 until your dog has taken several steps. Click and treat all backward movement. Take a brief break to get back into position.

5. Repeat Steps 3–4 two more times. End your training session.

When your dog reliably takes steps backward while you stay in the same spot, it's time to add the cue.

1. Get into position. Cue "Back Up" once, in a friendly voice. When your dog takes two steps backward, click and treat.

2. Repeat Step 1 until your dog reaches the end of your "hallway." Take a brief break to get back into position.

3. Repeat Steps 1–2 four times. Gradually work up to your dog's taking more steps before you click and treat. End your training session.

In future training sessions, work to where your dog will move backward for the entire length of your training area before you click and treat. When your dog is zipping along backward, it's time to make it more challenging by removing the area restrictions. How you do this will depend on how you set up your "hallway." For example, if you used a line of chairs, then remove one chair from the line for one repetition, then two chairs for a repetition, then three, and then the last chair.

Keep working against the wall at first—remove only one side of your training area at this point. Then, start positioning your dog farther from the wall. Gradually work to where your dog no longer needs the barrier in order to back up. When you reach that point, transition the click to your release cue, "OK!"

Balance Bone on Nose

This trick can make a great photo op!

Goal: Your dog will balance a dog treat on his nose until you cue him to eat it.

What You'll Need: Clicker, treats that you can balance on your dog's nose easily.

Preparation: Teach Sit-Stay first. Accustom your dog to your handling his muzzle so he is comfortable with your hands around his nose.

1. Cue "Sit."
2. Touch the treat to the top of your dog's nose. If he goes to take the treat, just pull it all the way back. Wait and try again. When he holds still, click and give him the treat.
3. Repeat Step 2 four times. End your training session.

When you can touch the treat to the top of your dog's nose without his trying to eat it, you're ready to move on to the next step.

1. Cue "Sit." Place the treat on the top of your dog's nose. Immediately remove it, click, and give your dog the treat.

A great trick is teaching your dog to balance a treat on his nose.

2. Repeat Step 1, gradually increasing the amount of time that the treat stays on your dog's nose before you click and treat. Keep your hand close in case you have to stop the treat from falling off. Repeat five times.

3. Cue "Sit." Place the treat on your dog's nose. Wait a few seconds and then click. See if your dog will try to get the treat himself. Know that many dogs won't automatically catch the treat in a flip off of their noses. Some dogs will develop the ability to catch the treat quickly; others will take many repetitions. Either way is OK. Repeat four times. End your training session.

At future training sessions, when your dog is reliably balancing the treat on his nose, transition the clicker to your release cue, "OK!"

Tip: *You don't necessarily need a verbal cue for this behavior. The act of putting a treat on your dog's nose can be the cue for him to hold still. If you want a cue, though, add it when the behavior is reliable. You could use "Hold" or "Balance" or whatever you want as long as you're consistent.*

Bashful

This trick is sure to get an "awwww" from your friends.

Goal: Your dog will put one paw on his nose.

What You'll Need: Clicker, treats, sticky note.

Preparation: Depending on what you want the final behavior to look like, teach Sit or Down first.

1. Cue "Sit" or "Down." Put a sticky note on your dog's muzzle.
2. Your dog will likely raise a paw to rub the sticky note off. When his paw touches his nose, click and treat.
3. Repeat Steps 1–2 nine times. End your training session.
4. Repeat Steps 1–2 three times. Click and treat all correct responses.
5. Wait to see if your dog will touch his paw to his nose without the sticky note. Give him a full minute. If he does, click and treat. If he doesn't, go back to using the sticky note for a few more repetitions and then try again.
6. Repeat Step 5 nine times. End your training session.
7. When your dog is reliably putting his paw on his nose, add the cue. Cue "Are you bashful?" or something similar, once, in a friendly voice. Click and treat all correct responses.
8. When your dog is reliably responding to the cue, add the release cue "OK!" to end the behavior.

Teach Sit or Down before attempting the Bashful trick.

Tip: *If your dog is uncomfortable or stressed about the sticky note, try to make it a positive experience for him. Give him treats and lots of praise, just for wearing the sticky note, until it is no longer a problem. If he continues to be stressed, try another trick instead. There is no need to distress your dog just for a cute trick!*

Crawl

Here's how to teach your dog to crawl.

Goal: Your dog will crawl across the ground.

What You'll Need: Clicker, treats.

Preparation: Teach Down first.

1. Cue "Down." Hold a treat right in front of your dog's nose. Wiggle it to entice him and then, very slowly, move it straight out, away from him, a couple of inches (cm). Keep it low to the ground. The second he stretches for the treat, click and give him the treat.

2. Repeat Step 1 two more times. Each time, when your dog starts to crawl forward, click and give him the treat.

3. With an empty hand, but holding your hand in the same position as if you had a treat, repeat Step 1. When your dog begins to move, click and give him a treat.

4. Repeat Step 4 five times. End your training session.

In future training sessions, gradually work up to where your dog will crawl a distance of several feet (m). Once your dog learns to reliably crawl several feet (m), it's time to add the cue.

1. Cue "Down." Cue "Crawl" and give your hand signal. When your dog crawls several feet, click and treat.

2. Repeat Step 1 five times. End your training session.

In future training sessions, when your dog reliably performs the behavior on cue, transition the clicker to your release cue, "OK!"

Don't click and treat the Crawl unless his rear is on the ground.

Tips: *If your dog keeps getting up instead of crawling, you're likely holding the treat too far in front of him or moving it too fast. Try going slower. Don't click and treat unless his rear stays on the ground.*

Dance

Dance is a great trick, but you've got to make sure your dog is strong enough to handle it.

Goal: Your dog will rise up on his hind paws and move in a circle.

What You'll Need: Clicker, treats.

Preparation: This behavior requires your dog to carry all of his weight on his hips and hind legs. Do not attempt this trick if your dog has any orthopedic issues that would cause him to experience pain during this behavior.

1. Hold a treat above your dog's nose. Wiggle it to entice him and encourage him to rise up, front paws off the ground.
2. The second his front paws leave the ground, click and give him the treat.
3. Repeat Steps 1–2 two times.
4. With an empty hand, but holding your hand in the same position as if you had a treat, repeat Steps 1–2. When your dog rises off the ground, click and treat.
5. Repeat Step 4 five times, gradually working to where your dog rises higher. End your training session.

Tip: *If your dog jumps off the ground, hold your hand lower.*

When your dog is reliably rising up on his hind legs, it's time to get him to move.

1. Use your hand signal to get your dog to rise up. Slowly move your hand in a circle so that your dog follows it. Click for even the smallest movement and then treat.
2. Repeat Step 1, gradually working up to a full circle, five times. Click and treat all correct responses. End your training session.

When your dog is moving reliably in a circle, it's time to add the cue.

1. Cue "Dance." Use your hand signal to get your dog to dance in a circle. Click and treat.

If your dog jumps off the ground while learning Dance, hold your hand lower.

2. Repeat Step 1 five times. For now, have your dog complete just one circle. Click and treat all correct responses.

In future training sessions, you can ask your dog to complete more than one circle. Your click ends the behavior. Go only as far as your dog is physically able and comfortable. When your dog is reliably dancing in a circle, transition the clicker to your release cue, "OK!"

Tip: *If you want to make this very fancy, you can train the Dance to fluency in one direction only and then start from scratch and train it the other way—just be sure to call it something else. So if a clockwise circle is "Dance," then a counterclockwise circle could be "Reverse." Or, you could name them different dances. One could be "Samba!" and the other "Polka!"*

Drop It

Drop It isn't just a trick; it could be helpful for getting your dog to drop something dangerous.
Goal: Your dog will spit out an item in his mouth.
What You'll Need: Clicker, treats. An item that your dog will take in his mouth.
Preparation: It helps if you have already taught Take It, but as long as the item is desirable to your dog, and he will put it in his mouth, it's not necessary.

1. Offer your dog the item. Let him hold it for a few seconds.
2. Hold up a treat right in front of him. He will likely spit the item out to get the treat. The second he spits out the item, click and then give him the treat.

Use an item that you know your dog will take in his mouth to teach Drop It.

3. Repeat Steps 1–2 two times.

4. Offer your dog the item. This time, hold your empty hand in front of your dog's nose, in the same position. When he spits out the item, click and give him a treat. This will fade the lure so that you and your dog don't become dependent on it.

5. Repeat Step 4 seven times. End your training session.

When your dog is reliably spitting out the item when you hold up your hand, it's time to add the verbal cue.

1. Offer your dog the item.

2. Cue "Drop It" once, in a friendly voice. Hold up your hand as you have before. When he spits out the item, click and give him a treat.

3. Repeat Steps 1–2 for a total of ten repetitions. End your training session.

Tips: *After you've introduced the verbal cue, you can fade your hand signal. Just make your gesture smaller and smaller until you no longer need it. If you find that your dog is so excited about the treats that he no longer wants to pick up the item, try using a higher value item and lower value treats.*

Fetch/Retrieve

It's not just retrievers who can learn this fun trick. You'll need to first teach your dog to Give. (The steps for teaching Give can be found later in this chapter under Give.)

Goal: Your dog will go to an item, pick it up, bring it to you, and deliver it to your hand.

What You'll Need: Clicker, treats. An item that your dog will readily take in his mouth.

Preparation: Teach Give first. Fetch is a chained behavior—there are several behaviors that are parts of the whole. It is easier if your dog learns the last part, Give, which is delivering an item to your hand, first.

Teach Give before you attempt Fetch.

1. Place the item near you, on the floor.

2. Click and treat for any interest your dog has in the item, even if he just looks at it.

3. Repeat Steps 1–2 for a total of ten repetitions. Your goal is for your dog to show such interest in the item that he picks it up, but you may not achieve

that during the first session, which is OK. If your dog does pick up the item, he will likely spit it out when you click, and this is also OK. The click ends the behavior, and you are rewarding him for picking it up.

When your dog is reliably picking up the item, it's time to add the cues.

1. Place the item near you, on the floor.
2. Just before your dog goes to pick up the item, cue "Fetch."
3. Just before he puts the item in your hand, cue "Give." When he places the item in your hand, click and treat.
4. Repeat Steps 1–2 for a total of ten repetitions. End your training session.

In future training sessions, gradually increase the distance that the item is from you. If at any time your dog drops the item too early, just go back to a point where he was successful at dropping the item in your hand and complete more repetitions there.

Tip: *As your dog gets reliable with the behavior, start practicing in different locations and with different items.*

Give

Give means that your dog will place an item in your hand. It's the end of the Fetch/Retrieve exercise, and it's also used when your dog picks up any item that you want him to bring to you. For example, if you are on a walk, and you can tell that your dog has something in his mouth, you can cue "Give," and he will place the item in your hand. Depending on the item, you might regret it, but it is better than his swallowing something that is dangerous for him. Teaching Give can help solve the problem of a dog's thinking that just because he has something in his mouth, he should run away with it and you should chase him.

Give means that your dog will place an item in your hand.

Goal: Your dog will deliver an item in his mouth to your hand.

What You'll Need: Treats, an item that your dog will readily take in his mouth. You will need two hands for this exercise, so you will not have a spare hand for a clicker. You can use a verbal marker, such as "Yes," instead of the click. Be sure that you "charge up" the verbal marker (as you did with the clicker when you first introduced it) so he understands that it means a treat is coming.

Preparation: Teach Take It first.

1. Cue "Take It."

2. Hold an open hand directly below your dog's muzzle. In your other hand, hold up a treat.

3. When your dog sees the treat, he is likely to spit out the item. Catch it. When he does, mark "Yes" and give him the treat.

4. Repeat Steps 1–3 two times.

5. Cue "Take It" and hold an open hand directly below your dog's muzzle. This time, hold your other, empty hand in the same position as you did when you had a treat.

6. When your dog drops the item in your hand, mark "Yes" and give him a treat.

7. Repeat Steps 5–6 seven times. End your training session.

When your dog is reliably dropping the item in your hand when it is held below his muzzle, then it's time to add the cue.

1. Cue "Take It."

2. Just before you hold your hand up to signal your dog to drop the item in your hand, cue "Give" once, in a friendly voice. Then hold up your hand. When he drops the item in your hand, mark "Yes" and give him in a treat.

3. Repeat Steps 1–2 for a total of ten repetitions. End your training session.

In future training sessions, you can fade your hand signal by making it smaller and smaller, so you can use just the verbal cue. In addition, start moving your hand around, just a few inches at a time, so that your dog has to move to deliver the item to your hand.

Tip: *When your dog is reliably responding to the Give cue and putting the item in your hand, start working with other items. Start with high value items that he is likely to put in his mouth, and then you can move on to other items.*

High Five

Teach your dog to give you a high five.

Goal: Your dog will raise one paw high and touch it to your open palm.

What You'll Need: Clicker, treats, paw target.

Preparation: Teach Sit and Paw Target first. Before you begin, decide how specific you want to be with this behavior. For example, do you want your dog to high-five your right hand with his right paw only? Or does it matter which paw he uses? Decide first, and then you will click and treat only the responses you want.

In the High-Five, your dog will raise a paw and touch it to your palm.

1. Cue "Sit." Hold the target in your hand, low to the ground, with your palm facing your dog. Cue "Paw."

2. When he touches his paw to the target, click and treat.

3. Repeat Steps 1–2 five times. Gradually hold the target higher and higher so that your dog has to reach to touch it.

4. Hold your hand in the same position, but without the target in it. Cue "Paw." If he touches your hand with his paw, click and treat. If he doesn't, wait at least a minute, just holding your hand still, to see if he understands. If he doesn't, put the target back in your hand for more repetitions.

When your dog is reliably touching his paw to your palm, it's time to add the cue.

1. Cue "Sit." Cue "High Five" once, in a friendly voice. Cue "Paw." When your dog touches his paw to your hand, click and treat.

2. Repeat Step 1 for a total of ten repetitions.

In future training sessions, use just the High Five cue, not "Paw."

Tips: *Be sure that you are not holding your hand too high for your dog to easily reach. Also, be sure that he is sitting on secure ground so he doesn't slip. If he starts to slide, he may not want to raise his paw because it will put him off balance.*

Jump into Your Arms

Get ready to catch your canine! Of course, always be sure your dog is physically able for any trick, but also check yourself! If you have a bad back or are not physically able to securely catch and hold your dog, please do not attempt this trick. Your dog needs to trust that you will catch and hold him safely. You also don't want to get hurt! This is not an ideal trick for very large dogs.

Goal: Your dog will leap from the ground into your arms for you to catch him.

What You'll Need: Clicker, treats. You will also need a chair for you to sit on.

Preparation: It can be helpful to teach Wait first (see end of chapter), so that your dog will wait until you cue him to jump into your arms.

Try This!

JUMP THROUGH YOUR ARMS

If you want your dog to learn to jump through your arms, then start the same process as for the hoop, except squat down and lay one arm down on the floor. You will eventually need both arms, so you may want to use a verbal marker for this exercise instead of a clicker. When your dog is reliably going over your arm, gradually add your other arm in an arc, forming a hoop with your arms. You may need to do this gradually so that your dog doesn't try to go around your arms instead of through. Click (or mark) and treat all correct responses. When the behavior is reliable, add the cue "Through!" or "Hup!"

1. Sit in a chair directly in front of your dog.

2. Encourage your dog to jump into your lap. You can pat your hands on your legs, talk sweet to him, do what it takes to encourage him. When he jumps into your lap, click. Toss a treat on the ground so he jumps off of the chair to get it and resets for the next repetition.

3. Repeat Steps 1–2 for a total of ten repetitions. End your training session.

4. Repeat Steps 1–2, except when your dog jumps into your lap, hold him briefly in both arms, in a manner that is comfortable for both of you.

5. Repeat Step 4 for a total of ten repetitions. End your training session. Repeat sessions until your dog is very comfortable jumping up into your lap and being held.

6. Stand up, facing your dog. Bend at the knees and encourage your dog to jump up. If he does, hold him, click, and release him gently to the floor, tossing a treat for him. If he hesitates, give him a minute to see if he will jump up. If he still doesn't, complete more repetitions with you sitting down again.

7. Repeat Step 6 for a total of ten repetitions. End your training session.

When your dog is reliably jumping up into your lap with your knees bent, it's time to put it on cue.

Have a little circus-like fun and teach your dog to jump through a hoop.

1. Position yourself in front of your dog. Cue "Hup!" or "Jump," or another verbal cue of your choice—just be consistent. Then encourage your dog as you have been doing to jump up into your arms. Click and treat all correct responses.

2. Repeat Step 1 for a total of ten repetitions. Gradually work until you are in a full standing position. Click and treat all correct responses. End your training session.

Jump through a Hoop

Teach your dog the classic trick of jumping through a hoop.

Goal: Your dog will jump through a hoop.

What You'll Need: Clicker, treats, hula hoop large enough for your dog to jump through comfortably.

1. Hold the hula hoop in front of your dog, on the ground. Click and treat for any interest in the hula hoop, even if he just looks at it.

2. As your dog shows more interest in the hula hoop, shape his behavior so that you click for one paw through the hoop, then two, then all four as he passes through the hoop. Do ten repetitions.

3. Repeat Step 2 until your dog is passing through the hoop. Be sure to allow your dog to approach the hoop from both sides so that he doesn't become dependent on going through only one way. For each training session, do ten repetitions.

When your dog is reliably going through the hoop, it's time to add the cue and raise the hoop.

1. Hold the hoop in front of your dog, on the floor. Cue "Through!" or "Hup!" once, in a friendly voice. Be sure that the cue is consistent and not similar to a cue for another action. Click and treat all correct responses.

2. Repeat Step 1 for a total of ten repetitions. Gradually hold the hoop higher and higher with each successful repetition, raising it just an inch (cm) at a time. Click and treat all correct responses.

Know Toys by Name

You can teach your dog to identify his toys by name and bring them to you.

Goal: Your dog will retrieve specific toys that you request.

What You'll Need: Clicker, treats, toys.

Preparation: Teach Fetch/Retrieve first.

1. Start with one toy (e.g., a tennis ball), placed a short distance away. Warm up with some Fetch cues. Click and treat all correct responses.

2. Start labeling the toy by cueing "Fetch Ball." Click and treat all correct responses.

3. Repeat Steps 1–2 nine times. End your training session.

You can teach your dog to identify his toys and bring them to you.

Trainer Tip

TOY NAMES
Make sure that the names you give the toys are distinct so that it will be easier for your dog to tell them apart.

4. Use a different toy, for example, a squeaky bear. Repeat Steps 1–3 with the new toy, calling it something different ("Fetch Bear"). End your training session.

5. Place the ball a short distance away from the dog and the squeaky toy about 2 feet (.6 m) away from the ball.

6. Face the ball. Cue "Fetch Ball." If your dog retrieves the ball, click and treat. If he goes to the squeaky toy, simply place the squeaky toy farther away and try again.

7. Face the squeaky bear. Cue "Fetch Bear." If your dog retrieves the bear, click and treat. If he goes for the ball, simply place the ball farther away and try again.

8. Repeat Steps 6–7 eight times, randomly calling out each toy. Don't always bounce back and forth between them; create an unpredictable pattern. End your training session.

In future training sessions, gradually move the toys closer together.

Tips: *When your dog can reliably differentiate between two toys, add a third toy. You'll follow the same process. Start by introducing the new toy by itself, then introduce it with just one toy, and then add the third toy. Only go as fast as your dog can be successful.*

Paws Up

Paws Up is a useful behavior when you want just your dog's front paws up on you or something, such as a bed. This is a good behavior for therapy dogs because it can make it easier for patients to reach them if they put their front paws up on a hospital bed.

Goal: Your dog will put only his front paws up on a person or object.

What You'll Need: Clicker, treats.

Preparation: Teach Paw Target and Off first. (The steps for teaching Off can be found later in this chapter under Up/Off). Make sure that your dog is orthopedically sound to support his weight on his rear end.

Paws Up is a good behavior for therapy dogs to learn.

1. Warm up with some Paw Target behaviors.

2. Stand next to a bed or chair. Cue "Paw." Click and treat. Cue "Off." Click and treat a correct response.

3. Repeat Step 2 three times.

4. Repeat Step 2, except once one paw is up, cue the other paw. Click and treat all correct responses.

5. Repeat Step 4 five times. End your training session.

6. Repeat Step 2, except withhold the click until your dog places both paws up. Click and treat all correct responses. Repeat a total of ten times and end your training sessions.

7. In future training sessions, add the cue "Paws Up" right before "Paw." After ten repetitions, you will just use the new cue "Paws Up."

Tip: *Practice this behavior in different locations.*

Play Dead

This might be the ultimate canine party trick.

Goal: Your dog will fall to the ground and lie on his side, holding still.

What You'll Need: Clicker, treats.

Preparation: Teach Down and the release cue.

1. Cue "Down." Once he is in position, hold a treat in your hand and start at your dog's nose. Slowly tuck the treat under his chin and then draw the treat across your dog's shoulder, at an angle, so that he stretches onto his side.

2. As soon as he is lying on his side, click and toss the treat to reset him for another repetition.

3. Repeat Steps 1–2 two times.

4. Repeat Steps 1–2, except this time, use an empty hand. Be sure to use the same hand gesture that you have been using. When your dog stretches out on his side, click and treat.

5. Repeat Step 4 seven times. End your training session.

Play Dead is a classic trick that's fun to teach.

6. Repeat Step 4, gradually extending the time that your dog lies on his side, a second at a time, until you click and treat. Work up to about five seconds. Do ten repetitions and then end your training session.

7. When your dog will hold the sideways Down for five seconds, it's time to add the cue. Just before you use your hand signal, cue "Bang!" or "Play Dead!" once, in a

friendly voice. Choose your cue and be consistent. Click and treat correct responses. End your training session after ten repetitions.

8. Work to where you can gradually stand up and signal your dog, rather than leaning down near him. For example, instead of stretching across your dog's shoulder, only stretch ¾ of the way and hold still, seeing if he completes the action on his own. In later repetitions, make this motion smaller so you only motion towards the shoulder. Then gradually work to where you are kneeling and motioning, then standing and motioning. If at any point he is confused, go back to the point at which he was successful.

9. When your dog is reliably working with you standing up, then substitute the release cue ("OK!") for the click. Continue to treat after your release cue.

Put Toys Away

There's nothing better than a little help around the house.

Goal: Your dog will put his toys away in a basket or box.

What You'll Need: Clicker, treats, toys, basket/box.

Preparation: Teach Fetch and Drop It first.

1. Have the basket directly in front of you. Scatter some toys around the room, not too far from you. Cue "Fetch." When your dog reaches you with the toy, cue "Drop It" and he will spit the toy into the box. Click and treat.

2. Repeat Step 1 until all the toys are in the box. Click and treat all correct responses.

3. Scatter the toys and repeat again, for a total of ten repetitions. End your training session.

Try This!

INTERACTIVE GAMES

Teaching your dog tricks helps engage his brain and keeps him mentally stimulated. Interactive games also provide healthy mental challenges for your dog.

There are games on the market that you can purchase to challenge your dog's creativity. Most require your dog to use his nose to find treats hidden within toys. Some are easier, such as a ball that you fill with kibble and that release the treats as the dog rolls it around. Others are harder, such as puzzles that require the dog to paw at levers or push blocks to reveal compartments hiding treats.

These games are good for occupying your active dog while you are busy doing other things. Just be sure that the specific toy is durable enough to leave with your dog unattended. Some will require supervision, depending on how destructive your dog is. Besides, part of the fun is watching your dog figure out the puzzles!

In future training sessions, gradually work farther and farther from the box.

Roll Over

Teach your dog how to roll over.

Goal: Your dog will lie down and roll completely over to return to his original position.

What You'll Need: Clicker, treats.

Preparation: Teach Down first.

1. Cue "Down." Hold a treat in your hand. Tuck it under his chin, then across his shoulder, and then all the way over his body so that he follows it and rolls over. Your dog may roll all the way over the first time. If so, click and treat. If not, click and treat for any stretch toward the treat. You will gradually ask for increasing stretches until he rolls all the way over.

2. When you have three successful rollovers, discontinue the treat in your hand, but use the same hand signal. Click and treat all correct responses.

3. Repeat Step 2 until you have ten total repetitions. End your training session.

4. When your dog is reliably rolling over, add the cue. Just before you give the hand signal, cue "Roll Over" once, in a friendly voice. Click and treat a correct response.

Shake

Prove how friendly your dog is by teaching him to shake hands.

Goal: Your dog will put his paw in your hand for you to shake.

What You'll Need: Clicker, treats, paw target.

Preparation: Teach Paw Target first.

During the Roll Over, your dog will roll over completely to return to his original position.

1. Hold the paw target in your hand, with palm facing up. Cue "Paw."
2. When your dog puts his paw on the target, click and treat.
3. Repeat Steps 1–2 two times.
4. Hold your hand in the same position, without the paw target. Cue "Paw."
5. When your dog puts his paw in your hand, click and treat.
6. Repeat Steps 4–5 six times. End your training session.
7. When your dog is reliably giving you his paw, add the cue "Shake" and then "Paw." After ten repetitions, you'll no longer need to use "Paw."

Sit Pretty

This is a fun trick, but you should probably skip it if your dog has any orthopedic problems.

Goal: Your dog will sit up.

What You'll Need: Clicker, treats.

Preparation: Teach Sit first.

1. Cue "Sit." Hold a treat just above your dog's head. Wiggle it, enticing him to reach up for it.
2. As soon as his front legs leave the ground but he's remaining in a sit, click and treat.
3. Repeat Steps 1–2 twice.
4. Repeat Steps 1–2, except hold your hand in the same position without a treat. Click and treat correct responses.
5. Repeat Step 4 six times. Each time, gradually shape your dog to where he picks his front legs up higher until he is holding the position you want. End your training session.
6. When your dog is reliably going into position, add the cue "Sit Pretty." Click and treat all correct responses for a total of ten repetitions.
7. When your dog is reliably responding to the cue and then add the release cue "OK!"

Teach Sit before you move on to Sit Pretty.

Speak

Teach your dog Speak, and your conversations with him won't have to be one-sided.

Goal: Your dog will bark on cue.

What You'll Need: Clicker, treats.

1. Do something that is likely to get your dog to bark. When he does, click and treat.
2. Repeat Step 1 five times. Click and treat all correct responses.
3. When your dog is reliably barking, add the cue "Speak!" Click and treat all correct responses.

Spin

Teach your dog how to spin in a circle.

Goal: Your dog will spin in a circle.

What You'll Need: Clicker, treats, target stick (optional).

1. Hold the target stick at your dog's nose level. You can use a hand if you prefer. Cue "Touch." Slowly move the target stick in a circle. If your dog will do a complete circle, click and treat. If not, just try a quarter circle at first. Click and treat a few repetitions at that level, then try a half circle for a few repetitions, then three-quarters of a circle, and then a full circle.
2. Repeat a total of ten times. End your training session.
3. When your dog will reliably complete a circle, add the cue "Spin" just before you motion with the target stick. Click and treat all correct responses.

Tip: *If you want your dog to keep spinning, then start to click for two spins, then three. Don't let your dog get dizzy, though! Add the release cue "OK!" so that your dog will know when to stop spinning.*

Teaching your dog to bark on cue is relatively easy.

Take a Bow

After learning these magnificent tricks, your dog deserves to take a bow.

Goal: Your dog will lower the front of his body down while his rear remains up.

What You'll Need: Clicker, treats.

1. With your dog in a standing position, hold a treat under his chin and move it straight to the floor, between his front legs. When he lowers his head, click and treat.
2. Repeat Step 1, working to where your dog will bend his front elbows. As soon as they bend, click and treat.
3. Repeat Step 2 two times.
4. Repeat Step 2, except hold your hand in the same position but without the treat. Click and treat a correct response.
5. Repeat Step 4 six times. End your training session.
6. When your dog is reliably bowing, it's time to add the cue. Just before you perform your hand signal, cue "Take a Bow!" once, in a friendly voice.
7. Repeat Step 6 for a total of ten repetitions. End your training session.
8. Repeat Step 6, adding the release cue "OK!"

Up/Off

You can use Up and Off to allow your dog up on furniture and then let him know when it's time to get down. You can also use Off to cue your dog to get off of you or others if he jumps up.

Goal: Your dog will get off of whatever he's on, with four paws on the floor.

After learning all of these tricks, let your dog Take a Bow!

PERFORMANCE DOGS

If you want to try your hand at show business, teaching your dog tricks is a good way to get started. Dogs are used in TV commercials, in videos, in movies, and as models for advertisements. Dogs are even on Broadway and in local theater productions.

In order to be a good canine actor, your dog will need to have solid obedience skills in addition to fancy tricks. He must also be confident and comfortable in a variety of environments. He may be expected to work under hot lights, with loud noises, big cameras, flashes of light, and strangers. Shy dogs, or dogs that take a while to warm up to situations, will be too stressed for this type of work. It takes a confident dog to be an actor!

Opportunities for stardom may be limited, depending on the area you live in. If you are in New York or Los Angeles, the opportunities may be greater, but with greater competition. Whether you approach a local advertising agency to use your dog as a model that can perform a handsome Sit-Stay, or interview agents to represent your dog for a potential TV career, don't hesitate to be a stage mom or dad. Never put your dog in situations that could harm him or frighten him. Even if the public falls in love with him, he's your best friend. Make sure that everyone you work with has his best interests and safety in mind.

What You'll Need: Clicker, treats

Preparation: Teach Hand Target first.

1. Decide where you want your dog to jump up, such as on the couch. Warm up with a few Touch behaviors.
2. Hold your hand up on the couch. Cue "Touch." When your dog jumps up and touches your hand, click and treat.
3. Hold your hand off the couch. Cue "Touch." When your dog jumps off the couch to touch your hand, click and treat.
4. Just before you present your hand on the couch, cue "Up" and then "Touch." When your dog jumps up, click and treat.
5. Just before you present your hand off the couch, cue "Off" and then "Touch." When your dog jumps off, click and treat.
6. Repeat Steps 4–5 eight times.
7. Repeat Steps 4–5 ten times but use only the new cues. You no longer need to use the cue "Touch" because you have replaced it with the new cues. End your training session.

Tip: *If you find that your dog is hesitant to jump up on the furniture, then initially click and treat for any stretching or movement toward jumping. Eventually, your dog will jump all the way up.*

Wait

Wait is not just a trick, it is polite behavior.

Goal: Your dog will hesitate in one spot until you tell him to do something else.

What You'll Need: Clicker, treats. If you are working at a doorway, have your dog on leash so that he doesn't run outside. You'll also need a doorway, crate, or gate.

1. Stand at the doorway. Start to open the door. If your dog starts to go outside, shut the door. Don't shut it on your dog!
2. Repeat Step 1 until your dog hesitates. Click and throw the treat over the threshold to encourage your dog to go outside.
3. Repeat Step 1 nine times. End your training session.
4. Repeat Step 1, gradually working to where you can open the door all the way and your dog will remain in position until you click and treat. Repeat a total of ten times. End your training session.
5. Repeat Step 1, gradually working to where you can step across the threshold but your dog remains in place until you click and treat. Repeat a total of ten times. End your training session.
6. When your dog is reliably waiting at the door, add the cue "Wait." Vary the amount of time he has to wait before you click and treat. After ten repetitions, end your training session.

Tips: *For Wait, it doesn't matter if your dog is sitting, standing, or lying down. Some dogs will choose to sit, which is fine but not necessary. Practice this behavior in different locations.*

Wave

Wave is one of the simplest tricks to teach.

Goal: Your dog will wave his paw.

What You'll Need: Clicker, treats, paw target.

Preparation: Teach Paw Target first.

Teach Paw Target before you teach Wave.

1. Hold the paw target in your hand, with palm facing your dog. Cue "Paw."
2. When your dog puts his paw on the target, click and treat.
3. Repeat Steps 1–2 two times.
4. Hold your hand in the same position, except just before your dog touches the target, pull your hand away. Click and treat.
5. Repeat Step 4 five times. End your training session.
6. When your dog is reliably waving, add the cue "Wave" before "Paw." After ten repetitions, you no longer need to use "Paw."

CHAPTER 13

GET OUT THERE AND SHOW OFF YOUR DOG!

With all the fun that you and your dog are having with training, why not take it further? There are so many activities that you can do with your dog. Check out the possibilities! Some of these activities and sports were originally created for dogs bred for specific purposes, but many sports allow any purebred or mixed-breed dog to participate. For whatever adventure you try, make sure that your dog is physically able for the task and having a good time.

Competing with Your Rescue Dog

If you adopted your dog, he may be a purebred dog or a mix of several different breeds. You may have registration papers for him with a breed registry, but most often you don't. In the past, having a mixed-breed or unregistered dog was a hurdle for entering your dog into competitive events, but not these days! Recently, even the traditional bastion of purebred dog shows, the Westminster Kennel Club Dog Show, embraced mixed-breed dogs competing in its agility competition.

Many organizations now allow mixed breeds to compete along with their purebred counterparts. So whether your dog has a classic fancy name, such as "Snowfall's Gallant Knight," or simply goes by "Hank," there's a place for him on the competitive field if you and your dog want to participate.

Each organization has its own rules and procedures for registering your dog for competition, so research them to find out how to start the process. Your dog's lineage or background won't stop him from becoming a blue-ribbon winner.

ACTIVITY	WHAT IT IS	WHAT DOG IS BEST SUITED
Agility	A sport in which a handler directs a dog through an obstacle course.	Fast, energetic dogs that are physically sound.
Barn Hunt	A sport that demonstrates a dog's vermin-hunting ability. (No rodents are endangered or injured during a barn hunt.)	Generally for dogs bred to hunt vermin, although any dog may show talent and enthusiasm for the sport. Dogs must be of a size to fit through an 18-inch (45.7-cm) gap through hay bales.
Bikejoring	A mushing activity in which a dog or team of dogs is harnessed to a tow line pulling a cyclist.	Any dog that is energetic, likes to run, and is physically sound.
Canicross	Cross-country running with one or two dogs, usually attached to a waist leash; popular in Europe.	Any physically sound dog that enjoys running over a distance.
Carting	A sport in which a dog pulls a cart containing supplies or people.	Large, strong dogs that are physically sound.
Conformation (Dog Shows)	An activity in which an expert in specific canine breeds evaluates individual dogs for how well they conform to their breed standards.	Purebred dogs.
Disc Dog	A sport in which a handler and dog compete in catching distance throws and choreographed freestyle disc catching.	Energetic dogs that like to catch and are physically sound.
Dock Diving	A sport in which dogs compete in jumping for distance or height from a dock into a body of water. The handler tosses a bumper or toy into the water for the dog to retrieve.	Dogs that like the water and who can swim and retrieve.

ACTIVITY	WHAT IT IS	WHAT DOG IS BEST SUITED
Earthdog	An activity that tests the working ability and instinct of dogs bred to hunt vermin through man-made tunnels. (No vermin are endangered or injured during trials.)	The American Kennel Club (AKC) allows specific breeds to participate in Earthdog trials.
Field Trials	A competitive event that has a variety of activities for retrievers, pointing dogs, and flushing dogs.	The AKC allows specific breeds to participate in field trials. Visit akc.org for details.
Flyball/Catchball	A sport in which teams of dogs race against each other over hurdles to a box. Dogs jump against the spring-loaded box to release the ball, which they must then carry back to the start line.	Any fast, energetic dog that is physically sound, likes balls, and can retrieve.
Freestyle	A competition in which dogs heel with their handlers to music. Some organizations focus on heelwork, while others add emphasis on creativity and theme-based choreography.	Any dog can participate.
French Ring	A sport that involves jumping, obedience, and bitework.	Energetic, high-drive dogs that are physically sound. In the United States, there are no breed restrictions, although in France only specific breeds can participate.
Herding	An activity and competition in which dogs demonstrate aptitude in herding livestock.	The AKC allows specific breeds to participate in herding trials.
Hiking/Backpacking	An activity in which a dog accompanies a handler on a hike, sometimes wearing a backpack.	Any dog can participate, although if he is going to wear a pack, the dog should be physically sound.
Nosework/Tracking/Search and Rescue	Activities, competition, and sport in which dogs follow their noses to find a specific scent or person. There are a variety of tracking activities, from competitions for ribbons and titles to working with rescue personnel to find lost people and cadavers.	Any dog can participate. There may be specific requirements for individual organizations, such as search and rescue organizations.

ACTIVITY	WHAT IT IS	WHAT DOG IS BEST SUITED
Lure Coursing	A sport in which dogs chase a mechanical lure.	The AKC limits competition to sighthounds, but all breeds can participate in a Course Ability Test.
Obedience	A sport in which handlers and dogs perform a set routine of obedience exercises.	Any dog can participate.
Rally	A sport in which handlers and dogs follow a path of signs in a ring, each sign indicating a specific exercise that they must complete.	Any dog can participate.
Schutzhund	A sport in which dogs compete in obedience, tracking, and protection.	Any energetic, high-drive dog can participate.
Skijoring	A sport in which a dog or dogs pulls a person who is on skis.	Any energetic dog that loves to run and pull and is physically sound.
Sledding/ Mushing	An activity/sport in which a team of dogs pull a sled.	Any energetic dog that loves to run and pull and is physically sound.
Therapy Work	An activity in which a handler and dog visit people in health-care facilities, libraries, schools, and other places. Animal-assisted activities are those in which teams bring cheer, while animal-assisted therapy is prescribed by a health-care professional for a patient to achieve specific goals.	Any confident dog that is extremely social with people and is trained to respond to obedience cues in a variety of settings can participate.
Treibball	An activity and sport in which dogs herd large exercise balls into a soccer goal.	Any dog can participate.
Weight Pulling	A sport in which dogs pull a cart loaded with weights.	Any dog that is physically sound can participate.

PART IV

SOLVING
TRAINING AND
BEHAVIORAL
ISSUES

CHAPTER 14

DEALING WITH INAPPROPRIATE BEHAVIOR

Your "NOOOOO!" can be heard 'round the block. Your dog has done something bad again. Of course, your instinct is going to be to yell at him ... but is that the most effective way to fix the problem? The answer is ... No!

Yelling and physically punishing your dog may make you feel better because it's a release for your frustration and anger. It's just not terribly constructive. For example, your dog gets hold of your shoe and runs off with it. You yell at him to come to you. He cowers and crawls over to you. You grab the shoe away and swat him on the rear. You show him the shoe and yell, "Leave this alone! Don't take my shoe! Bad dog! BAD DOG!" You're probably thinking that you've made it clear that he should never touch your shoes again. Not exactly.

Instead, you punished your dog for coming to you. The next time he's in the yard and you call him to come inside, he may not. The next time you call him to come to you because you have to give him important medication, he may avoid you. This is because you've actually taught him *not* to come to you. He has associated coming to you as a negative experience. You also may have taught your dog to go hide with the shoe next time so he can tear it to bits under the table without your seeing him. These are not behaviors that you want to teach your dog.

Yelling and physically punishing your dog for problems is not constructive.

What could you have done instead? You could have trained your dog some behaviors that would have been very helpful. If you saw your dog headed for the shoe, you could have used Leave It so that he never picked it up in the first place. If you were too late, and he already had the shoe, you could have used Drop It so that he'd spit it right out.

If you hadn't trained your dog yet, there still were better options. You could have encouraged your dog to come to you, then calmly taken the shoe, and then praised him for giving it to you. That would have taught him that it is rewarding to come to you … and bring you things! It could be the start of a nice retrieve.

The Cost of Corrections

Dogs need rules and boundaries. You should be a leader in your home; you just don't have to be a tyrant to achieve leadership status. There is a big difference! If you use harsh methods to correct your dog when he makes mistakes, the price you pay may be further problems.

- **Swatting, spanking, "pops on the rear," slapping, scruff shakes:**
  - Can cause fear, especially fear of hands or approaching humans, and resulting aggression. Depending on the dog, these corrections can cause the dog to shut down. This is called "learned helplessness," in which the dog is too fearful to try any action, for fear of punishment.
  - The idea of rolling up a newspaper and swatting your dog to disassociate the action with your hands is a myth. Your dog knows that you're holding the newspaper!
- **Collar grabs, dragging dog:**
  - Can cause fear, especially fear of hands or approaching humans, and resulting aggression. This could be a problem if you ever need to grab the dog's collar for safety issues. It would be better to train your dog to positively associate your grabbing his collar with treats and praise.
  - Can cause aggression so that dog bites when someone reaches for collar or head. This is a common cause of bites to children when they reach for their dogs' faces.
  - Pulling a dog in one direction automatically causes most dogs to pull back. This is called an oppositional reflex, and it makes it even harder to move the dog in the direction you want to go.
- **Alpha rolls (flipping the dog over onto his back to show that you are dominant or the boss):**
  - Can cause confusion at best, fear and resulting aggression at worst. This correction can cause fear of hands or human approach. It can cause a dog to be so frightened that he will urinate. This will not necessarily teach him to stop doing what you didn't like. It is likely to teach him that you are unpredictable and can't be trusted—that you become aggressive randomly.

Grabbing your dog's collar can cause fear and resulting aggression.

- Based on the inaccurate belief that wolves force their subordinates to flip upside down to show respect. This is not true. Lower-ranking wolves roll over of their own volition to a higher-ranking wolf. Dogs are not wolves. Dogs also realize that you are not a wolf, either. You don't pin him with your muzzle. Therefore, the alpha roll does not accomplish what is intended.

■ **Yelling, screaming:**
  - Depending on the dog, could cause fear and resulting aggression. A human temper tantrum, with yelling and screaming, can cause some dogs to be so afraid that they will urinate. This will not necessarily teach your dog to stop doing what you didn't like, but it is likely to teach him that you are unpredictable in your anger. Some may start growling, feeling a need to protect themselves.
  - With other dogs, yelling is ineffective. You could scream all day and they'll just ignore you.

■ **Spraying water or vinegar from a bottle:**
  - Can cause aversion to water, which is unfortunate when it's bath time!
  - Your dog learns to obey you only when you carry a spray bottle.

■ **Doing something unpleasant to your dog until he does what you want (negative reinforcement):**
  - Can cause fear and resulting aggression; can cause the dog to shut down.
  - Depending on the application and the dog, can cause aversion to other things. For example, one method of teaching a dog a retrieve (for competition or field training) is to pinch his ear firmly, often against the buckle of a collar, until he takes the item in his mouth. Once he does, you release the pressure. This is called a "forced retrieve" or "conditioned retrieve." Does it work? It can. But it can also teach your dog to dislike retrieving. And it's not necessary to use this method to get a reliable, consistent retrieve—even for competition and field trials.

The most effective way to stop problem behaviors is to manage and train your dog.

  - This doesn't mean that you should never discipline your dog. It doesn't mean that there are no consequences for "bad" behavior. When you use positive methods to train your dog, however, you're just smarter about it. You can avoid the negative consequences that come with physical punishment and still have a well-behaved dog.

So, if your dog does something that you don't like, what should you do? It depends on the infraction. If the dog is about to hurt someone or himself, a sharp "No!" can interrupt the behavior. If you use positive training methods with your dog, a single, sharp "No!" can be extremely effective because your dog doesn't hear it all the time. If you are constantly yelling at your dog, it just becomes background noise.

If your dog is just being annoying and isn't doing something dangerous, ignoring him is extremely effective. Ignoring behavior that you don't like is one of the best ways to discipline him. Dogs hate to be ignored! They thrive on attention. For example, if your dog is bounce, bounce, bouncing by the door, waiting for you to open it, just ignore him. Don't move, and don't open the door. The second he stops bouncing, you open the door. He'll learn that door will never open if he's airborne.

The most effective way to stop problem behaviors is to manage and train your dog.

The Management Plan: Controlling the Paycheck and Benefits

Modern dog trainers talk a lot about management. The concept is simple, but the execution can sometimes be a challenge. Once in place, however, it's a very powerful tool for preventing problem behavior. Prevention is the key word—with a good management program, you prevent your dog from misbehaving.

The more that your dog practices a behavior, the better he will get at it. So if he's practicing behaviors that you don't like, he's getting very good at them! What starts as a few repetitions of an annoying behavior will quickly turn into a habit. Habits are harder to change, for people as well as for pets. This is why it's easier to train Walking Nicely on Leash to a puppy that's never walked on leash before than it is to train an older dog that's been dragging people around for years.

The less training your dog has, the more management you have to do. If your dog hasn't yet learned to chew on appropriate toys, you need to be sure to keep everything out of his way that he may find tempting to gnaw on until you teach him which items are OK. If your puppy isn't house-trained, you need to confine him until you teach him where you want him to potty. If he's counter-surfing, you can block off the kitchen area until you teach him to stop it. The more you teach your dog the behaviors that you prefer, the less management he will need. There is truly something special about an older dog that completely understands your rules and routine! That's the goal—you just have to train your dog to get there.

If your dog pulls like a sled dog, turn and walk the other way instead.

Take Control

A humane, effective way to deal with your misbehaving dog is to control all of the good stuff in his life. Once your dog learns that you control all good things, you have his attention and respect! It's also so much easier than trying to muscle him into doing what you want.

Your dog already knows that you're the one who can get into the dog-food bag and the refrigerator. You're the one who can attach his leash and take him outside for adventures. All of these are very rewarding to him. Once you begin a positive training program, your dog will learn that you are a source of fun and treats. He will want to earn the treats, so he'll pay closer attention to you and learn how to enjoy working for you.

If he doesn't do what you ask, no paycheck. If he acts inappropriately, he loses benefits. For example, your dog starts shredding one of his toys. You take the toy away from him—too bad! He doesn't get to play with it anymore. Does he start barking like crazy when you reach for the leash? You step away from the leash instead. Too bad! You don't attach the leash to his collar if he's barking. He needs to be quiet instead. While on a walk, he starts dragging you to a spot on the side of the road. You put on the brakes. Too bad! He doesn't get to sniff that spot. If he walks nicely, he can go in that direction. If he continues pulling like a sled dog, then you'll just turn and walk the other way instead, and he loses the opportunity to sniff that enticing spot altogether.

You will find that your dog pays quick attention to what is working and what doesn't. If you do let him shred toys, bark, and drag you down the street, then he'll continue to do so. By withdrawing the reward, you can teach him that those things really aren't very fun after all.

You can still maintain your leadership if you let your dog eat before you do.

Does the Devil Make Them Do It?

What makes your dog misbehave? It may not even really be misbehaving. Normal dog behaviors, such as eliminating, chewing, digging, barking, and jumping, are often considered annoying by people, but dogs engage in these behaviors because they come naturally to them. You just have to train them to understand when these behaviors are appropriate and when they are not.

The Dominance Myth

A common myth is that dogs misbehave because they are trying to be "dominant." It's as if your dog aspires to be the ruler of your household—the "alpha"—and make you and your family his loyal subjects. The truth is that dogs aren't that complicated. They don't spend hours plotting intricate maneuvers to storm your castle. You know how your dog will be happily running to you one second and then get distracted by something in the dirt? How is that creature capable of masterminding a takeover?

Some of this myth stems from early concepts that dog behavior was overly similar to wolf behavior. In a wolf pack, there is an alpha male and alpha female, who determine pack rules and responsibilities. Other wolves in the pack have varying ranks, and there can be jockeying for position at times. Popular myths of the alpha wolf have trickled down into our relationship with our domestic dogs, which are leagues away from their lupine cousins.

You may have heard that the alpha wolf always eats first, so, before feeding your dog, you should always eat something first, in front of him, to maintain your leadership position. This is simply not true. The alpha wolf in a pack does decide who gets to eat first, but it isn't always him. Alphas often let the youngsters eat first, out of practicality—young wolves need the nutrition to survive much more than their older relatives.

Your dog already knows that he can't eat without you. You control the food he eats, when he eats it, and where he eats it. Munching on a cracker in front of him right before you present his food bowl is irrelevant.

Dogs do not steal things, chew things, pee or poop on things, bite, pull on leash, bolt out the door first, or many other behaviors because they are dominant. The reason why they do those things is much simpler. They're dogs. These behaviors are rewarding to them. Dominance is also not a personality trait. A dog can be social, shy, or a goofball, but he can't be dominant as a personality descriptor.

Some dogs growl when they play tug-of-war, but this type of growling is not threatening.

So is there such a thing, then, as dominant aggression? Yes. Dominance is defined in animal behavior as a relationship between individuals that is established by force, aggression, and submission in order to determine who has priority access to resources such as food, preferred resting spots, and access to mates. If your dog is on his bed, and he growls at another dog that tries to lie down next to him, this is dominance. He is saying that the bed belongs to him, and he doesn't want the other dog on it.

If your dog runs out the door ahead of you, however, what is the resource that he is challenging you for? The door? Access to outside? This makes no sense. He just wants to go outside because it's exciting out there, or maybe he really needs to eliminate.

Don't mistake normal puppy and dog play for dominance. Some dogs growl when they play tug-of-war, and they are not threatening you at all. They're playing. If your dog nabs a toy and runs off, looking over his shoulder for you to chase him, this is not dominance, either. He wants you to chase him and play. True instances of dominant aggression occur less frequently than common culture would have you think. So if your dog misbehaves, please don't assume that he's trying to outrank you!

Triggers

Sometimes, dog behaviors have triggers. Some dogs bark furiously when looking out the windows of their houses. Or, you may take your dog out for a ride and he barks when someone approaches the car. Some dogs growl when children approach. Some dogs only pee in the house during a thunderstorm or fireworks. Some of the reasons may be behavioral in nature; for example, it's not unusual for fearful dogs to eliminate inappropriately or act aggressively. Sometimes, the reason is physical.

Dogs settle comfortably into routines, so any changes could be stressful for them.

If your dog exhibits a sudden change in behavior, rule out physical problems. For example, if your dog hasn't peed in the house in years and suddenly starts peeing on your carpet, a vet check is in order. Or, if you've been picking up your little dog forever, and one day she suddenly snaps at you, take her to the vet. If the problem is physical, then no amount of training or behavior modification is going to help until the physical problem is addressed first.

Once your veterinarian eliminates any physical problems, then you can consider whether the trigger for your dog's behavior is

IF YOUR DOG DOES THIS ...	TRAIN THIS INSTEAD
Jumps up on you	Sit
Pesters you when you are eating	Settle (on his bed or a mat)
Chases the children, the cat, or squirrels	Leave It
Bolts out the door	Wait
Steals your socks	Leave It or Retrieve

something else. For example, are there any stressors in your home that could cause your dog to start peeing in the house? Something that seems minor to you, like a change in your work schedule, could be stressful to your dog. If you used to always come home at 5:30 p.m., but a work project has you staying late every night until 8:00 p.m., this is a disruption in routine. Dogs settle comfortably into routines, so this could be stressful for him. When dogs get stressed and upset, they can urinate or chew destructively.

When your dog does something you don't like, ask yourself, "Is this normal? What caused it? Can I fix it?" You may never know why your dog does certain things, but some educated guesses might be very helpful in guiding you to a solution.

Train What You Want

Once you identify any triggers that may be causing your dog's undesired behavior, you can address them. Instead of getting angry all of the time and telling your dog what you *don't* want him to do, you can train your dog to do things that you want him to do. "No!" just isn't very specific. Telling your dog to stop doing something is different from telling him what *to* do.

An effective method is to train an incompatible behavior. This is a behavior that, when performed, makes it impossible for the dog to do the behavior that you don't like. The chart on the top of the page shows some common problem behaviors, along with alternatives that you can teach your dog instead.

Think about other things that your dog does that bother you. What can you teach him to do instead? Train those desired behaviors to fluency so that they become better habits for your dog.

Techniques to Help Frightened Dogs

If your dog is afraid of something, there are two techniques often used to help him develop more positive associations with the scary item. You can also use these techniques for dogs that don't like certain activities, such as nail clipping or bath time. If your dog is so frightened that he eliminates, or is behaving aggressively, it's best to work with a canine professional who uses reward-based methods and has experience working with your dog's specific behavior issue.

Desensitization

Desensitization is the process of increasing an animal's tolerance to a stimulus by gradually increasing the presence of the stimulus. You start at the point at which your dog can perceive the scary thing but does not show signs of stress. This is called "under threshold." If your dog shows stress, you are already exposing him to too much of the item. This is called "over threshold."

For example, your dog is afraid to ride in the car. If he is standing next to the car, he starts to look away, yawn, and whine. If he is 3 feet (.9 m) from the car, he starts to become tense. But he can be at your front door, looking at the car in the driveway, with no problem. So you would start at the front door. You would take one step toward the car and make sure that your dog was still OK, and then proceed another single step, and so on. Desensitizing your dog to the car may take one session or many sessions.

Counterconditioning

Counterconditioning is the process of pairing a stimulus that causes a response with another stimulus that causes an opposite response. The first stimulus then starts causing the second response. You give something to your dog that he really likes when he's exposed to something he really doesn't like. He then builds a better association with the thing he doesn't like, so he grows to like it.

Don't give your dog a food-stuffed toy only when you leave the house, or he will come to associate the toy with your leaving.

With the car example, every time your dog looked at the car you could give him a treat. He would start looking at the car more often. As he approached the car on his own, you would give him a treat so that he would start moving closer to the car. He would start to associate the car with treats and start looking forward to being near the car.

You must be careful with counterconditioning that you don't proceed too fast or push the dog too hard. It can backfire if you're not careful. The dog could have the opposite reaction than what you intended, developing a negative association with the item you were

WHEN SHOULD YOU CONSULT A VETERINARY BEHAVIORIST?

If your dog is exhibiting a behavior issue that concerns you, how do you know when you need help from a veterinary behaviorist as opposed to a professional dog trainer? Veterinary behaviorists are educated to deal with both minor and severe behavior problems. Lore Haug, DVM, MS, DACVB, CPDT-KA, CABC, of Texas Veterinary Behavior Services in Sugar Land, Texas, explains that there are certain situations in which contacting a veterinary behaviorist can provide valuable insight into a behavior-change program. These include situations in which an animal may have a medical problem that is causing or contributing to the problem.

"The veterinary behaviorist can help manage the medical issues to maximize the animal's response to a behavior-modification program," Dr. Haug says. "Additionally, veterinary behaviorists are uniquely trained to manage cases in which psychoactive medications are needed or indicated—for example, animals with marked fear, anxiety, or repetitive behaviors. In short, veterinary behaviorists are one of the few professionals who are trained to address *all* aspects of an animal's health and well-being."

It can be hard to find a board-certified veterinary behaviorist in your area because there aren't that many of them. Don't give up, though. Dr. Lore adds, "Owners living in areas that do not host a veterinary behaviorist can still benefit from their knowledge by encouraging their pet's regular veterinarian to contact a veterinary behaviorist by phone or email for assistance in managing difficult cases."

using as a good thing. For example, your dog could start not liking the treats you are using because they now remind him of the scary car.

This is why you should not give your dog a food-stuffed chew toy only when you leave the house. Most dogs love food-stuffed toys. But if your dog only gets one when you leave, and he doesn't like it when you leave, then he will start associating that toy with the negative experience of your going away. Giving your dog food-stuffed toys randomly when you are at home can prevent this.

More Powerful Together

Desensitization and counterconditioning are often used together, and they work very well together. You can often make faster progress by pairing the two techniques together.

You start under threshold, the point at which the dog is not exhibiting stress. You then start rewarding the dog with something he finds wonderful, such as treats or playtime with a toy. You gradually move closer to the scary item, continuing to offer rewards. As long as the dog does not exhibit stress, you are still under threshold and performing desensitization correctly.

CHAPTER 15

PROBLEMS WITH HOUSE-TRAINING

House-training problems are one of the top complaints of dog owners. Many dogs get relinquished to shelters because they have accidents in the house. It's not their fault—they were probably never taught properly.

House-training is the same process whether your dog is a puppy or an older dog. The main difference is that an older dog will not need as many potty breaks as a puppy does. Other than that, the concept is exactly the same.

If you're having a challenge with house-training, there are two main categories to consider. First, has your dog ever been successfully house-trained? A gauge to use is three months—has your dog ever gone without an accident for three months? If not, then he's not house-trained. Second, is the problem sudden? Has your dog been accident-free for months or years and suddenly started eliminating in the house again?

If your dog is not successfully house-trained, there could be several reasons. It's humbling to realize, but the first place to look is in the mirror. Here are some questions to ask yourself:

- **Are you following the house-training program to the letter?** Review the section on house-training carefully and see if you are following the plan.

- **If you are diligently following the process, is everyone else who interacts with your dog?** For example, you may confine your dog when you're not home and supervise him closely when he's loose in the house, but does your spouse? If everyone isn't being consistent, it will be harder for your dog to learn.

Here are common reasons why house-training problems occur:

- **The dog has been given too much freedom, too soon.** The solution is to go back to more stringent confinement. Go back to the beginning of crate training. When your dog stops having accidents for one month, confine him to one room. When you've had another successful month, allow him one room and a hallway. Slowly work up to the entire house if that is your goal. Any time your dog has a setback, go back to the last step at which he was successful and stay there until you've had a month of success before moving on to the next step. It's not uncommon for dogs to have accidents if they are given too much space before they completely understand that they have to to eliminate outside.

- **The dog does not have enough supervision.** This goes hand in hand with confinement. If you let your dog out of his crate, you need to watch him diligently. If you turn your back for a minute, and he has an accident, you allowed it to happen because you let down your guard. Your dog will not learn if you don't keep a close eye on him and interrupt him before he makes a mistake.

  The solution is to supervise your dog more closely. If you watch your dog, you can prevent accidents from happening by stopping him and rushing him to his elimination spot, where you can praise him. Remember, every time your dog has an accident in the house, he's practicing that behavior. You want him to have many more chances to practice the behavior of elimination in his designated elimination area.

- **The dog is not getting enough potty breaks.** Puppies and seniors need more frequent potty breaks than the average dog. Some toy breeds also seem to need more breaks. And you may just have a dog that needs to go more often. The solution is to add another potty break or two to the schedule to see if that makes a difference.

There are other issues that can cause house-training headaches. Sometimes it's an age thing—a puppy is just slow to learn, or an adult dog regresses. You may adopt a rescue dog that is OK for a month or so and then starts eliminating in the house. Some dogs only pee in the house when they greet people. Male dogs can start lifting their legs to mark furniture. There are positive, effective ways that you can deal with each of these issues.

Confused Puppies

You may think that your puppy will never understand the house-training concept. Some puppies just take longer to figure it out, but there are definitely things you can do to accelerate the process.

Keep a house-training log, tracking four key items:

1. The specific time you give him each potty break.

House-training problems may occur if you give your dog too much freedom too soon.

2. What happens during the break—does he pee, poop, or do nothing?

3. Any time he has an accident, and what it is. If you find the evidence later and don't know when he did it, just mark the approximate time. And don't leave your puppy unsupervised!

4. His exact feeding and water schedule.

Keep the log for about one week and see if you notice any patterns. Is he OK at night, but not in the afternoon? Find the times when he has accidents frequently and add at least one more potty break during that time.

Also look for unusual frequency in elimination. Does your puppy pee every half hour? This is not normal. Are his stools very loose, or does he have diarrhea? This is not normal.

For example, an Alaskan Malamute puppy drinks a lot of water. He just can't seem to get enough of it. He pees every half hour, and a large amount each time. The urine is almost clear. Sometimes, when he's playing, he even leaks urine. The owner calls the breeder, who assures the owner the puppy is fine, and that Alaskan Malamutes are just "stubborn" and hard to house-train. Finally, the owner has had enough and consults the puppy's veterinarian. The vet diagnoses the pup as having juvenile renal disease. There really was something wrong with the puppy.

If your puppy is healthy and just seems to be slow in understanding the house-training program, you will need to get more black and white. Be super vigilant and supervise all moments that your puppy is loose. Keep to the confinement training. When you take your puppy to his elimination spot, and he eliminates there, really pour on the praise! Give your puppy several treats, one after the other. Praise him. Pet him. Have a party! Sure, your neighbors will think you're overly excited about pee and poop, but who cares? You are making it really obvious to your puppy that you are ecstatic when he eliminates in the spot you've chosen for him.

Not giving your dog enough potty breaks may be the cause of house-training problems.

Be consistent. Be persistent. Some puppies just take longer than others. The effort you put into this now will mean a lot fewer messes throughout the life of your dog.

Adult Regression

Sometimes adult dogs that have been house-trained for months or years will have setbacks. In adolescence, this is not unusual. If it's a sudden issue, always consult your veterinarian first. If the vet clears your dog of any health problems, then go back to your house-training program and start from scratch, as if your dog were a puppy. Dogs usually pick up the routine quickly again.

Sometimes a change in routine will confuse or stress your dog and cause him to have house-training regression. For example, moving to a new home, or visiting another home, can often trigger house-training incidents. Just because your dog has learned not to eliminate in your home doesn't mean that he knows not to eliminate in another home. Your new home's previous inhabitants also may have included a dog that had house-training issues. Even though you can't smell old pee in the carpet and carpet pads, your dog certainly can.

For example, a family moves into a house and, within a week, their previously house-trained dog begins peeing in the living room and in the hallway. They take their dog to the vet, and he checks out OK. They figure that he must be stressed from the move, as they all are, so they start confining him more and begin a house-training refresher program. He persists in peeing in those spots. They meet the neighbors, who tell them that the previous owners had an elderly Poodle who peed in the house all the time. This explains why the family's dog is having accidents … he can smell where the other dog eliminated, so he thinks that's the doggie bathroom. If you suspect that this may be the case, get the carpet professionally cleaned. You may have to replace it altogether, if the problem persists.

If you adopt a rescue dog that is allegedly house-trained, it's still a good practice to implement a house-training program right from his first day home. It will help him learn your expectations right off the bat.

Being at a shelter can be very stressful for dogs, so don't be surprised if your rescue dog has house-training accidents. The shelter may have been given misinformation about the dog's abilities, the dog could be stressed at all the recent changes in his life, or the dog just never learned to generalize house-training to all indoor places. Be patient and train him as if he were a puppy.

If your adult dog is having house-training problems, take him to the veterinarian.

Piddly Greeters: Submissive Urination

Some dogs leak urine when greeting people or other dogs. This is common in puppies and in some breeds, such as Cocker Spaniels. This is actually not a house-training problem. Your dog may perfectly understand to eliminate only in his elimination area. When a dog urinates during greetings, it's actually a sign of respect. It's called submissive urination.

Dogs leak to show respect for others. Some dogs do it for all people, while others do it only for tall people, or men, or people with deep voices. If it wasn't so messy, you might find it a compliment!

Here is how to address submissive urination.

1. When you come home, completely ignore your dog for at least ten minutes. Don't even make eye contact. Just casually take off your coat if you're wearing one, put away your keys or purse, check your mail, change clothes, and the like. When you first come home is when your dog is the most excited and has the least control over his bladder.

2. After about ten minutes, casually let your dog out of his crate. Do not make eye contact and do not pet him. Immediately take him outside to eliminate. You can still give him a treat and/or praise him when he eliminates outside.

3. Bring him inside and ignore him for at least five more minutes.

4. You can now acknowledge your dog. Be very calm and do not loom over him to pet him. Do not pet him on the head because this is an assertive gesture. Instead, scratch him on the chest. The more excited and exuberant your greeting, the more likely you will cause your dog to pee. So keep it calm.

5. Whenever guests visit your home, confine him just before guests arrive to help give him space away from the excitement of your arriving guests.

Tips: *This laid-back greeting style could be challenging for you. You love your dog, and you're happy to see him. You want to make a big deal out of greeting him. This will not help your dog if he is a submissive piddler, though. It will just make things worse. So control your emotions and be very calm and casual about all greetings. You should not have to do this forever. Once your*

Vet Tip

HEALTH-RELATED ISSUES

If your dog exhibits a sudden change in his house-training habits, take him to a veterinarian. Many sudden changes in behavior often have a physical reason. Dogs that suddenly start peeing in the house may have urinary tract or kidney infections. Some medications also cause an increase in thirst and, therefore, an increase in urination. No amount of house-training will help you if your dog suffers from a physical problem. So take your dog to the vet and get him checked out before you try training as a solution.

dog learns that he doesn't have to show his respect all the time and he learns to control his bladder, you can gradually resume more exuberant greetings.

Marking

Marking is most common in intact males reaching adolescence. Neutering your dog early may help prevent marking, but you may have reasons for not neutering or waiting to neuter your dog.

Marking is really just a house-training issue. Instead of being able to allow your dog more freedom as he reaches the teenager stage and learns the house-training program, you will have to remain vigilant.

Testosterone levels are higher in adolescent dogs than in adult dogs. Between four and ten months of age, a male puppy's testosterone levels may be up to five times that of an an adult male. This is when your intact male teen may start lifting his leg and marking territory. He's not trying to irritate you; his hormones are telling him to do this.

Dogs only eliminate in the house because you allow them to. If your boy starts to lift his leg, immediately interrupt him and rush him outside to his elimination spot. Praise him for going outside; make a big deal about it. Be sure to clean any messes thoroughly with an enzymatic cleaner.

For management purposes, you may also consider getting a belly band. This is a fabric wrap that goes around his body and penis; you insert a feminine pad in it to absorb any urine. He will lift his leg, but the urine won't mark anything. However, this will not solve your problem! You will still need to train him, but belly bands can come in handy when you are taking your adolescent male dog to a friend's house or an unfamiliar place.

To stop your dog from marking, you need to be vigilant with your supervision and confine him when you can't watch him. You can absolutely have an intact male dog in your house that doesn't lift his leg on your furniture or belongings. You just have to train him not to do it.

With a dog that submissively urinates, try to be calm and casual about all greetings.

CHAPTER 16

SOLVING SPECIFIC PROBLEMS

Dogs can make our lives better, but it's not always without some challenges. Whenever you bring different species together, there are bound to be some bumps in the road. Positive trainers are creative trainers. By using positive methods, you'll have a lot more tools in your toolbox to figure out solutions that work for you and your dog.

Attention-Demanding

Some dogs learn to pester you when they want something, usually because this behavior proves to be rewarding. If your dog barks at you, and you give him what he wants, he'll continue to bark because it worked. If he noses you, and you pet him, he'll continue nosing you. If he drops the ball in your lap and noses your hand until you throw it, and you do, he'll continue bringing you the ball. If he paws at you to get you to do something, and you do it, he'll continue pawing at you.

One thing that can make attention-demanding worse is being overly fussy over your dog, showering him with constant attention, and letting him sleep with you in your bed. Some dogs can sleep in the bed with you just fine, with no side effects. Others can get overly dependent. This is not a healthy attachment for your dog, and it can lead to separation anxiety and create a nervous, stressed dog.

Some dogs learn to pester you when they want something.

You can love your dog and provide for him without spoiling him rotten. If your dog is showing signs of attention-demanding or an inability to leave you alone, you need to address it now, before it gets worse.

Your dog will never learn to stop demanding your attention unless you stop giving it to him. At first, it will be hard. Both of you will be changing your habits. Behavior generally increases before it extinguishes—this is normal. This means that if your dog barks for attention, and you've been giving it to him for a while, his barking will get worse when you suddenly stop. You have to wait him out. If you give in, it will be that much harder for him to break the habit.

Another helpful tip is to work on your training. With regular training sessions, your dog will learn that he gets your attention by performing behaviors for you.

Barking

Barking dogs can drive you barking mad. They can wreck relations with neighbors and embarrass you in public. There are lots of reasons why dogs bark:

- Some dog breeds, such as those in the Herding Group, are natural barkers, so there can be a strong genetic component to the problem.
- It can be rewarding. For example, if your dog barks at you and you pay attention to him, he'll increase that behavior because it worked.
- They are announcing something. Alarm or alert barking occurs when a dog senses something and feels a need to announce it. This can include a cat outside the window or someone approaching the house.
- Fear.
- To engage you or another animal to play.
- Frustration.
- Predation or when chasing something.
- Boredom.
- In greeting.

In order to stop the barking, the first thing you must do is determine why your dog is doing it, if you can. If it's something you can manage or prevent, that often solves the problem. For example, if your dog barks only at the window at people or other animals, just block your dog's access to the window. You want to prevent your dog from practicing the behavior. If he keeps it up, it can become an ingrained habit.

Some dogs in the Herding Group are natural barkers.

BEHAVIOR OFTEN GETS WORSE BEFORE IT GETS BETTER

Any time you change the rules on your dog, you could see an increase in the behavior you're trying to change. This is normal and is called an "extinction burst."

For example, your dog always barks when you pick up his leash. So, one day, you decide that you're tired of it and are not going to leash him while he's barking. You pick up his leash and wait for him to stop barking. He doesn't! He barks and barks and barks, and it seems to be getting worse. This is because barking has always worked for him before. Any time he barked, you put on his leash and he got to go on an adventure. So he keeps at it because it's always worked in the past.

How do you deal with an extinction burst? You have to ride it out. If you leash your dog anyway, you're just reinforcing the barking behavior, and it will be even stronger than before. So have lots of patience, and wait your dog out. Then consistently follow up from that point on—don't ever leash your dog while he's barking. Your dog will learn to be quiet instead, which is your goal. You just have to get through the extinction burst first!

If the problem isn't fear-related, and your dog is just barking because he is excited, you can train your dog to hush on cue.

Goal: Your dog will be quiet when you cue him.

What You'll Need: Clicker, treats.

1. Do something to encourage your dog to bark. Then wait for him to stop on his own.
2. The second he stops, click and treat.
3. Repeat Steps 1–2 nine times. End your training session.

When your dog is reliably stopping his barking very quickly, it's time to add the cue.

1. Do something to get your dog to bark.
2. Just before you think he will be quiet, cue "Hush" or "Quiet"—be consistent. Use the cue one time, in a friendly voice. If you shout at your dog, he likely will just bark louder, thinking that you're joining in!
3. When your dog is quiet, click and treat.
4. Repeat Steps 1–3 nine times. End your training session.

Begging

Dogs beg for food for several reasons. If you ever feed your dog from the table, he learns that it's rewarding to hang out near you while you eat. He can start pestering you for more food. Dogs can also learn that the dining area itself is rewarding if there are crumbs on the floor.

If your dog begs at the table, be sure that no one in your family is feeding him from the table. If the begging continues, and people give in, your dog will not learn to leave people alone while they are eating. Then, train your dog to Settle so that he learns to go to a mat or his bed while you are eating. While he is on his mat, give him a food-stuffed toy so that he can enjoy a treat while you do, too.

Car Anxiety/Carsickness

Dogs can get nauseated and carsick just like people can. You don't want a car ride to be miserable for your dog. Talk to your veterinarian about medications that may help ease his symptoms. You can train your dog to better enjoy car rides, but you may need the medication to help with the process.

Goal: Your dog will enjoy car rides.

What You'll Need: Clicker, treats.

Start at this step if your dog gets anxious just approaching the car.

1. Start at the point just before your dog experiences anxiety. When your dog shows any interest in the car, or even looks at the car, click and treat.

2. Take a small step closer to the car. When your dog looks at the car, or if he moves toward it, click and treat.

3. Repeat Step 2 several times, but stop before your dog exhibits stress. The point at which he exhibits stress will vary, depending on your dog, so pay attention to his signals.

In future training sessions, work up to where you can get your dog in the car and secured in his crate or seat belt, and he is not stressed.

When your dog is happily going into the car, continue with the following steps. Because you'll be driving, you won't be able to use treats safely. Plus, since nausea is often a factor, you don't want to feed your dog and make the nausea worse.

1. Start the car while your dog is in it. Let it run for two seconds while you praise your dog. Turn the car off and remove your dog from the car. Getting out of the car will be a reward for your dog.

2. Repeat Step 1, gradually increasing the amount of time that your dog is in the running car. Work up to a couple minutes. If your dog exhibits stress, you are working too long. Repeat no more than five times, fewer times if your dog is anxious.

3. When your dog is comfortable with Step 2, put your dog in the car, start the car, move the car down the driveway, drive back to the car's original position, turn off the car, and remove the dog. Praise your dog while the car is moving. Repeat no more than five times, fewer times if your dog is anxious.

4. When your dog is comfortable with Step 3, repeat it, gradually taking longer and longer

Use a crate or a doggy seatbelt to secure your dog in the car.

drives. The first time you leave your property, you may only go around the block. For each repetition, when you return to your driveway, turn the car off and remove your dog from the car. Repeat no more than five times, fewer times if your dog is anxious.

Tips: *These short driving sessions can gradually acclimate your dog to car rides. The way you secure your dog in the car may also help. Dogs should always be secured in cars, never allowed to be loose. If your dog dreads car rides, and he is normally crated, try a canine seatbelt. Conversely, if your dog gets carsick and is normally in a seatbelt, try a crate. The change may have an impact on helping him feel more secure in the car.*

Chasing or Herding

Chasing is extremely rewarding to most dogs. Some breeds are genetically programmed to chase. If your Corgi chases the kids, it's simply because his DNA is telling him to! That doesn't mean that you have to allow your natural chaser to go after things.

Teach Leave It. A great foundation in Leave It will help teach your dog that *not* chasing after something can be just as rewarding. Also introduce your dog to the fun of chasing a flirt pole toy instead of your kids.

Management is the first step toward preventing counter-surfing.

Counter-Surfing

If you have a tall dog that can reach the counter, sooner or later he may go exploring. These explorations are often quite rewarding. The first time your dog lands himself a ham sandwich, he'll discover that the counter is a treasure trove.

Management is the first step toward preventing counter-surfing. Block your dog's access to the counter unless you are there to supervise his behavior. Otherwise, you are just giving him a chance to practice his new behavior. Keep your counters clear of anything that he could find tempting.

Train Leave It, and use it when you see him about to jump up and put his paws on the counter. When you want to try him unsupervised in the kitchen, leave several food-stuffed chew toys on the floor. The goal is to redirect your dog's attention to the floor, rather than to the counter.

Digging

Just as some dogs are born to chase things, others are born to dig. Terriers, for example, were originally bred to hunt and kill vermin. Digging is a desirable trait in an animal bred to go after mice and voles. Dogs also dig because it's fun. It can sometimes be hard to believe that two little front paws can dig holes that deep! It's a behavior, however, that many people find annoying and destructive.

To stop your dog from digging, you have to be supervising him to interrupt and redirect the behavior. If you're not, then you can't teach him not to dig. This means that you will have to manage the situation. Instead of keeping your dog outside while you are away from home, bring him inside. You can always crate-train him if you have concerns that he will have accidents or be destructive if left alone indoors.

When outside, redirect your dog to behaviors that you like better than digging. Give him toys, and rotate the toys frequently so that he doesn't grow bored with them.

Try This!

MAKE A DIG PIT

A dig pit can be a good solution if you have a very persistent digger. Create a defined area in your yard where you will allow your dog to dig. You can fill it with sand or loosen the dirt to encourage him. You can even hide toys in there. When you catch your dog digging in an area that you don't like, cue "Leave It." Then, run with your dog over to his designated dig pit and encourage him to dig there instead. Praise him when he does! Repeat every time you catch him digging in an area that you don't like. With repetition and consistency, your dog should transfer his desire to dig to his own area.

Door-Darting/Escaping the Yard

Dogs escape because it's fun. There's a whole world of adventure out there, and they want to explore it. It is also powerfully rewarding, with all of the scents and excitement, so once it starts, it can be challenging to fix.

Door darting, or dashing through yard gates, is easier to fix than escapes from the yard when the dog is unattended. There are several incompatible behaviors that you can teach your dog to prevent him from dashing outside. You can teach Wait so that he has to wait for you to cue him before he goes outside. You can teach Down-Stay on a mat or his bed for times when company comes and you have to answer the door. A simple Sit also works well. If he is sitting, he's not running away.

If your dog is escaping from your yard, this is very challenging to fix. The behavior is rewarding to your dog, but it's also dangerous. Your dog could easily get hit by a car or otherwise hurt.

Keep your dog inside when you are not home to supervise him. Reinforce your fence. If he's digging under the fence, reinforce the bottom of your fence with chicken wire, extending it several feet into the yard and burying it. If he's going over the fence, string some wire across the top through PVC piping so that when your dog reaches the top of the fence, his paws will just roll on the PVC rather than gain purchase. Provide toys for your dog to enhance his experience in your yard; rotate them daily so he won't grow bored with them.

Eating Inappropriate Things (Coprophagia and Pica)

Some dogs eat inappropriate things, such as poop or other objects. Coprophagia is the act of a dog eating feces, whether it's his own or another animal's. While we find it disgusting, it's a very normal behavior for dogs, especially puppies. Mothers lick their puppies to stimulate them to eliminate and then lick them clean afterwards.

Some puppies will outgrow the habit. Others carry it into adulthood. Some can be quite persistent! A dog will follow another dog around, waiting for him to poop so that he can eat it right away.

There are several theories about why dogs enjoy eating feces, but there hasn't been any scientific evidence to back them up. Some theorize that a dog is missing certain nutrients or that the dog's diet is too rich and, therefore, nutrients are passing into the feces, making them appealing to the dog to eat.

If your dog is escaping your yard, it is a challenging problem to fix.

The only way to stop a dog from eating poop is to be there and prevent him from doing it. If you leave him unattended in a yard where there are feces, he will be able to eat them and continue his habit. Here are some things you can do:

- Go out with your dog and pick up the feces right away. If your dog is too fast for you, then put him on leash.
- Feed your dog a good-quality, easily digestible food. If he absorbs all of his nutrients, he may be less interested in feces.
- Teach Leave It.

Pica is the consumption of nonfood items. Puppies will chew on anything, and they can ingest things if not supervised closely. Dogs will also exhibit pica out of boredom. If a dog is bored, he'll start gnawing on something and may ingest it. For some dogs, this can become more of an obsession, such as those dogs that go out of their way to eat rocks. Some dogs can successfully pass items that they ingest through their digestive systems, but some items may get stuck and require surgery. This can be very dangerous.

You can help calm an excitable dog by giving him regular, adequate amounts of exercise.

If your dog is randomly eating things that he shouldn't, keep a safe environment for him. Either confine him when you can't supervise him or make sure that there is nothing to tempt him, except appropriate toys, when he is unsupervised. Provide a good variety of appropriate toys, including food-stuffed interactive toys. Rotate them so that he doesn't grow bored. Teach Leave It.

If you think that your dog may have a compulsive disorder, then consult your veterinarian. You may need professional help.

Excitability/Nervousness

Some dogs can get so bouncy that you swear that they may have attention deficit hyperactivity disorder. Some of this is inherent in the breed or breed mix. For example, the typical Boston Terrier is going to be a lot more excitable than the average Basset Hound.

You can help with excitability by giving your dog regular, adequate amounts of exercise. Games of fetch; long, brisk walks; and playing with another dog are all good options, depending on your dog's health. (Always consult your veterinarian if you have concerns.) You'll notice that on the days you miss the canine workout, your dog will be less focused and more likely to be hyper.

Teaching your dog to relax is just as important as exercise. When you are starting, schedule your training sessions for times when your dog is naturally more tired. Dogs are crepuscular animals, which means that they are most active at dawn and dusk.

First, exercise your dog to take the "edge" off. Then, settle with your dog in your lap or next to you. Gently start rubbing his ears and then his neck, chest, and sides. Make it a soothing massage. If your dog is not used to being handled, incorporate the Handling exercises from the Puppy Training section. Make it a positive experience for him. Keep the sessions short if he is too fidgety. Work up to gradually longer sessions until your dog learns to readily relax.

You can also teach Down-Stay to help your dog learn to relax. Give your dog a food-stuffed toy to reward him for settling on his mat or bed or in his crate.

When assessing your dog for excitability, be sure it really isn't nervousness. A stressed dog can sometimes come across as a hyper dog. A nervously hyper dog will be showing signs of stress, such as lip licking, clinginess, whining, and the like. If your dog is actually nervous, then you will need to find out what his triggers are—what is making him so concerned? Work on addressing his fears. The relaxation exercises can also help.

Turning away is a sign of fear.

Fear

Some dogs can be shy or fearful. If a dog's parents were shy or skittish, the puppies can be, too. Often, fearfulness is due to a lack of proper socialization during a puppy's critical socialization period. Sometimes the signs are obvious, such as a tucked tail, cowering, and whimpering. Other signs may be harder to recognize if you don't have experience with fearful dogs. They include:

- Lip licking
- Yawning
- Whining, barking
- Trembling
- Turning away
- Wet paw prints
- Urination

During the critical socialization period, proper socialization can help reduce or eradicate a puppy's fear. Desensitization and counterconditioning can also help with puppies and dogs. There are other options as well. The method you use will depend on the individual dog and the trigger for the fear. If your dog is so fearful or shy that he has a reduced quality of life, please consult a professional trainer. The trainer should use positive methods and have experience working with shy dogs.

There are other things that you can try to help ease your dog's fear. Along with behavior modification, these may help as additional options to try. The Thundershirt, a snug-fitting jacket, has been shown to help some dogs. Rescue Remedy, a Bach Flower Remedy, is used to help dogs in extreme stress (people use it, too). There are also dog-appeasing pheromones (DAP), offered via diffusers or in sprays, which are supposed to mimic a mother dog's pheromones and may comfort your dog.

You may also consider medication to help your dog. Always consult your veterinarian for assistance. Medication to help address fear is not the same as tranquilizers. If your dog is extremely shy due to a chemical imbalance, the medication may help balance your dog's blood and brain chemistry and make it easier for the behavior-modification training to take hold.

Never force a dog to confront his fear. This is called "flooding," and it can seriously backfire. If you make a dog be near something that he is afraid of, it could erode his trust in you. Why should he trust you if you put him in the midst of the thing that terrifies him? It could cause your dog to freak out and try to flee or bite.

Understand the Challenges

When training a fearful dog, please know that it can provide unique challenges. Fearful dogs are *not* stupid! They may take longer to learn exercises, however, because they have more issues that they are dealing with than a confident dog. For example, you are in a group class trying to teach your dog to Down. He is eager for the click and treat, but he is hesitant to lie down. He will not look at you, but he keeps looking around the room. He keeps staring at the dog and handler working next to you. He flinches slightly when someone scrapes a chair across the floor.

Your dog is concerned and stressed about the environment, and lying down is a very vulnerable position. He is watching for monsters and trying to pay attention to you at the same time, which is really hard.

Flower essences can be used to help dogs in extreme stress.

Your patience will help him learn that he can successfully learn the exercise and not get hurt.

This example doesn't mean that your dog should never attend a group class. It really depends on the level of fear that your dog is battling. If he is so terrified that he would not even take treats in a group setting, then private lessons would be better for your dog. Or, find a class that is specifically geared toward shy and fearful dogs. Other shy dogs, however, can do fine in a group class, and it can be a very empowering experience for them as they learn that they can actually have fun in different surroundings. Only work with an instructor who understands shy dogs and how to effectively work with them in a group-class setting.

Having a shy dog is challenging, frustrating, and also rewarding. You will experience setbacks, and this is normal. You will seem to make great progress at times, and then your dog will seem to backslide, which is very frustrating. Watching a dog come out of his shell, however, is joyous. A dog that previously was frightened of people and learns to willingly approach strangers with confidence is truly heartwarming.

Fear Biting

Most aggression is due to fear. If a dog is fearful and feels a need to defend himself, he can bite. It doesn't matter what breed. All dogs have teeth! If your dog has bitten someone, or you're concerned that he may bite someone, please consult a trained professional who uses reward-based methods. One of the best things you can do for your fearful dog is to help protect him from the things he fears until you can teach him that he does not need to be so afraid. If he's so afraid that he feels a need to bite, completely limit his interactions with people who frighten

Be patient with a shy dog!

him. Some dogs are social and outgoing with family but not with people outside the family. Other dogs are OK with only certain members of the family.

Don't put your dog in a position where he is forced to be around people who he finds frightening. Some people make the mistake of thinking that they need to socialize a fearful dog by taking him to places where he will meet people. This often backfires because the dog becomes completely overwhelmed. If your dog is afraid of people, limit his interactions, don't increase them. Wait until you have clear directions from a professional, who can help you introduce your dog to people properly.

As you work with a professional, you can also train your dog to happily wear a muzzle. You can use the desensitization and counterconditioning techniques we've covered as part of your overall behavioral modification program.

Jumping on Furniture

Can you blame your dog for getting up on the furniture? It's comfy! If you don't want your dog to jump up on the furniture, be sure you don't confuse him by allowing him up sometimes and then getting angry at him at other times. Set the rules right from the first day.

Some dogs just discover that furniture is comfortable without their owners allowing them up there. Or, you may adopt a rescue who was allowed to get up on the couch in his previous home, so he doesn't understand you don't want him to do so in your home.

If you are not in the room to supervise your dog, you can't guarantee that he won't get up on the furniture if allowed access. You can block his access to the room if this is an issue. Or, if that's not convenient, you can put something on the couch, such as boxes, to keep him off. It doesn't make for very attractive decor, but if no one's home at that time anyway, does it matter?

Train your dog the Off cue. If your dog gets up on the furniture while you are there, cue "Off." You can also use your Hand Target to get him off of the furniture and then reward him when he's off. As he approaches the furniture, you can also use Leave It.

If you don't want your dog on the furniture, enforce the rule from day one.

Another option is to teach your dog that he can only get up on the furniture if you allow him to. You can do this in several ways. You can indicate he can get up by putting a throw blanket on the piece of furniture he's allowed on. You can purchase a nice pet throw in a variety of pet-supply catalogs, or you can just use a sheet or blanket. First, teach Down-Stay on the throw while it is on the ground. When he's settling on it reliably, put the throw on the furniture and cue "Down." This will teach him that he can settle on the blanket on the piece of furniture. If he gets on a piece of furniture that doesn't have the throw, then use the Off cue, followed by leading him to the correct spot and cueing "Down."

You can also use the Hand Target to cue him when he's allowed up on the furniture with you. Use your Hand Target up on the furniture so that he jumps up. If he jumps up on his own, do not let him stay there. Immediately give the Off cue. Practice this in a training session. With consistency, he'll learn that he can only get up on the furniture when given the cue.

Jumping on People

Most dogs jump up on people to greet them. It's a social behavior, and usually means a dog is friendly and trying to say hello. It's not always welcome, though. Be sure you are not accidentally rewarding your dog for jumping up on you. For example, if you are sitting down on the couch and your dog puts his front paws on you, and you pet him, you are rewarding your dog for paws on people. If you are standing and your dog jumps on you and you push him off or give him any attention at all, you're rewarding him. Some dogs love to bounce off you! So be sure you are not giving your dog a reward for this behavior, or it will be very hard to fix.

Make sure that you are not rewarding your dog for jumping up.

To fix this problem, teach your dog something else you like better. You can cue your dog to Sit, or teach your dog Sit for Greeting.

Goal: Your dog will automatically sit when approached by people.

What You'll Need: Clicker, treats. Other people.

Preparation: Teach Sit.

1. Have the person approach your dog. As your dog sees the other person and the person draws next to your dog, cue "Sit." The person should not pet your dog. When your dog sits, click and toss the treat to reset him for the next repetition.

2. Repeat Step 1 nine times. End your training session.

3. At future training sessions, work to where your dog will start automatically sitting when the person approaches.

When your dog automatically sits upon a person's approach, it's time to move onto the next step.

1. Have the person approach your dog. Your dog should automatically sit. Have the person allow your dog to sniff his hand, then scratch briefly behind your dog's ear. After just two seconds of petting, click. Toss the treat to reset the dog for the next repetition. The person should stop petting your dog when you click.

2. Repeat Step 1 nine times. End your training session.

3. At future training sessions, gradually work up to your dog being able to sit longer for petting.

Tips: *Only teach this behavior with people your dog finds comfortable and not scary. If you have a fearful or shy dog, for example, never make him sit when strangers approach. This is too much for a fearful dog, and could cause him to growl or bite.*

Mounting/Humping

This is a behavior that often horrifies and embarrasses people. You're sitting around having a lovely cocktail party and your dog starts humping his toy right in front of everyone. Or worse, a guest! Mounting, or humping, is a natural dog behavior. Male and female dogs can exhibit mounting behavior, even if they are spayed or neutered. Males can mount other males, females can hump other females, some dogs hump inanimate objects. Yes, it can be sexually oriented, but not always. Puppies will often hump each other in play. And it's often just a sign of frustration or high excitement.

If your dog starts mounting, simply and calmly remove the source. If you give the dog attention for the behavior, that's a reward. For example, if your dog starts humping his toy, take away the toy. Redirect your dog's attention to a chew toy or food-stuffed toy instead.

Redirect mounting behavior with a chew toy.

If your dog is humping another dog, cue "Leave It." Separate the dogs. If it's a person, cue "Leave It" and remove your dog from the person. You can always leash him or confine him if necessary. If your dog is humping due to overexcitement, learn the triggers for the behavior and try to stop the situation from escalating so your dog doesn't reach that level of frustration.

Mouthing/Nipping

Puppies mouth because they are teething, and they are trying to engage you in play. Please see the Bite Inhibition section for information on how to teach a puppy not to mouth.

If bite inhibition is not taught when a dog is a puppy, it can continue to adolescence and adulthood. This is more serious, as the bigger the dog, the bigger the mouth! Some dogs only mouth when they get excited. For example, a retriever may mouth you when overly excited. Even if it is infrequent, don't encourage the behavior. You may not mind if your dog takes your arm in his mouth, but someone else could be startled or frightened by this behavior. If your dog is mouthing you out of excitement, use Leave It. Redirect your dog to an appropriate item and praise him for chewing on that, instead. If your dog is so overly excited that he doesn't listen, confine him until he calms down. Also see the Excitability section for tips.

Puppies mouth because they are teething.

Some dogs learn that mouthing gets them what they want. These dogs are not being dominant. They have just learned that if they chomp on you, it's rewarding. For example, you go to leave your dog in the backyard, but your dog doesn't want you to leave. He starts nipping at your arms, grabbing your pants leg, maybe even going after your shoes. Some dogs nip so hard you get bruises. You yell at him and push him away, which just makes things worse. Any attention you give him at this point is rewarding. You also can't leave very quickly, since he's attached to you! So he's learned that his exuberant nipping is effective. For this type of problem, really work on your regular training behaviors—Sit, Leave It, Down-Stay, Sit-Stay, etc. This will teach your dog more effective, acceptable ways to earn rewards. If you have concerns your dog will hurt you with his mouthing, then consult a professional trainer who uses reward-based methods.

Phobias

A phobia is an extreme fear. When a dog is that afraid, he may bolt in terror. The dog is not able to think clearly, and will even run out in front of traffic as he flees what terrifies him. Some dogs have been known to leap through plate glass doors, or leap out of windows, during thunderstorms or fireworks. Dogs will injure themselves, chewing their way out of crates. Dogs can urinate or have diarrhea. Seeing a dog experience a phobic reaction is a heartbreaking experience.

Noises

Even dogs that are normally very confident can sometimes develop phobias to noises, especially thunderstorms or fireworks. Some dogs react to smoke or other alarm noises, while some get worried about traffic noises.

See the Fear section for general tips in dealing with your dog's fear. In addition, desensitization to noises can be helpful. You can purchase special effects CDs that have noises on them, and start playing them at levels that your dog does not react. You can gradually increase the level, and give your dog treats, taking each session slow to get your dog acclimated to the sounds.

With thunderstorms, know that it may not always be the noise that causes your dog to react. There are some theories that a dog is really reacting to a drop in barometric pressure, or the increase in static electricity.

Household Things

Sometimes it doesn't take something as dramatic as a thunderstorm to send a dog into a panic. Some dogs will freak out at the sight or sound of a vacuum cleaner. Dogs can be frightened of everyday household things—hair dryers, fireplaces, the dishwasher, swimming pool, hoses—you name it.

If your dog is afraid of something, don't make him confront it. This can make his fear much worse. Instead, you can help him learn to like the object better.

Goal: Your dog will approach a scary item and learn it is not so scary.

What You'll Need: Clicker, treats.

Reward your dog for showing any interest in the object that frightens him.

1. Put the object far enough away so your dog is not exhibiting stress. Stay still. Any movement towards the item should be initiated by your dog. If the item makes noise, such as a vacuum cleaner, have it turned off.

2. Watch your dog for any interest in the item. Even if he just looks at it, click and treat. As you continue to click for your dog looking at it, he will start approaching it. For each step your dog takes towards the object, click and treat.

3. Repeat Step 2 nine times. End your training session.

4. At future training sessions, continue to click and treat for any interest or movement towards the item. This may take few sessions or many sessions, depending on how afraid your dog is of the object. Gradually work up to where your dog will approach the item confidently.

When your dog is confidently going up to the item, it's time to move it around. Something as small as movement can frighten your dog again. In this step, you'll also add noise for applicable objects. You will do these introductions separately, to make it easier for your dog to adapt.

1. Warm up by your dog approaching the item a couple times. Click and treat each approach.

2. Pick up the item and move it, just an inch or two, either laterally or away from your dog. Do not move it towards your dog, as this could be too scary. Watch your dog's reaction. Does he flinch? Don't move it so much next time. Does he back up, then approach again? Click and treat any confident response or movement towards the object.

3. Repeat Step 2 nine times. End your training session.

4. At future training sessions, work to where you can move the object around and your dog remains confident. After ten repetitions, end your training session.

5. If the object makes noise, you may need to back your dog up across the room, depending on how sound sensitive he is to the object. Turn the object on for one second, then turn off. Watch your dog's reaction. Click and treat any confident response or movement towards the object.

6. Repeat Step 5 nine times. As your dog grows more confident, gradually increase the amount of time the object is turned on. End your training session.

7. At future training sessions, start combining the object turned on with movement. Click and treat any confident responses or movement towards the object. After ten repetitions, end your training session.

Expert Tip

IS HE PULLING ON THE LEASH?

Dogs pull for many reasons, mainly because it's rewarding to them. Pulling is fun! Some dogs are bred to pull, such as Siberian Huskies.

Dogs don't understand that pulling is an issue until you teach them. Teach them to walk with you, instead of in front of you. To address the issue, teach your dog to Walk Nicely on Leash.

Tips: *In this exercise, the dog shows all initiative. Let him process the experience and gain confidence on his own. Do not lure him with treats. Only click when he shows bravery, and then give him a treat as a reward. If you use treats to lure him, he may follow them, but then grow overwhelmed at his proximity to the scary object. You don't want the enticement of food to overshadow the event, as that won't teach him to be confident.*

People

If a puppy was not properly socialized to a variety of people before his critical socialization window closed, he may be fearful of people. Bad experiences with people can also cause a dog to be fearful. See the Fear section for tips on how to address this issue. Desensitization and counter-conditioning are often used to help dogs grow more confident with people.

Remember that fearful dogs can lash out in self-defense. While that may just make a dent in your vacuum cleaner, it can be more serious when a person is the recipient! Manage your dog to avoid potentially scary situations with people. Do not take your dog to public places to "socialize" him—that's not the correct way to do it! Don't allow people to pet your dog just because they ask, or are convinced they can "fix" your dog. If your dog is afraid of people, the nicest person in the world could approach him and he would think that person was a monster. Don't take a chance on a bite. Get professional help from a trainer who uses reward-based methods.

Resistance to Handling

Some dogs do not like you touching their paws. Some dogs are very sensitive about you touching their ears, mouth, or other body part. This is not uncommon, but it's something that you should definitely address. You should be able to touch your dog all over his body, because throughout his life you will need to care for him. If he is ever injured in a sensitive area, you can't forego treatment just because he doesn't tolerate handling.

If a puppy was not socialized to a variety of people during the critical socialization window, he may be fearful of people.

You could force your dog to put up with it, but that could cause him to distrust you and make him actually hate it worse. Instead, teach your dog to enjoy handling. Review the Handling exercises in the Puppy Training section. This technique can be used with dogs of any age. Just keep in mind that if you have an adult dog that has been intolerant of handling for many years, it will take you longer to change his mind about it. It can be done! You just have to be extra patient with him.

Also be sure you're not teaching your dog that handling is a bad experience. For example, if you grab your dog's collar to punish him, he will learn that a collar grab precedes punishment. Likewise, if your dog is having a playdate with another dog and you grab his collar to leash him up and take him home, you're teaching him that a collar grab means the fun is over. Instead, teach him to come to you and sit so you don't have to go grabbing for him.

Separation Anxiety

Separation anxiety is a heartbreaking condition. Dogs are truly terrified to be left alone. They are so frightened that they will hurt themselves in order to escape confinement. Separation anxiety is a serious condition.

Some people think their dog has separation anxiety if he exhibits stress when they leave him alone, but that is not necessarily the case. Just because your dog gets a bit stressed doesn't mean he has real separation anxiety. The condition should be diagnosed by a veterinarian. Here are some of the symptoms:

Stress over being alone is not the same as separation anxiety.

- **Drooling**. When you return home, you may find puddles of drool on the floor. (This is often mistaken for urine at first, until you realize there is no urine smell.)
- **Self-injury**. Your dog will hurt himself to escape.
- **Anorexia**. Your dog will not eat while you are gone. If you leave him a food-stuffed chew toy, he will ignore it until you return.
- **Destructiveness around escape routes**. Dogs that tear up entire rooms are usually not suffering from separation anxiety. The hallmark of the condition is destruction around doorways or windows.

Your veterinarian may prescribe medication for your dog, which works best with combined with a behavior modification program. The program really requires the help of a professional trainer, veterinary behaviorist, or certified applied animal behaviorist, depending on the severity. In general, it will take time, patience, and dedication to help your dog with his separation anxiety. You cannot leave your dog unattended during the course of treatment, which can be challenging for many. The good news is with the right medication and treatment plan, you can see success with your dog.

There are things that you can do to help and to hinder your dog's progress. If your dog is already so clingy that he can't bear to be apart from you, don't let him sleep on your bed with you. Some dogs can sleep on the bed and be just fine, but others can become insecure. The bed is a place of high privilege, and it contains a lot of your scent since you spend so much time there. Some dogs can become abnormally attached to you (or in the case of some dogs, to the bed). If your dog has a behavioral issue, such as fear and aggression, he should not sleep on the bed until it is resolved. And afterwards, you should still carefully monitor him to ensure the behavioral issues don't creep back again. This is not to say a dog will become "dominant" when sleeping on the bed! It's just that some dogs can't handle it without having issues.

Another thing that can make the problem worse is to overly shower your dog with attention, and fuss over him like an overprotective parent. This can create a highly insecure dog. If you are so upset and hovering about everything, surely something must be wrong? But your poor dog can't figure out what it is, so he can live in a state of constant worry, wondering why you're so agitated and smothering. If your dog suffers from separation anxiety, take an honest look at how you interact with your dog. You may have accidentally helped create the problem. If so, surely you didn't mean to! People who do this usually have big hearts and just feel a need to spoil a dog out of love, but this is not healthy for your dog. You can love your dog without smothering him.

If you fuss over your dog like an overprotective parent, you may create a highly insecure dog.

One thing that you can do to help is train your dog. Train him to do anything—Sit, Down, Walk Nicely on Leash, High Five—pick a behavior! By learning he can earn rewards, your dog will gain confidence. Dogs with separation anxiety lack confidence, so boosting his confidence through training will help him build a stronger foundation.

Shyness

Some dogs are not quite fearful, but take a while to warm up to things. They are more shy than downright terrified. Some dogs are specific about their shyness. They may only be shy with people, or in new environments.

If you have a shy dog, it's important to recognize his signs of stress. If he is licking his lips, yawning, hanging back, getting clingy, whining, turning away, or hesitant, respect these signals as indicators he is concerned about something. Displacement signals can be other indicators. These are behaviors that are perfectly normal, but out of context. For example, you are about to take your dog into a new pet supply store. You go through the sliding doors and your dog stops and starts scratching at his collar. Does he suddenly have an itch? Maybe, but not likely. His scratching is a displacement signal. It's normal for him to scratch himself, but it's odd that he chose that place and moment to do so. Displacement signals can be signs your dog is stressed.

If your dog is exhibiting stress, determine what the cause is. Keep him well away from it so he can acclimate as his own pace. Don't force him into a situation in which is he uncomfortable.

A good management plan can help prevent a lot of stealing.

It will help you to review the Fear and Phobia sections for tips on helping fearful dogs. Your dog's reactions may not be as extreme, but the same tips apply. Your dog could also benefit from the desensitization and counter-conditioning information, especially if your dog is very specific about things that trigger his shyness. For example, if your dog is only shy around men, you could work on this issue by associating men with your dog's favorite treats.

Stealing

Dogs steal because it's rewarding. If they steal food and eat it, it's a reward. If they steal an item and you chase them, it's a reward. If they steal an item and get to chew it up, it's a reward.

A good management plan can help prevent a lot of stealing. Don't give your dog access to things he likes to steal. This means you may have to teach your kids to put away their toys and clothes, and you may have to teach yourself to put them away, too!

While you implement a management plan, teach your dog Leave It. You'll use this when you observe him heading for something you don't want him to have. Teach Drop It for when he already has an item, and you want him to spit it out. You can also teach the Retrieve if you want your dog to bring you the item.

Try This!

STEALING FOOD
If your dog is stealing food off the counter, check out the Counter-Surfing section for tips.

Whining

Whining can drive you crazy. Some dogs are excellent whiners, and can reach shocking pitches of sound that feel like they cut through your brain. There are some people who don't even mind if their dogs bark, they just don't want them to whine!

Dogs whine for many reasons. They can whine when they are upset, afraid or stressed. They can also whine when they are excited. Some dogs will whine when you're angry or upset, trying to appease you. Some dogs just happen to be more likely to whine than others.

There are several things you can do to help stop your dog from whining. If your dog is whining because he is stressed or afraid, then try to determine what it is that is upsetting him. Yelling at him won't help him be any less stressed, and will likely make the whining worse. Please review the Fear and Phobia sections for tips. Your dog may not be as afraid as a really frightened dog, but the same tips will work for a dog that is slightly stressed or upset.

Also, be sure you are not rewarding the whining. If your dog whines because he wants to get out of his crate, and you let him out of his crate, then you are paying him. If he whines for you to throw the ball, and you throw the ball, you are paying him. If he whines for you to let him outside and you do, you are paying him. With your payments, you're teaching your dog that whining is very successful. If your dog is whining to get something, don't give him a reward until he is quiet. This includes giving your dog access to things that can trigger whining. For example, if your dog whines at the window when he sees something outside, don't give him access to the window if his whining bothers you.

This is different from comforting a dog that is afraid! It is a complete myth that you shouldn't comfort a dog that is frightened, because you're just rewarding that behavior. Fear is an emotion, not a behavior. If your dog is afraid, you should comfort him and make him feel safe and protected. Your dog looks to you for help and a safe harbor, and there is nothing wrong with offering it to him.

CHAPTER 17

AGGRESSION

Aggression can be one of the most heart-wrenching, frustrating, and frightening issues to experience with your dog. It's so upsetting that many people live in denial about their dog's aggression until the problem escalates to where they can't ignore it any more. Excuses abound, from "He must have been abused before we got him, so he doesn't like men" to "He didn't mean to bite me, and I could tell he regretted it." Puppies are not that good at gauging the damage that their teeth can do, but adolescent and adult dogs are. When a dog uses his teeth to make a point, it's not an accident. He means it. Dogs have exquisite control over their teeth and can move lightning fast. You are not quick enough to get out of the way. If your dog snaps and misses, he meant to miss. If he bites, he meant to bite.

Aggression takes several forms. Growling is a form of aggression. If your dog growls over a bone or his place on the bed, it's aggression. If he growls when your child approaches, it's aggression. Barking and lunging can be signs of aggression. When the fur rises on your dog's shoulders and back, called piloerection, it can be a sign of aggression. Snapping and biting are signs of aggression.

Get Help!

If your dog exhibits these behaviors, do not wait to get help. Aggression does not go away on its own; more often, it worsens the longer it goes on. The best practice is to get professional help because aggression is complicated to resolve and has tremendous liability issues. Choose a professional trainer who uses only reward-based methods, not the old-fashioned choke chains, prong collars, or electric collars, or the outdated "dominance theory," which can make aggression much worse.

Choose a professional trainer who has proven experience and education in dealing with aggressive dogs—interview the trainer carefully to ensure that he or she is qualified. A professional trainer can ensure that you are following the behavior-modification program properly. If there are children involved, please contact a veterinary behaviorist or a Certified Applied Animal Behaviorist (CAAB). An animal behaviorist is different from a regular trainer, even a trainer with great credentials.

Children and dogs can be a beautiful team—or a trip to the emergency room. If your dog growls at your children, then do not hesitate to get help. Ask your veterinarian for a referral to a veterinary behaviorist or a CAAB today. You may have to travel to find one, but many also offer Skype and phone consultations.

There are some general tips to keep in mind when dealing with aggression.

- **Recognize it as aggression and admit that there is a problem.** It is hard to admit that your dog may not be perfect or may even be "mean." But admitting a problem is always the first step to fixing it. Just because your dog may growl over toys or snap at your boyfriend doesn't mean that he is a bad dog. It also doesn't mean that your only option is euthanasia, which is at the heart of many people's concerns. With the surge in positive training methods over the last decade, there are more solutions than ever to help aggressive dogs.

- **Do not punish your dog for growling.** This is a common mistake. You don't want your dog to growl, so you punish him for it. You're embarrassed when he growls, so you punish him for it. Big mistake. A growl is a warning. Your dog is telling you that he is upset about something. If you punish him for growling, you could successfully stop him from doing so … but you haven't eliminated the thing that he's upset about in the first place. So, in effect, you've eliminated the warning system. Never punish your dog for growling. You want to know when he's upset! It's better to hear about it in a growl than for your dog to feel that he needs to go straight to a bite.

- **Do not use harsh physical punishment.** You've already read about the consequences of physical punishment. They are even more pronounced in aggression cases. Do not treat aggression with aggression, as you will likely make the problem much worse.

If you shouldn't use physical punishment to "correct" your dog, what can you do? There are extremely helpful tools that you can use, depending on what type of aggression you are dealing with.

Territorial Aggression

Territorial aggression occurs when a dog is protecting an area that he considers his. Some dogs will attack and bite a person who enters the home. Others will act aggressively when anyone enters the yard. Others are territorial about vehicles or their crates. Studies have shown that dogs that are chained in yards have an increased amount of territorial aggression.

Some people like it when their dogs are territorial, but this is a slippery slope. A dog does not automatically know who is a bad person and who isn't. If your dog is protecting

Never punish a dog for growling, as it's valuable communication.

your home by acting aggressively, he is just as likely to act that way toward your neighbor's daughter who comes to visit as he is toward a criminal.

Different areas have different laws about whether you will be liable if your dog bites or injures someone when they are on your property. Don't assume that you will not be held responsible; check your local area's ordinances. Even if the law says you're in the clear, you would feel awful if an innocent person was injured by your dog.

Some people think that their dogs are exhibiting territorial aggression when, in fact, they are actually scared of people. The dog is barking and growling not because he wants to protect his property, but because he thinks that people are scary and wants them to go away. How can you tell the difference? The dog will normally exhibit the same territorial behavior elsewhere, in areas other than what you would consider his "home turf."

If your dog is exhibiting territorial aggression, management is your best tool until you can implement a behavior-modification program with a professional trainer. Ensure that your fence is tall and secure, and consider putting a lock on it so unauthorized people will find it harder to enter.

Do not use an underground fencing system. The use of electric shock is not recommended in general, but it can also cause aggressive behavior to escalate. A territorial dog's aggressive behavior is already escalated, and the additional punishment of an electric shock can trigger an attack.

If you know that guests are coming over, confine your dog. After your guests are settled, if your dog has a history of accepting people in your home, bring your dog out on leash for extra control. Use your clicker and treats to reward relaxed, social behavior.

If your dog is protective of his crate or the car, here is how you can train your dog to have a better response than aggression.

Goal: Your dog will not exhibit aggression when people approach his crate or your car.

What You'll Need: Treats, other people to help you.

1. Have the other person walk past the crate or car, several feet (m) away.
2. As soon as your dog sees the person, start feeding him treats, even if he growls or lunges. If he is so agitated he will not eat the treats, start over with the person farther away.
3. As soon as the person has walked by and your dog can no longer see him or her, stop the treats. Ignore your dog.
4. Repeat Steps 1–3 nineteen times. End your training session.

Most aggression is based on fear.

AGGRESSIVE RESPONSES CREATE AGGRESSIVE DOGS

According to a veterinary study published in the *Journal of Applied Animal Behavior* (2009), if you're aggressive to your dog, your dog will be aggressive, too. The highest frequency of aggression occurred in response to these interventions:

- Hitting or kicking the dog (41% of owners reported aggression)
- Growling at the dog (41%)
- Forcing the dog to release an item from his mouth (38%)
- "Alpha roll" (forcing the dog onto his back and holding him down) (31%)
- "Dominant down" (forcing the dog onto his side) (29%)
- Grabbing the jowls or scruff (26%)
- Staring the dog down (staring at the dog until he looks away) (30%)
- Spraying the dog with water pistol or spray bottle (20%)
- Yelling "no" (15%)
- Forced exposure (forcibly exposing the dog to a stimulus—such as tile floors, noise, or people— that frightens the dog) (12%)

Tips: *You are trying to change your dog's opinion of people approaching his crate or car. This is why you feed him even if he is growling or lunging. Just rapidly feed him as long as the person is within his sight. You will find that his outbursts become less volatile as he starts to anticipate food instead of worrying about the person's approach. This may take many sessions, depending on how long your dog has been practicing this behavior.*

Aggression toward People

Most aggression is based in fear. Dogs that are frightened of people often act aggressively—growling, barking, snapping, snarling, biting. Punishing your dog won't get rid of the fear. You need to teach your dog that people are nice and are nothing to be afraid of. This must be done very carefully, and gradually, preferably with the help of a professional.

Do not force your dog to confront his fear. This will make the fear much worse. For example, if your dog is scared of men, don't hand your dog's leash to a man or make your dog approach a man. The man could be a wonderful person, but in your dog's eyes, you just handed his leash over to or made him approach a monster.

THE MIRACLE OF MUZZLES

Muzzles get a bad rap. It's true that when people see your dog wearing a muzzle, they may react negatively. But to an aggressive dog and his owner, a muzzle may be your best friend. Training your dog to happily wear a muzzle keeps everyone safer. If you know that your dog can't hurt someone, you'll feel less apprehension.

Choose a basket muzzle that will allow your dog to pant, drink water, and take treats. If your dog will need to wear the muzzle for an extended period of time, you don't want it to constrict his ability to breathe.

Slowly introduce your dog to the muzzle. Smear peanut butter or cream cheese in the bottom, and encourage him to stick his nose into the muzzle to get the treat. When he's happily poking his nose into the muzzle, fasten it briefly and then immediately remove it. Gradually work up to where your dog wears the muzzle for longer periods of time.

If your dog is aggressive at the veterinarian's office, then your vet will appreciate you acclimating him to a muzzle beforehand. Put the muzzle on before you enter the facility. When the veterinary staff needs to muzzle an aggressive dog that isn't used to one, it's much more stressful for the dog.

A muzzle can also be an added safety net to your management program. If you have your dog behind a baby gate and he is wearing a muzzle, you have some added protection if he somehow gets out of the gate.

If your dog is aggressive toward strangers, implement a stringent management plan until you can get professional help. Keep him away from strangers. If you have guests over, you can put him in his crate, in another room, or behind a secure baby gate so that he can't reach your guests and become overwhelmed.

If he's crated or behind a baby gate where you can easily reach him, you can toss treats to him while your guests are over. You can give him a bully stick or food-stuffed chew toy. Do not let your guests give him treats. A very food motivated but fearful , dog could get overwhelmed, so he will approach a stranger to take a treat but then become overwhelmed by the proximity. This can lead to a bite.

Aggression toward Other Dogs

Some dogs are great with people, but they are aggressive toward other dogs. This can be due to fear. Dogs that haven't been socialized with other dogs can be fearful of them and act aggressively as a result. Some dogs are also antagonistic toward other dogs. Certain breeds historically were bred to fight other dogs, and even though dogfighting is no longer legal, their DNA may still tend toward dog aggression.

Some dogs can learn to love other dogs, while others can learn to tolerate them. Others may never learn to be in the presence of other dogs without being aggressive. It depends on the individual dog, the dog's socialization history, how long the dog has been aggressive toward other dogs, the training methods used to address his aggression, and other factors.

Until you can get professional help, carefully manage the situation so that your dog does not encounter strange dogs. Taking your dog to a dog park to "socialize" him is not wise and will likely make the problem worse ... not to mention cause problems for the other dogs there.

Resource Guarding

Aggression over food, toys, and other items is called resource guarding. Growling is not the only symptom; other signs include tensing when you approach, turning away from you and getting in between you and the item, carrying the item away, or, if it's food, eating faster.

There are tons of clips on video websites showcasing dogs growling over objects, much to the amusement of the public. These are not funny. Even the tiniest of dogs growling over a bone can deliver a bite. What if he bites a child? A dog that growls over an object is stressed. He growls to let you know that he's upset. If you persist and try to take the object from him, he may feel that he needs to elevate his communication to a bite.

If your dog is growling over objects, keep a list of everything that he growls over and remove them from his environment until you get professional help. The list will help you determine how to address the issue—you will start working with least valued items first.

For example, your dog doesn't growl over plastic chew bones. He tenses and gets in between you and tennis balls. He growls over bully sticks. You would start with the plastic chew bones. Here is an example of the beginning training process.

Goal: Your dog will not resource guard.

What You'll Need: Treats. Item that your dog does not resource guard.

1. Give your dog the item. Let him chew on it for a few seconds.
2. Show your dog a treat. When he drops the item, give him the treat.
3. Repeat Steps 1–2 nine times. End your training session.

Tip: *What this does is teach your dog that if he drops an item, he gets paid for it. This is the foundation for more complex versions of this exercise, with which a professional trainer can assist you. You want your dog learn that it's OK to share!*

Dogs that haven't been socialized with other dogs can be fearful of them.

CHAPTER 18

SOLUTIONS FOR REBELLIOUS TEENS

If you've waited to train your dog until he is a teenager, or if you adopted an adolescent dog, you may have your hands full. Your dog has had months and months to build unwanted behaviors. On the other hand, even if you started training your puppy at a tender age, when he enters adolescence, you may wonder if someone replaced your angel puppy with a rebellious teenager.

Shelters and rescue organizations are full of adolescent dogs; this age can be a very trying time for pet parents. People bring home puppies that are relatively easy, and then all heck breaks loose when the puppy reaches adolescence—and people get frustrated.

Teenage dogs are work. They still require supervision, sometimes even more so than when they were puppies. They can get into much more trouble. Short little puppy legs can't reach the kitchen counter, but the lanky legs of a teenager can. Those legs also propel dogs much faster, so when a teenage dog runs, there's no way that you can catch him.

It's understandable that people get frustrated during this challenging time. Unfortunately, some give up, and the dogs end up in rescue or shelters. That doesn't have to be the answer. There are solutions to surviving your dog's adolescence.

The best approach is to understand what's actually going on. Your dog really isn't rebelling against you. He's just growing up. When a dog hits adolescence, many things happen at once.

Teenage dogs have senses that are much sharper than when they were puppies. They want to explore their environments. They can have a lot of energy! Those sweet naps they used to take as puppies are long gone. With some dogs, you may feel that you exercise them enough to run a marathon, but they still aren't tired.

Hormonal levels in intact dogs are extremely high, even higher than those in an adult dog. A dog that is ruled by hormones is not always a dog that makes good decisions. A male dog can run right out into traffic if he's following the scent of a female dog in heat. He won't think to stop and look both ways! It is estimated that a dog can smell a female dog in heat up to three miles away.

Male dogs can be consumed by scent, especially where other dogs have peed. This means that his entire body is focused on what he is smelling, not on what you are saying. It's not personal; it's hormones.

Female dogs that come into heat can become agitated and can whine or be irritable. They may become extremely interested in other dogs and scents. Some can even go into a false pregnancy and start carrying toys around and nesting. If this is happening to your little girl, she may not listen to you as much as she used to because her hormones are talking louder to her.

Know that hormones can also cause some dogs to get snarky with other dogs, even dogs they consider to be friends. Same-sex dogs can compete for resources or for the attention of a dog of the opposite sex.

As your dog goes through his adolescent period, don't despair. Just as with puppyhood, it's a brief blip on the radar of your dog's life. This, too, shall pass! Learn to understand your hooligan teenager and how to deal with this phase of his life.

Training? What Training?

A common issue with teenage dogs is that they may act like you've never trained them a day in their lives. You could have taken your dog to puppy kindergarten through advanced classes. Then, he hits adolescence, and one day you cue him to Down, and he looks at you like you've sprouted two heads and started babbling in an alien tongue. This is really not unusual.

Don't get frustrated or angry. And don't feel as if you've failed your dog, either. Instead, go back several steps in your training. Review your lesson plans again, and start from the point at which your dog performs well. Start from scratch if you have to. It won't take you as long to bring your teenage dog back up to speed as it did with your initial training. The fact that you have been training your dog all along will help you, as he will catch up again more quickly.

Teenage dogs can have tons of energy!

New Behaviors that Aren't Nice

Adolescence can be a time when dogs discover new things about the world around them, such as that it's really fun to steal socks. Or to get up on the couch that they ignored before. Sometimes these behaviors are just annoying, but sometimes they can cause concern. For example, you go to bed one night, and your dog growls when you approach the bed or reach for his collar.

If your dog is developing new, undesirable behaviors, training can help with many of them. For example, if your dog suddenly decides to try a career as a thief, teach Leave It. If he's hopping up on the furniture, and you don't want him up there, teach Down on a better spot, such as his bed. Give him an alternative behavior to perform that you like better.

The Fear Factor

Adolescent dogs sometimes also experience fear periods. There are different theories about fear periods in dogs. Some maintain that there are several fear periods, starting in puppyhood and going into adolescence, and the timetable varies from theory to theory. Some dogs seem to go through periods of unusual fear, while others just sail through their teens.

What you may notice is that your dog is suddenly frightened of something when he wasn't before. For example, you travel frequently, and your puppy is used to seeing you tote your suitcase on a regular basis. One day, you bring the suitcase out of the closet, and he starts

A common issue with teenage dogs is that they may act like they've never been trained.

barking at it furiously, backing up, with the fur raised on the back of his neck and shoulders.

What happened? Your dog could be going through a fear period. This, too, isn't rebellion. It's just a phase. If a dog is frightened, he is much less likely to respond to your cues. He's too afraid.

Give your dog a few days. Check the section on fear in Chapter 16 for tips on handling a fearful dog. If this is just a fear period, your dog will likely bounce right back in a week or so. Remember not to scold him for his actions because that will just worsen his fear, and then you may have an extended problem.

Testing Boundaries

Your puppy may have always waited patiently outside the dining room while you ate but, as a teen, decide to come jumping up to check out the dining-room table. Or, you are holding a brush and reach for your dog's ear, and he backs away, even if you've brushed him since you brought him home.

Adolescent dogs can test boundaries—they are learning what they can and can't do. If you think about it, they often get away with it. You throw the ball and, instead of bringing it back, your dog runs and runs all over the yard. You chase him down. You go to put on his leash and he dashes all over the house, dancing away just out of reach, so you fall into a daily routine of "chase the dog."

Please be assured that your adolescent dog is not trying to dominate you or take over the world. He's just a teenager, and he's exploring boundaries. This doesn't have to be a challenge. Just go back to your training and reduce his privileges until the phase passes and you establish the rules once again.

For the dog that's interrupting your dinnertime, go back to teaching Down. If he persists, you can crate or tether him until your training becomes a habit again. For the dog that doesn't want to be groomed, review the section on handling in Chapter 7 and make it a more positive experience for him so he doesn't avoid it.

Adolescent dogs can test boundaries.

Most of all, be consistent. If your teenage dog is testing boundaries, you can stick to your rules and teach them again, just as if he were a puppy. If you chase your dog all over the house, trying to get a leash on him, this is a great game to your dog. Just don't play it. He won't go outside if you don't let him. This is a lesson that he can quickly learn if you are consistent and patient. Teach him to always sit when you attach a leash.

Be aware that sometimes, when your teenage dog acts as if he's pushing boundaries or testing you, he may actually have a physical problem. Please never assume stubbornness or defiance. For example, the dog that doesn't want you to brush his ears may have an ear infection. Brushing his ears hurts him.

If your dog starts stopping on walks, refusing to budge further, he may have an orthopedic problem. Hip dysplasia can manifest itself in adolescence, and your dog may be experiencing pain on his walks. This can be the same dog that runs in the park, which often confuses people. The reason for this is that the park is very exciting to your dog, so he'll play past the pain. An everyday walk around the block may not be enticing enough to push through it.

If you suspect that your dog's behavior may be physically rooted, please take him to your veterinarian. It's better to rule out a physical problem first and then treat it behaviorally if your veterinarian says that your dog is OK.

Manage your teenage dog to help prevent issues.

Helping the Transition

You may experience only a few issues during your dog's teenage phase, or you may experience an avalanche. It really depends on the individual dog. But you *can* survive your dog's teenage period! Here is a summary of tips to help you get through it and help your dog transition to a successful, adult canine family member.

- **Training**. Even if you've trained your dog up until this point, it's normal for dogs to backslide in adolescence. Just go back to your lesson plans and commit to the training program.

- **Consistency with rules and boundaries**. You can keep rules in your house without being harsh about them. Stick to your rules and train your dog to follow them. With positive methods, your dog will learn that it's much more fun for him to do what you want.

- **Manage and redirect behavior**. Because teenage dogs get distracted by smells and new experiences, redirect them to activities that you prefer. For example, if your dog won't come in from the yard because he's sniffing every clump of dirt, go out with him on leash so you can better control his movement. Continue to work on his Recall training—make it more rewarding for him to come to you, so you can compete with the dirt! (Which is humbling, but don't feel bad. It's not unusual. Dogs love to smell dirt.) Another example is a dog that starts exhibiting undesired behavior, such as counter-surfing. Redirect his attention to the floor with food-stuffed chew toys. As your dog goes through adolescence, you will just need to be a more vigilant parent.

- **Patience and understanding**. Your dog is not trying to be the "alpha" or dominate you. The sweet puppy you brought home and cherish is still in there. Remember all of the reasons why you fell in love with your puppy. Don't let your frustration and anger lead you down the slippery slope of physical punishment, or you could create more severe behavioral problems. If your dog does something that really upsets you, calmly crate or confine him until you can breathe again and think through the issue. Remember, your dog is still young. He's still learning!

- **Veterinary assistance**. If your dog's behavior is puzzling you or suddenly changes, consider consulting your veterinarian. Your dog may be actually experiencing a physical problem.

- **Professional training assistance**. If you are at your rope's end, tie a knot and call a professional, reward-based trainer to help you. It is better to call for help when problems first arise rather than waiting until they become ingrained habits.

CHAPTER 19

TRAINING A RESCUE DOG

Rescue dogs are not "broken" or "damaged goods." Dogs end up in rescue for many reasons. Honestly, most of them end up in rescue for acting like … dogs.

People sometimes have unrealistic expectations for dog behavior. A big problem is lack of research before purchase. They fall in love with a cute dog on TV or in a movie, and they bring home a lovable puppy that starts growing up to be a dog that acts like a dog. If you don't really understand what it's like to live with a 200-pound (90-kg) dog, then when that little wrinkly puppy grows up to be a Mastiff, it may not be what you expected. Dogs are a big responsibility and a financial commitment, and everyone who brings home a dog is not prepared for this.

You may not have a lot of background on your rescue dog.

Some dogs also end up in rescue because of life circumstances. If a spouse loses his job and can barely afford rent and food, there is no spare money for the family dog. Senior citizens pass away, and sometimes there isn't anyone who can take their dogs, so they get turned over to local shelters.

Do dogs get turned into rescue due to behavioral problems? Yes. Lack of house-training is a very common cause. Rambunctiousness is another, along with lack of manners, such as jumping on people, mouthing them, and dragging people while on leash. All of these issues can be solved with proper training.

Other dogs do have issues with fear or aggression, which causes them to end up in rescue or shelters. Most aggression is based in fear. A good rescue will give you full disclosure on the dog's behavior, including any aggression issues. This dog may not be a liability or a project that you are willing to take on.

The challenge with rescue dogs is that you may not have a lot of background on them. You may not really know if they are good with children, or if they are truly house-trained, or if they have ever bitten someone. If you work with a rescue organization that is lucky enough to use foster homes, you can often get a better idea of how a dog will react in a home setting. Keep in mind, though, that the foster-home environment is still different from your home.

Just because you don't know about a dog's past doesn't mean that you can't forge a wonderful future together. No matter your dog's background, there are things that you can do to help ease him into becoming your companion. If your dog is a puppy, start by building a solid foundation. Review the Puppy Training chapter, and you'll be off to a great beginning. If you've adopted an adult dog, there are other considerations to keep in mind as you help your dog adjust.

Bonding With and Socializing Your Adult Rescue Dog

Don't be surprised if your new dog doesn't listen to you at first. He may not have had any training. Even if he did, he may not have learned to respond to anyone other than the person

---

Rescue Tip

THE HONEYMOON PERIOD

You'll often hear professional dog trainers and rescue volunteers talk about the "honeymoon period" with a newly adopted dog. When dogs enter a new home, they are often on their best behavior at first. It's only after they start feeling comfortable in their new routines that behavior problems may arise. Your new rescue dog that never chewed up anything the first few weeks starts gnawing on the coffee table. Or, your new family member who got along with your other dogs suddenly growls over a bone.

Behavior problems popping up after about a month are common. You can help prevent them by establishing a confinement and training routine right from the start as good preventative measures. Your honeymoon doesn't have to be over!

who trained him. He also really isn't invested in you yet. Some dogs are naturally very social and friendly. Your new dog may have greeted you like an old friend the first second he met you, but that doesn't mean that he's really bonded with you yet. One of your initial tasks after adopting your new friend will be to work on building a good relationship with him. Spend time with him, play with him, love him. Get to know who he is and what he likes. Does he feel so-so about tennis balls, but he loves squeaky toys? Does he go nuts for liver treats, but he turns his nose up at cheese?

An effective bonding technique, and one that also establishes you as someone who controls all of the important things in your home, is to hand-feed your dog all of his meals initially. Hand-feeding teaches your dog many great things. For example, all dogs need to eat to live. If every piece of kibble or spoonful of wet food comes from your hand, your ranking as an important person elevates pretty quickly. It also teaches your dog that hands approaching him are positive things. Every time your hand offers him a piece of food, you build a positive association with that hand. This will make it easier for you to groom him, take care of him, help him with future injuries, pet him, and more.

You don't have to wait to start training your rescue dog.

Hand-feeding is a helpful technique with dogs that may be shy or fearful of you. You may have adopted a dog that needs to work on his shyness, and this technique will help teach him that you are not so scary. If your dog is too timid to take the food from your hand, simply roll the piece of kibble gently across the floor to him. (Don't throw it, or that could startle him.) Hand-feeding does take more time out of your day because you have to sit with your dog and feed him his meals, but it can go a long way towards building your relationship.

Training your dog is a wonderful, effective way to bond with your dog. You will learn how to better communicate with each other, you will be teaching him behaviors that you prefer, and he will learn that he gets rewarded for working for you. You don't have to wait to start training your rescue dog. Once you learn what he finds rewarding, you're ready to start.

Dealing with Bad Habits

Your dog may have come along with habits that you don't like. For example, your new dog may have been allowed up on the furniture in his previous home or foster home, but you prefer that your dog not get up on the furniture. However, when he sees your favorite recliner, he may hop up there and make himself comfortable. Your dog may jump up to kiss your face, which you may not prefer. Or, he may beg at the table, which annoys you.

All of these issues are easily handled by training your dog alternate behaviors that you find more appealing. Review the Basic Cues chapter and start teaching your dog better manners.

The Benefits of Structure

Bonding with your rescue dog doesn't mean that you should be permissive from the start, only to change the rules later. It can be tempting, especially if you have a dog that is shy or that you suspect has been abused, to feel sorry for your rescue dog. Dogs like structure and routine, so one of the best things you can do for your dog is to set your house rules right from the start. For example, you feel sorry for your rescue dog, so you let him sleep on the bed when he first comes home. If, a few weeks later, you decide that he's settled in and should sleep on his own bed on the floor, you will just confuse him. Or, if your dog is very thin and you feed him from the table because you can't bear what he went through in his past, then don't get upset when he learns to beg at the table.

Of course, you love your dog, and you adopted him to give him a wonderful life. You can absolutely do that without pitying him. Your dog is lucky to have found a home with you! Determine what your house rules are, and use positive methods to teach these rules to your dog. The person who had your dog before may not have trained him, which is why your dog may have ended up in rescue in the first place.

Determine what your house rules are and use positive methods to train your dog.

Helping the Shy Dog

Your dog may be a fearful dog, or he may just be initially shy in his new environment. You can help your dog by taking note of the things that frighten him and watching his body language for signs that he is stressed. Reading the section on fear and phobias in Chapter 16 will help you learn what to recognize and how to work with your dog.

For example, your new rescue dog cowers and is hesitant to walk on your hardwood floors. He's fine on carpet, but the hardwood floors seem to terrify him. Your dog probably has never walked on this type of floor before, so he is scared of it.

You can help him by making the floor a positive experience. Use treats not to lure him, but to reward him for any confident approaches to the floor. Over the weeks, feed him his meals near the floor, then a couple of inches onto the floor, then a foot onto the floor, and so on. Only progress as far as your dog is comfortable. Don't force him to go on the floor. If he has to walk across the floor to get to the door leading outside, then consider putting a carpet runner on the floor until he grows more comfortable.

It can be tempting when you rescue a dog to show him off to all your friends and family right away. If he is a shy dog, however, keep the new introductions limited and brief. Only invite one or two people over at a time, and see how it goes. Let your dog set the pace. This will also teach you the types of people that he warms up to quickly and the ones he doesn't. For example, is he really hesitant around men? He may not have been socialized to men previously, so you will be able to work with him to make men less scary to him.

> If dogs are abandoned by their owners, they can develop intense attachments to subsequent owners.

Dealing with Common Issues

There are some common issues that are reported by those who adopt rescue dogs. Knowing about them ahead of time can help you be prepared in case you encounter them.

Separation Anxiety

If dogs lose or are abandoned by their owners, they can develop overly intense attachments to subsequent owners. If you take a week off to be with your new dog, spending all your time with him, and then head off to work the next week, this dramatic shift can be too much for some dogs and trigger separation anxiety. It's great if you want to take extra time to be with your new companion, but part of that time should be used to train him to be OK with time by himself.

Don't smother your new dog with attention when you first bring him home. You will want to! But if you shower him with attention, invite all of your friends and family to come see him, and take him everywhere with you, you are setting him up for a rude awakening when the party is eventually over. You could be causing separation anxiety.

Instead, give your dog attention, but in more realistic doses. You will have your new companion for the rest of his life, so don't try to introduce him to everything in the first month. Pace yourselves. Don't let him sleep on the bed at first. Take a couple of months to see how he settles in and adjusts before you get him used to sleeping on your bed. From the start, crate him for a few minutes, even when you are home. Gradually work up to longer periods of time so that he gets used to being apart from you. (If he is not yet crate-trained, start on that right away.)

If you think that your dog is showing signs of separation anxiety—clinginess to you, whining when you prepare to leave, refusing to eat when you are gone, drooling, destructiveness around escape routes—don't wait. Contact a professional to help you before the problem gets more pronounced and ingrained.

House-Training Issues

It is very common for a rescue dog to have accidents in his new home. The dog may never have truly been house-trained. Even if he learned not to eliminate in his previous home, he may not necessarily transfer that behavior to your home.

Prepare a rescue dog's new home with you by learning about common issues that can occur.

You can prevent this from becoming a problem by implementing a house-training program right away when you bring your new dog home. Pretend that he isn't house-trained, even if you have been assured that he is. If he is house-trained, you will sail through the program quickly. If he isn't, then you'll be preventing accidents from ever getting started.

CHAPTER 20

TRAINING
SENIOR DOGS

I t is never too late to train a dog! Older dogs have much better attention spans than puppies do. If you are just bringing home an older dog, you can start training him the basic cues and work from there. If you have had a dog for years, and he is just getting older, it's still fun to teach him new things.

Keeping the Mind Bright

Teaching an old dog new tricks provides mental enrichment and stimulation. This is the case, especially if you've had a dog for years and have done many activities with him. Maybe you've had to retire him from agility. Maybe he's developed arthritis, so you can't take him running like you used to. Or maybe you've gotten a new puppy that requires a lot of your attention. Your senior dog still probably has the heart to keep up with you, even if his body no longer can. Teach him some new things. It will keep his mind fresh and make him very happy to keep working with you.

Choose tricks or activities that your dog can physically perform without discomfort. If you have doubts or concerns, consult your veterinarian. Keep in mind that new activities don't have to be complicated. A senior dog can still learn to retrieve the newspaper or put away his toys.

Training Aids

As your dog ages, his hearing will naturally fade, and it's common for arthritis or other orthopedic issues to arise. Here are some things that you can do to help in your training, communication, and adventures with him.

- **Use hand signals if your dog has trouble hearing you.** Your dog may still hear the sharp sound of a clicker as his hearing starts to diminish. If you suspect that he can't hear the clicker, then you can use a hand-signal marker instead. For example, you could start with a closed fist, open your hand to flash all five fingers, and then close your hand quickly again. Follow immediately with a treat so that your dog learns the new marker signal.
- **If your dog's sight is starting to go, there are still fun games to play.** A dog's sense of smell is usually the last to fade, so play some scent games! For example, teach a version of the

shell game. Hide a treat under one cup. When your dog noses the cup, lift it so he can get the treat. After he does this reliably, add another cup to the scenario. Hide one treat under one cup. If your dog noses it, lift the cup for him to get the treat. If he noses the wrong cup, just do nothing. He'll soon learn he has to find the treat by using his nose.

■ **Make it easier for your dog to travel with you.** If you still want to take your senior dog places with you, then consider getting a dog ramp for your car. A dog ramp is a portable ramp that you can tuck in your car to make it much easier for an aging dog to get in and out of the car, preventing him from jumping and hurting older joints and bones.

Treasuring Your Bond

Those flecks of gray on your dog's muzzle are all memories of his time with you. Take lots of pictures and video. All of your training, efforts, and love are wrapped up in that sweet senior canine package. By using positive methods to train your dog, you've built a lifetime together with mutual respect and affection. What a journey you've made together!

Choose tricks or activities that your senior dog can do comfortably.

RESOURCES

Breed/Dog Sport Organizations

American Kennel Club (AKC)
8051 Arco Corporate Drive, Suite 100
Raleigh, NC 27617
Telephone: 919-233-9767
Email: info@akc.org
Website: www.akc.org

Canine Performance Events (CPE)
P.O. Box 805
South Lyon, MI 48178
Email: cpe@charter.net
Website: www.k9cpe.com

International Disc Dog Association/Skyhoundz
660 Hembree Parkway, Suite 110
Roswell, GA 30076
Telephone: 770-751-3882
Email: info@skyhoundz.com
Website: www.skyhoundz.com

North American Dog Agility Association (NADAC)
24604 Dodds Road
Bend, OR 97701
Website: www.nadac.com

North American Flyball Association
1333 West Devon Avenue, #512
Chicago, IL 60660
Telephone: 800-318-6312
Email: flyball@flyball.org
Website: www.flyball.org

United States Dog Agility Association (USDAA)
P.O. Box 850955
Richardson, TX 75085
Telephone: 972-487-2200
Email: info@usdaa.com
Website: www.usdaa.com

World Canine Freestyle Organization (WCFO)
P.O. Box 350122
Brooklyn, NY 11235
Telephone: 718-332-8336
Email: WCFODOGS@aol.com
Website: www.worldcaninefreestyle.org

Therapy Organizations

Pet Partners
875 124th Avenue NE, Suite 101
Bellevue, WA 98005
Telephone: 425-679-5500
Email: info@petpartners.org
Website: www.petpartners.org

Therapy Dogs, Inc.
P.O. Box 20227
Cheyenne, WY 82003
Telephone: 877-843-7346
Email: therapydogsinc@qwestoffice.net
Website: www.therapydogs.com

Therapy Dogs International (TDI)
88 Bartley Road
Flanders, NJ 07836
Telephone: 973-252-9800
Email: tdi@gti.nt
Website: www.tdi-dog.org

Training and Behavior

American College of Veterinary Behaviorists (ACVB)
College of Veterinary Medicine, 4474 TAMU
Texas A&M University
College Station, TX 77843
Website: www.dacvb.org

Association of Professional Dog Trainers (APDT)
104 South Calhoun Street
Greenville, SC 29601
Telephone: 800-PET-DOGS
Email: information@apdt.com
Website: www.apdt.com

International Association of Animal Behavior Consultants (IAABC)
565 Callery Road
Cranberry Township, PA 16066
Email: info@iaabc.org
Website: www.iaabc.org

National Association of Dog Obedience Instructors (NADOI)
7910 Picador Drive
Houston, TX 77083
Telephone: 972-296-1196
Email: info@nadoi.org
Website: www.nadoi.org

Behavior: Any action that an animal does.

Bite inhibition: A behavior in which an animal learns not to bite down hard.

Capturing: A method of marking and reinforcing behavior that a dog performs on his own, without lures.

Classical conditioning: The process of associating a neutral stimulus with an involuntary response until the stimulus triggers the response.

Clicker: A box-shaped training tool that emits a "click" sound when you press it on one side.

Clicker training: A system of teaching that uses a clicker to mark desired behavior, followed by positive reinforcement.

Conditioned response: A learned response to a previously neutral stimulus.

Conditioned stimulus: A previously neutral stimulus that comes to evoke a conditioned response.

Counter-conditioning: The process of pairing a stimulus that causes a response with another stimulus that causes an opposite response.

Cue: A word or physical signal that you use in order to get a dog to perform a specific behavior.

Displacement signal: A normal dog behavior that is performed out of context. Also called a cutoff signal.

Dominance: A relationship between individuals in which one individual establishes by force and aggression that he or she has priority access to multiple resources, such as food, preferred resting spots, and access to mates.

Fluency: The level of training at which your dog will perform a behavior with distractions, in different environments, under different conditions.

Luring: A hands-off method of guiding a dog through a behavior.

Marker: A signal used to mark a desired behavior the second that it occurs. The "click" sound is a marker.

Modeling: A method that uses physical manipulation to get a dog to perform a behavior.

Negative punishment: A method in which something pleasant is removed after a behavior, which makes the behavior decrease.

Negative reinforcement: A method in which something unpleasant is removed after a behavior, which makes the behavior increase.

Operant conditioning: The process of changing an animal's response to a certain stimulus by manipulating the consequences that follow right after the response.

Pheromones: The chemicals that dogs excrete to attract other animals.

Piloerection: A condition in which the fur on a dog's shoulders, and sometimes back, rises. This can be due to aggression, fear, or high excitement.

Positive punishment: A method in which something unpleasant is added after a behavior, which causes the behavior to decrease.

Positive reinforcement: A method in which something favorable is added after a behavior, which causes the behavior to increase.

Shaping: Training that involves building behavior by reinforcing progressive parts of the behavior.

Target: Something that an animal is taught to touch with a part of his body, such as his nose or paw.

Target stick: A long stick used for targeting. Some are telescopic.

INDEX

Photo Credits

Shutterstock: holbox, 1; Anita Nes, 4; Barna Tanko, 5; Andresr, 7; Solovyova Lyudmyla, 8, 48; Siriseeho, 11; Eric Isselee, 12, 188, 189; Jagodka, 13; Susan Schmitz, 13, 121, 160; Pavel Hlystov, 13; Nata Sdobnikova, 12; Erik Lam, 12, 61, 150, 156; Szekeres Szaboics, 13; Otsphoto, 15; Derek R. Audette, 16; Javier Brosch, 18, 45; Annette Shaff, 19, 105, 198, 212, 222, 224, 225; sianc, 21; Cynoclub, 23, 125, 141; athurstock, 24; PathDoc, 25; Anke van Wyk, 26; Solovyov Vadym, 27; Dimedrol68, 28; Ivaschenko Roman, 33; Michelle D. Milliman, 34; Nikolai Tsvetkov, 35; WilleeCole Photography, 37, 70, 87, 139, 147, 172, 208; Barna Tanko, 39; RiumLab, 40; Jadimages, 41; gwb, 42, 151; Rock and Wasp, 43; Lars Tuchel, 44; AnetaPics, 46, 62; Rob van Esch, 47; Adele D, 50; Rita Kochmarjova, 51, 63, 75; johannviloria, 52; dezi, 53, 161, 218; Zeljko Radojko, 54; ITALO, 56; Violet blue, 58, 162; Dora Zett, 59, 99, 119, 197; Andrey Arkusha, 65; Suzi Nelson, 66; Bianca Lagalla, 68; LauraVI, 71; tiggra, 74; Daria Filimonova, 77; mikeledray, 78, 136; Bellephoto, 80; Dariush M, 84; Anneka, 83, 85; Duncan Andison, 86, 134; Ermolaev Alexander, 89, 122; jiraphoto, 90; oliveromg, 92; gurinaleksandr, 94, 96; kees luiten, 98; Eldad Carin, 100, 180; Petrenko Andriy, 102; mezzotint, 103; Julija Sapic, 107; eurobanks, 106; jessicakirsh, 109; Liukov, 110; leungchopan, 111; Mat Hayward, 112, 152; Dragon Images, 115; Ambito, 117; artjazz, 118; Pelevina Ksinia, 120; BlueSkyImage, 123; Denisa Doudova, 124; iko, 126; J Paget RFPhotos, 127; Pavel Hlystov, 128; Jesse Kunerth, 129; Stefano Tinti, 131; iofoto, 132; Paul Shlykov, 133; lightpoet, 135; Jari Hindstroem, 138; bluecrayola, 142; Ksenia Raykova, 143; Jeanne McRight, 144; Jeff Thrower, 146; Pelevina Ksinia, 148; otsphoto, 149; Russ Beinder, 151; dwphotos, 153; padu foto, 157; Monkey Business Images, 157, 169; Aseph, 158; tsik, 163; ra2studio, 165; debby wong, 166; Anke van wyk, 167; Henri Faure, 168; Linn Currie, 168; gilmar, 169; Ksenia Raykova, 170, 171; Sakhorn, 173; Antonio Gravante, 174; Csehak Szabuks, 175; Jaromir Chalabala, 176, Lunja Photography, 177; Copycat37, 178; mcarper, 183; A Whitmore Photography, 184; MilanMarkovic78, 185; Leigh J, 187; Monika Wisniewska, 191; Yuri Kravchenko, 192; Ratikova, 194; gorillaimages, 195; Pushish Donhongsa, 196; Anna Koychuk, 199, 201; Paul Cotney, 200; Fnsy, 202; Anna Ri, 203; michaeljung, 205; Mark Herreid, 206; Sophie Lousie Davis, 207; Kuricheva Ekaterina, 211; Psheninam, 215; DragoNika, 217; Vitaly Titov & Maria Sidelnkova, 219; Jeroen van den Broek, 220; ARENA Creative, 226; Ivonne Wierink, 229

Ian Kahn, 227

Author photo: Ryan Dawkins

Front Cover: Javier Brosch/Shutterstock

Back Cover: Solovyova Lyudmyla/Shutterstock

Teoti Anderson, CPDT-KA, KPA-CTP

Teoti Anderson, a Certified Professional Dog Trainer and Karen Pryor Academy Certified Training Partner, has been a professional dog trainer for more than 20 years. She is the vice president of A Dog's Best Friend training company in southern Florida and the author of multiple dog training books. She also has a radio show, Get Pawsitive Results, on Pet Life Radio, is a regular columnist for *Modern Dog* magazine and has appeared in *Southern Living*, the *New York Times, DogFancy, Puppies USA, Whole Dog Journal* and other national publications. A popular workshop presenter, she has given presentations to pet owners and other canine professionals across the United States and in Japan.

Teoti is Past President of the Association of Professional Dog Trainers (APDT). The APDT, founded by renowned veterinarian, behaviorist and author Dr. Ian Dunbar, is the largest organization of dog trainers in the world. She also serves as a consultant on canine training and behavior for local and national dog rescue groups.